Published by *A Spicy Touch Publishing (Canada) Inc.*
1629 – 12th Avenue SW
Calgary, Alberta T3C 0R3
Phone: (403) 263 • 4101 / Fax: (403) 245 • 8302
E-mail: noorbanu@aspicytouch.com
Website: www.aspicytouch.com

Library and Archives Canada Cataloguing in Publication

Nimji, Noorbanu
A spicy touch III: a fusion of East African and Indian cuisine / Noorbanu A. Nimji

Includes index.
   ISBN: 978–0–9693159–1–9

   1. Cookery, Indic—Northern style.   2. Cookery, African.   I. Title.

TX724.5.I4N57 2007   641.595   C2007–901594–8

Technical Credits:
Editing: Sylvia Sikundar, Ganges, Saltspring Island, British Columbia
Research, Structural Editing, Design & Project Management: Jeremy Drought, *Last Impression Publishing Service*, Calgary, Alberta
Photography: Todd Patterson and Bill Bishop, *Ridge Rock Studios*, Calgary, Alberta
Front Cover: *Lamb Rhogan Josh* (see p. 87–88), by Todd Patterson and Bill Bishop, *Ridge Rock Studios*, Calgary, Alberta
Proofreading: Sandy Gough, Calgary, Alberta
Indexing: Brenda Belokrinicev, Athabasca, Alberta
Printed in Canada by *Friesens Corporation*, Altona, Manitoba

a Spicy Touch

VOLUME III

a Fusion of East African & Indian Cuisine

Noorbanu Nimji

A SPICY TOUCH PUBLISHING (CANADA) LTD.

CALGARY, ALBERTA

Dedication

When I wrote my other books, my husband was a constant source of encouragement and inspiration to me. Now it is his memory that is my source of inspiration and I dedicate this book to him.

ABDULMAJID NIMJI, 1928–2004.

Acknowledgements

SINCERE THANKS ARE EXTENDED FIRST to Sylvia Sikundar and Sikundar Umedally who deserve much of the credit for this book. Sylvia invested considerable time during the early stages of editing and her unwavering faith, cool and calm attitude, and constant inspiration kept me going. Without Sylvia's assistance and Sikundar's encouragement, this book would not have been possible.

My thanks and appreciation are also acknowledged for the support from my immediate family. Thanks to my son Akbar, for his incredible encouragement and support throughout this endeavour. Thanks to my daughters Khadija, Rosie, and Nazlin, and my sons-in-law Nasir and Hassan and my six grandchildren—especially Tahira, Faraha, and Khalil for direct assistance—all of whom still greatly enjoy my cooking.

I would also like to acknowledge my friends—especially Leila Kassam, Gulshan Lalani, and Kheirun Mohamedali, all of whom have encouraged me and made themselves available, from time to time, to both sample and critique the food.

Lastly, but certainly by no means, the least, my husband Majid who, in spirit, has encouraged me to publish this book.

My thanks too, to the following professionals, all of whom helped me to bring this book to publication. Jeremy Drought from *Last Impression Publishing Service*, for his additional research, structural editing, and design. Todd Patterson and Bill Bishop from *Ridge Rock Studios*, for their food photography and the portrait of the author. For the essential final round of proofreading, Sandy Gough, and for compiling the Index, Brenda Belokrinicev. My thanks to Calgary food writer, chef, author, culinary editor and poet, dee Hobsbawn-Smith for writing the Foreword. Thanks also to our printer of choice, *Friesens Corporation*, in Altona, Manitoba.

Noorbanu Nimji
Calgary, Alberta
March 2007

Contents

Foreword
by dee Hobsbawn-Smith

WHEN I WAS A TEENAGE VEGETARIAN living in a coastal Canadian city, I invited a man to dine, *chez moi*. He was older than me, and quite sophisticated; I thought to woo him with food. When he, unabashedly stalling, inquired what would be on the menu, I blurted out an uncomfortable lie, spontaneously ditching my simple plans of messy-but-yum carrot curry rolled inside warm chapattis. Crepes, I said, filled with something French and elegant and rich. The man never showed; I ate alone. Maybe if I had told the truth, he would have showed up, if only for the curry. But I was young and impressionable, and I still thought that swanky French food was the only sure way to a man's heart.

The story with a lie at its heart reveals a lot about those times and its food, the man, and me. But—in truth—if I had told the truth, my anonymous would-be date would have learned more. The truth was that before I accumulated even 20 years on the planet, I was already enamoured of the complexities of Indian food. Already, I routinely rolled chapattis and seasoned raita, slow cooked carrots and chickpeas with coconut milk and cracked cumin seed, and steamed pots of the world's most elegant rice, basmati, as the backbone of my preferred vegetarian diet. In fact, those were the very dishes I had planned to cook on that star-crossed day before the doubting lie fell out of my mouth. The subtleties and variety, the intense flavours and varied textures, superimposed on a vibrant colour palette to make Van Gogh drool—all the intricacies of East Indian cuisine captured my youthful attention as surely as I had hoped to capture that elusive man's interest. It would have been deeply connecting, and intensely satisfying, to share the tastes that really owned my heart and palate.

In this era, East Indian cuisine is *the* au courant flavour trend. Cookbook shelves, cutting-edge spice racks and canny cooks' pantries are elbow-deep in all things East Indian, to the joy of those who have loved its nuances for years. Cutting-edge restaurants are illuminating the flavours of the subcontinent, in a variety of menu styles, from true regional portrayals to Indian ingredients embedded in a fusion-embracing context. Tamarind, paneer, Moghulai spices, coconut milk, and garam masala have all migrated into modern culinary parlance, often side-by-side with those vaunted French ingredients and techniques that I had thought to use for craven carnal reasons as a younger woman.

[Of course, it is yet possible to use Indian cuisine for those cravenly carnal means. Little is as silkily seductive as a pan of rogan josh or unctuous lentils, their luxurious textures backed by the earthiness of ginger, garlic, garam masala, and the hopefulness of romance. And eating with one's hands opens the door to all kinds of possibilities. Serve a little imagination with the chapattis, and watch what may transpire!]

Noorbanu Nimji's latest book, *A Spicy Touch III*, has tapped most perfectly into the current zeitgeist. Her words are inspiring: this very second, stand up, walk to the kitchen, Polly put the kettle on, make a pot of chai. Steep it with cardamom, cloves, and cinnamon, sweeten it with milk and sugar.

Her raitas, reminding Noorbanu herself of cool oceans and hot sands, will convert many a non-yogurt-fan into the soothing pleasures of a smidge of seasoned yogurt beside nearly anything savoury. Just the mention of jaggery, or cane sugar, is a singularly headturning experience, invoking the tropics, and sun, and the heat of chili, smoothed by ghee, accentuated by the sour bite of tamarind.

Underscoring it all, Noorbanu's deep river of knowledge makes this book a reassuring tool to use. She draws on decades of easy familiarity and intimate knowledge to effectively demystify ingredients in a detailed glossary, and her recipes explain techniques clearly, accessible to novice and accomplished cook alike. Complexity without complication or confusion is reassuring, regardless of one's skills. To my great pleasure, there are many vegetarian recipes, and Noorbanu's use of oil is restrained and sensitive. But she never diminishes the primary importance of using good ingredients. Any beginning cook who wishes to learn how to create authentic cuisine in the style of the Gujarati traditions will learn how to do just that, with very little fuss, froufrou or fanfare. Any thoroughly grounded cook will find within Noorbanu's recipes inviting layers of flavour that beg to be tasted, shared, and made again in the cook's own style.

It was thrilling to learn that my teenaged chapattis are in fact roti, or rotli, in the Gujarati language. And as I closed the book, I realized that any young woman brave enough to invite a date to share a meal would, by offering dishes from within this collection, proffer a gift as complex as the young woman herself.

dee Hobsbawn-Smith
Calgary, Alberta
March 2007

introduction

ACROSS THE SUB-CONTINENT OF INDIA AND BEYOND, to wherever Indian people have settled, the variety of ingredients used and the spectrum of techniques employed in the preparation of their cuisine is truly astounding.

To those of you who have tried and enjoyed Indian cuisine, the notion of learning how to cook the food of that tradition, even to those who are comfortable and competent in the kitchen environment, might be judged as intimidating if not completely inaccessible. This will not be the case in this third volume of recipes by Noorbanu Nimji.

Following the success of her earlier books, *A Spicy Touch, Volume I* in 1986 and *Volume II* in 1992, both now out of print, Noorbanu Nimji was moved to action by the number and frequency of requests for a new book.

Indian cuisine is delicious regardless of its precise geographical origins— and those origins are both ancient and diverse, in geographical, cultural, and religious terms.

With combined sales figures of about 200,000 copies, the recipes in *Volumes I* and *II*, well known to many, were primarily those Noorbanu learned within the Ismaili community in East Africa.

Indian food has always been a fusion and the recipes in *A Spicy Touch III* are no exception. In this, her third volume, the author has drawn together the influences of Northern Indian, East African, British and Canadian living, arising, not least, from the very practicalities of adapting family recipes according to what was available for purchase at the time, wherever she has made her home.

Having made Canada her home for the past three decades and witnessed both an explosion of interest in Indian cuisine and more widespread availability of hithertofore hard to find ingredients, Noorbanu has taken note of these trends and further informed her own understanding of Indian cuisine through several visits to India. In *A Spicy Touch III*, she offers a more extensive range of recipes from other areas of India and East Africa, all with an emphasis on healthy eating.

If you are new to Indian cooking, there is no longer any need to be intimidated by the widespread use of herbs and spices in these recipes. Most of the ingredients are available in your local supermarket and, of the few still hard to find ingredients, these will surely be available in a specialized Indian or Asian grocery store, found in the majority of urban centres pretty much anywhere in the world.

Noorbanu has kept the recipes simple and presented them in the way she prefers to cook which is with an emphasis on low fat and vegetarian cuisine. Readers should probably start by trying the recipes in the manner in which they have been presented. When it comes to using herbs and spices, there are very few hard and fast rules and with some experience under your belt, feel free to experiment with and vary the recipes to suit your own palate and the tastes of those for whom you toil in the kitchen. Whether recipes are mild or hot, you can vary the amount of chilies to suit your palate. The recipes in this volume use reduced amounts of butter, fat and oil, in keeping with current recommendations for healthy eating. Chicken is usually skinned and visible fat is removed from all meats making them all low fat versions.

The book contains 134 recipes, of which two dozen offer variations and 90 are vegetarian. All recipes are presented with English names although, where appropriate, traditional names for ingredients and particular dishes are provided in Gujarati (the language of Gujarat in northwestern India) and/or Kiswahili (the official Bantu language of Kenya, Tanzania and Uganda). The book is organized in six sections:

- **BASICS** (Masalas, Pastes & Sauces)
- **ACCOMPANIMENTS** (Pickles, Chutneys, Raitas & Salsa)
- **APPETIZERS** (Salads, Snacks & Bhajia)
- **MAIN DISHES** (Chicken, Beef & Lamb, Seafood, Vegetables & Pulses)
- **STARCHES** (Rice & Bread)
- **DESSERTS** (Sweets & Drinks)

Recipes presented at the front of the book provide stock ingredients for many subsequent dishes. Preparing them and having them on hand will make the further preparation of this cuisine far less complex and more time efficient.

A detailed glossary and background notes specific to any unusual ingredient in a particular recipe will help you understand what you require and then look for on the shelves of your neighbourhood store.

A few helpful tips are included to make your cooking experience more successful and enjoyable, as is a list of must-have equipment. Don't miss the handy weights and measures conversion charts on the inside of each of the cover flaps. If you need to, fold them out and refer to them while you are cooking.

Essential Kitchen Equipment

- selection of heavy-bottomed pots and frying pans, all with close-fitting lids (either seasoned or nonstick, your choice).
- ovenproof casserole dish with a close-fitting lid
- selection of cookie trays and cake tins
- wok or *karahi* (the version used in India and Pakistan)
- food mill or processor
- juice blender
- spice grinder (a dedicated coffee grinder will work as a substitute)
- electric kettle
- selection of sharp knives
- selection of wooden spoons
- toaster oven
- microwave oven
- hand-held grater
- citrus juice press and zester
- vegetable peeler
- garlic press
- bamboo or metal skewers
- rolling pin, pastry board and flour sieve
- slotted spoon
- small and large strainer or colander
- selection of measuring cups and spoons
- lots of airtight, screwtop jars suitable for cupboards and fridge/freezer storage

a Few Helpful Tips

General Cooking and Equipment Maintenance

- To disguise strong food odours while cooking, simmer a small pot of vinegar on top of the stove.
- To prevent discoloration of pots when boiling water for steaming foods, add 1 to 2 tsp of lemon juice or vinegar.

On Eggs and Dairy Products

- Blend cottage cheese in a blender until it's smooth, then you can use it in dips, instead of sour cream.
- Before adding sour cream to a sauce that must boil, stir 1 tsp of flour into the cream. The sauce can then be boiled and the flour will prevent the sour cream from curdling.
- Cheese wrapped in a cloth dampened with vinegar will keep fresh and free from mold.
- For best results when whipping fresh cream, chill the bowl, beater and cream before whipping.
- When boiling an egg, add 1 tsp of vinegar to the water to prevent the egg from cracking.

On Herbs and Spices

- The key to successful Indian cuisine does not reside only in the recipe. The quality and freshness of herbs and spices is critical.
- Where fresh herbs are called for, try to find a reliable source. The flavour of most fresh herbs (e.g., coriander leaves [cilantro], mint, and curry leaves) changes significantly when they are dried. Tips on how to keep fresh herbs and spices in good condition for as long as possible are provided in the glossary. Do not make inappropriate substitutions when a particular ingredient is not available (e.g., curry powder for curry leaves; they are altogether different from each other and curry powder is not made from curry leaves).
- Unless otherwise noted, the recipes in this book use pure dried, ground chili peppers. It is not the same as the chili powder you usually find in chain grocery stores which is blended for TexMex cooking and dishes like *Chili Con Carne*. For further information, consult the Glossary, under **Chili**, on p. 168–9.
- For all other dried herbs and spices, it is best to purchase them in the least refined or manufactured of states and, regardless of their state, it is

always advisable to keep them in airtight containers in a cool and dark environment.

- Wherever it is possible and practical to do so, it is far better to purchase ajowain, cardamom, cinnamon, clove, coriander, cumin, dill, fennel, fenugreek, mace, mustard, nutmeg, poppy, saffron, and star anise in pod, seed or stick form, as opposed to ground or powdered. Most herbs and spices contain an essential oil or oils, their active ingredient, which is often the primary source of both their culinary magic and health or medicinal value. As such, all oil will oxidize and denature over time, therefore the fresher, the better. Roasting and grinding your own spices from pods and seeds to make masalas and as ground or powdered ingredients in other recipes helps liberate what oils remain at the time of use. Purchase a spice grinder or have an extra coffee grinder dedicated to the task available so you can roast and grind spices as you need them.

On Oil

- If time is short and you have no ghee on hand, nor time to make it, you can prevent butter from burning when sautéing by adding a small amount of oil. Butter alone burns easily, but the combination of the two does not. Vegetables and meats will be golden brown.
- When frying sweet dishes use fresh oil or oil previously used only for frying sweet dishes.

On Rice

- When washing rice do so very rapidly, using cold water and rubbing the grains between fingers and palm. Change the water several times until it runs clear. After washing do not handle or rub the rice any further as after being in water for more than a couple of minutes it becomes quite fragile. Excessive handling will guarantee mushy rice when it is cooked.
- If cooking more than 2 cups of rice, reduce the amount of water from the usual 2:1 ratio of water to rice by ¼ cup for each additional cup of rice. (e.g., to cook 3 cups of rice use 5¾ cups of water, 4 cups of rice use 7½ cups of water, etc. In some recipes, I may advocate using even less water: 1½ cups to 1 cup of rice whenever you are bringing the rice to a boil quickly and then turning down the heat, covering the rice with a lid and simmering it until it is cooked. The lid, the lower heat, and the simmering means less of the water evaporates and yet the rice still absorbs a sufficient proportion to be properly cooked.

Basics
masalas, Pastes & Sauces

Garam Masala (Basic)

Garam Masala (Special Blend)

Chaat Masala

Kashmiri Masala

Chai Masala

Paan Masala

Chili Paste

Garlic Paste

Ginger Paste

Curry Sauce

Tomato Sauce

Garam masala (Basic)

Ingredients

½ cup cinnamon sticks

2 tbsp green cardamom pods

1 tbsp black peppercorns

1 tbsp cloves

1 tsp grated nutmeg

Time

30–40 minutes

Yield

¾ cup,
approximately

Method

1 With the exception of the nutmeg, place all of the spices on a baking tray and lightly roast them for 10 minutes in an oven preheated to 300°F.

2 Turn the oven off, remove the spices and let them stand for 10 minutes.

3 Once cooled to room temperature, add the grated nutmeg and grind everything to a fine powder in a spice or coffee grinder.

4 Placed in an airtight glass container, this masala will remain sufficiently fresh for several weeks when stored in a cool, dry, dark place on the counter or in a cupboard, and up to several months in the refrigerator.

Garam masala (Special Blend)

Ingredients

4 green cardamom pods

3 × ½" sticks of cinnamon

2 tsp fennel seeds

2 star anise

½ tsp nutmeg, ground or grated

½ tsp black peppercorns

8 cloves

1 tsp cumin seeds

1 tsp coriander seeds

Time

30–40 minutes

Yield

3 tbsp

Method

1 With the exception of the nutmeg, place all of the spices on a baking tray, and lightly roast them for 10 minutes in an oven preheated to 300°F.

2 Turn the oven off, remove the spices and let them stand for 10 minutes.

3 Once cooled to room temperature, grind everything to a fine powder in a spice or coffee grinder.

4 Placed in an airtight glass container, this masala will remain sufficiently fresh for several weeks when stored in a cool, dry, dark place on the counter or in a cupboard, and up to several months in the refrigerator.

Notes

• This blend is used wherever you want extra flavour and spiciness.

Chaat masala

Method

1 Lightly roast the cumin seeds, black peppercorns, cloves and coriander in a broad-based cast iron pan over medium heat, stirring constantly to avoid burning, or bake in an oven preheated to 300°F for ten minutes.

2 Remove the pan from the heat and allow the contents to cool.

3 While the spices are still warm, add the dried mint leaves and grind together in a spice or coffee grinder. Add the mango powder, chili, ginger, salt and asafoetida and mix well.

4 Placed in an airtight glass container, this masala will remain sufficiently fresh for several weeks when stored in a cool, dry, dark place on the counter or in a cupboard, and up to several months in the refrigerator.

Ingredients

1 tsp cumin seeds

1 tsp black peppercorns

2 tbsp dried mango powder

1 tsp ground chili

1 tsp ground ginger

1 tsp salt

Optional

2 whole cloves

1 tsp dried mint leaves

1 pinch asafoetida powder

1 tsp coriander seeds

Time

20–25 minutes

Yield

¼ cup

Notes

• *Chaat Masala* is the essence of Indian street food. Although there are many ready-made varieties, it is most gratifying to make your own, varying the amounts of the ingredients to achieve your own unique taste. Chaat masala usually has a pungent smell and tastes both sweet and sour, and typically consists of dried mango powder, cumin, black salt, coriander, dried ginger, salt, black and red pepper. Best made fresh in small quantities, it can be used generously in chaat dishes, but sparingly on fresh fruit salads and cooked tandoori meat.

• **Asafoetida** (*Hing*): Also known as Devil's Dung, Stinking Gum, Asant, Food of the Gods and Giant Fennel, is a brownish, bitter, foul-smelling resin-like gum which comes from the dried sap extracted from the stems and roots of several species of the genus *Ferula* (*F. asafoetida*). It grows mainly in

Iran, Afghanistan and Kashmir. It is used in many Indian dishes and can be found commercially in powdered or lump form although it is most commonly available as a compound of 30% asafoetida resin, combined with rice flour and gum arabic. Asafoetida has a fetid, garlicky smell and is used only in small quantities. The spice is used as a digestive aid, in lentil and eggplant dishes, and in pickles. Its odour is so strong that it must be kept sealed in an airtight container although, upon cooking, its smell becomes milder and presents an onion-like taste. In India, it is used especially by the Brahmin caste of the Hindus and by adherents of Jainism, who are not permitted to eat onions.

Kashmiri masala

Ingredients

Dry
½ tsp paprika
1 tsp ground cumin
¼ tsp ground chili
¼ tsp *Garam Masala* (see p. 2)
¾ tsp salt
pinch saffron

Wet
1½ tsp *Garlic Paste* (see p. 8)
1½ tsp *Ginger Paste* (see p. 8)
2 tsp tomato paste
1½ tsp *Chili Paste* (see p. 7)

Time
15 minutes

Yield
2 tbsp, approximately

Method

1 Combine all of the wet ingredients and fold in the dry ingredients to produce a dryish paste.
2 Placed in an airtight glass container, this masala will remain sufficiently fresh for 1 week in the refrigerator and for several weeks if kept in the freezer.

Serving Suggestions

• You can increase the quantities of this masala three or four fold if you wish to make it in bulk.
• If you find a masala dish is not as spicy as you like, add one teaspoon, or more of this *Kashmiri Masala* to enrich the flavour according to your taste.

Chai masala

Method

1 Break the cinnamon sticks into small pieces. Roast cinnamon, cardamom, cloves, and pepper on a cookie tray in a preheated oven at 300°F for 10 minutes.
2 Remove roasted spices from the oven and allow them to cool to room temperature.
3 Blend spices in a spice or coffee grinder. Add the ground ginger, ground nutmeg and saffron, and mix well with a spoon.
4 Best when made fresh, this masala will remain sufficiently fresh in an airtight glass container for several weeks, when stored in a cool, dry, dark place on the counter or in a cupboard, and up to several months in the refrigerator.

Ingredients

¼ cup cinnamon sticks

1½ tsp cardamom seeds

1 tsp cloves

½ tsp black or white peppercorns, freshly ground

2 tbsp ground ginger

½ tsp ground nutmeg

¼ tsp saffron, optional

Time

20–30 minutes

Yield

7 tbsp (sufficient for 60 cups)

Paan masala

Method

1 On a baking sheet, under the broiler, lightly toast the coconut until it is dry but not browned.
2 Turn off the broiler, remove the coconut and set it aside to cool to room temperature.
3 Put all the other dry ingredients in a bowl, add the coconut, and mix them together using a spoon.
4 To prepare for 10 servings, add 1 tbsp of rose syrup to 5 tbsp of the above mixture. The rose syrup should be added a few hours before serving. Once combined with the rose syrup, the mixture stays fresh for a short time only.
5 Placed in an airtight glass container, the balance of the dry ingredients of this masala will remain sufficiently fresh for several weeks when stored in a cool, dry, dark place, either on the counter or in a cupboard, and up to several months in the refrigerator.

Ingredients

1 cup sweet shredded coconut

1 × 7 oz pkt rangola masala

4 tbsp dhania daal, roasted

2 tbsp fennel seeds, roasted

3 tbsp candy coated fennel

2 tsp cardamom seeds

4 tbsp sliced almonds, optional

rose syrup

Time

20 minutes

Yield

3–4 cups

Notes

- **Rangola Masala** is a commercially available mixture commonly found in Indian grocery stores.

- There are many different kinds of rose syrup on the market. Look for one which is the heaviest or most viscous of syrups.

- **Dhania daal** is derived from the core of the coriander seed. Seeds are split into two to extract the kernel that is then flaked and lightly roasted and salted. Dhania daal has a nutty flavour that blends well with other ingredients used in Mukhwas (mouth fresheners/digestive chews) of which *Paan Masala* is an example. *Paan Masala* (or *Paan Supari/Soparee* or *Sada Paan*) usually includes coarsely ground betel nuts and a variety of other spices.

- Mukhwas are a mixture of spices, fruits, and sugar combined to create a palate cleanser and are usually served after meals. They are also offered to guests and visitors as a sign of hospitality and eaten at cultural events.

- Paan leaves are actually the leaves of the Betel plant that is widely grown in many parts of India. There are several different types of Betel leaf which are made into a wide variety of Paan by adding different ingredients (masalas) and folding them into triangular-shaped morsels called *Bidas*.

Chili paste

Method

1 Wash the chilies, remove the stems and put them into a food processor with the lemon juice or vinegar or water.

2 Blend the mixture to a fine paste and put into sterilized containers with airtight lids.

3 Use just enough liquid to make a fine paste. If more fluid is required, simply add more water.

Variations

- You can use a mixture of green and red chilies, or make individual batches of red or green chili paste.

Notes

- Chili paste can be stored in sterilized, screwtop, airtight containers in the refrigerator for 8 to 10 days. It can also be frozen and stored for up to a year.

- Care should be taken when handling chilies. Gloves can be worn to prepare them. If the chilies are too hot, add sweet banana peppers or any other variety of pepper which are not as hot to reduce the heat.

- See the Glossary under **Chilies**.

Ingredients

½ lb fresh chilies

½ cup lemon juice
or white vinegar
or water

Time

20 minutes

Yield

1 cup

Garlic paste

Ingredients
1 lb fresh garlic

½ cup lemon juice
or white vinegar
or water

Time
30 minutes

Yield
2 cups

Method
1 To peel garlic, break the bulbs into separate cloves and put them into the freezer for about an hour.

2 Subsequently, the peel can be removed far more easily and quickly.

3 Cut off the root end of each clove and put all of the garlic into a food processor with just enough lemon juice or vinegar or water to make a fine paste. Add water if more fluid is required.

Notes
• Garlic paste can be stored in sterilized, screwtop, airtight containers in the refrigerator for 8 to 10 days. It can also be stored frozen for up to a year.

• See the Glossary under **Garlic**.

Ginger paste

Ingredients
1 lb ginger root, young and fresh

½ cup lemon juice
or white vinegar
or water

Time
30 minutes

Yield
2 cups

Method
1 Rinse the ginger to remove any dirt in the crevices.

2 Cut off all of the scars and hard parts. Scrub with a dry food brush to remove the outer skin.

3 Slice the root thinly and put it into a food processor with water or vinegar or lemon juice to blend to a fine paste. Add water if more fluid is required.

Notes
• Ginger paste can be stored in sterilized, screwtop, airtight containers in the refrigerator for 8 to 10 days. It can also be stored frozen for up to a year.

• Thin slices keep the ginger fibres from forming long "hairs" in the paste.

• See the Glossary under **Ginger**.

Curry Sauce

Method

1 Mix all the ingredients together.

2 To make a chicken curry, heat 2 tbsp of olive oil, add one portion of the sauce for each pound and a half of meat, and cook until the oil separates.

3 Then add the chicken and cook until chicken is tender.

4 Add a little hot water if required.

5 Add fresh chopped coriander leaves before serving.

6 If serving the curry with rice, add up to 2 cups of hot water to the chicken to make gravy.

7 For a beef or lamb curry, cook either with even more hot water as both beef and lamb take longer to cook than chicken.

Notes

• Keep this sauce on hand, and meals for which it is an ingredient can be prepared quickly. It will keep in the freezer for several months. One portion is sufficient to make a curry with 1½ lb of meat such as chicken, beef or lamb. It can also be used in vegetable dishes. For vegetable curries, omit the fried onion and garam masala. If you make curries only occasionally, make a single portion for immediate use. If you make curried dishes more frequently, make up a large batch of six portions, or more, saving one, or more, for immediate use, and freeze the balance in freezer appropriate containers.

• Derived from the southern Indian Tamil word "kuri," meaning "sauce," curry has become a catch-all term used to refer to any number of hot, spicy, gravy- or sauce-based dishes made with vegetables or meat and usually eaten with rice. In India, the word curry is rarely used. Most dishes

Ingredients

1 Portion

2 tbsp sunflower or olive oil

¼ tsp *Garam Masala*
(see p. 2)

½ cup canned,
crushed tomato

2 tsp *Garlic Paste*
(see p. 8)

2 tsp *Ginger Paste*
(see p. 8)

½ tsp turmeric

¼ tsp ground chili

2 tsp ground cumin

½ tsp ground coriander

¼ tsp paprika

1 tsp tomato paste

2 tbsp fried onion

¼ cup water

Basics

6 Portions

12 tbsp sunflower or olive oil

1½ tsp *Garam Masala*
(see p. 2)

3 cups canned,
crushed tomato

4 tbsp *Garlic Paste*
(see p. 8)

4 tbsp *Ginger Paste*
(see p. 8)

3 tsp turmeric

1½ tsp ground chili

4 tbsp ground cumin

1 tbsp ground coriander

1½ tsp paprika

2 tbsp tomato paste

12 tbsp fried onion

1½ cups water

Time

15–20 minutes

Yield

1 or 6 portions,
sufficient for 1½ to 9 lb
of meat

involving lentils are called daal or else are referred to by a name specific to the spices used in the preparation. Meat and vegetable dishes may either be named according to the method of cooking or the particular spices employed in the recipe. To make any curried dish easier to prepare, a curry sauce can be prepared in advance.

• Commercial curry powder is not the same as this curry sauce. It is a spicy mixture of widely varying composition, originally developed by the British before independence as a means of approximating the taste of Indian cuisine at home. Typically it is a yellowish powder, with the main ingredients being ground turmeric, dehydrated onion, red pepper and chili powder, (itself a mixture of chili peppers, cumin, coriander, salt, orageno, garlic powder and cloves), as used in the dish *Chili Con Carne*.

• Beware that commercial fried, dehydrated onions are coated with flour or starch which will change the consistency of the curry sauce significantly. Better results are achieved by making your own fried onions. One cup of freshly chopped, raw onion yields about 3 tbsp of fried, drained onion.

Tomato Sauce

Notes

• All of the tomato sauce used in this book is of the canned variety and should not be confused with tomato ketchup, the sugar-rich condiment. It is best to select the higher quality brands of tomato sauce as cheaper brands can impart a more acidic flavour to this cuisine.

Accompaniments
Pickles, Chutneys, Raitas & Salsa

Peppers in Balsamic Vinegar

Apple & Carrot Pickle

Apple & Mint Chutney

Sweet Mango Chutney

Coconut Chutney

Date & Tamarind Chutney

Homemade Yogurt

Yogurt & Mint Chutney

Mango & Yogurt Chutney

Peach & Mint Raita

Mint & Coriander Raita

Cucumber Raita

Peach Salsa

Peppers in Balsamic Vinegar

Ingredients

1 red bell pepper

1 yellow bell pepper

3 red or green chili peppers

1 tbsp olive oil

2 cloves garlic, finely chopped

¼ tsp salt, or to taste

2 tbsp balsamic vinegar

½ tsp ground chili, optional

1 tsp sugar

Time

20 minutes

Yield

2 cups

Method

1 Wash, remove the stems and julienne (cut into long thin strips) the bell and chilie peppers (seeds removed).

2 Heat the olive oil in a frying pan.

3 Add the bell peppers and chilies and sauté for 3 to 4 minutes.

4 Stir in the chopped garlic and salt, and sauté for 1 minute.

5 Stir in the balsamic vinegar, sugar, and ground chili if desired.

Serving Suggestions

• Serve with any main dish. This dish will keep in the refrigerator for up to two weeks.

Apple & Carrot Pickle

Method

1 Cut the apple, carrots, chilies and bell pepper into long strips (julienne) and put them in a bowl.
2 In another bowl, mix all the ingredients for the dressing.
3 Pour the dressing over vegetables and toss so all are well coated.

Serving Suggestions

- This pickle goes well with many main dishes and will keep in the refrigerator for up to two weeks.

Ingredients

1 Granny Smith apple

2 large carrots

2 green chili peppers, or to taste

½ green bell pepper

½ red bell pepper

Dressing

½ tsp salt

1 tsp ground cumin

1 tsp ground coriander

½ tsp ground chili

½ tsp paprika

1 tbsp white vinegar

1 tbsp olive oil

1 tsp sugar

Time

15–20 minutes

Yield

8–10 servings

apple & mint Chutney

Ingredients

1 or 2 whole red or green
chili peppers

½ tsp salt

1 tart apple, peeled,
cored and chopped

1 tbsp lemon juice

½ cup fresh mint

2 cups fresh coriander leaves

1 tsp sugar

1 tsp olive oil

Time

15 minutes

Yield

1 cup

Method

1 In a blender, purée the chili peppers, salt, apple and lemon juice.

2 Add the mint, coriander leaves, sugar and oil.

3 Blend to a fine paste.

Serving Suggestions

- This chutney is very versatile and can be served as an accompaniment for many entrees or snacks. One or two teaspoons can also be mixed into a cup of yogurt to make a creamed chutney.

- Without the yogurt, this chutney will last for 10 to 12 days in the refrigerator and can be frozen for up to a year.

Notes

- Enjoy the fragrance of summer at any time of year with this easily prepared chutney that goes well with many snacks and barbequed dishes.

Sweet Mango Chutney

Accompaniments

Method

1 Ensure the grated mango measures 1 cup after the liquid is expressed.
2 In a heavy-bottomed pan, heat the oil. Add the cumin seeds, mustard seeds and chilies.
3 As soon as the seeds begin to pop, stir in mango.
4 Cook the mixture for 3 to 5 minutes until the mango is transparent and most of the liquid has evaporated.
5 Add the sugar and cook until the mixture becomes a syrup of one string consistency. Take care not to overcook.
6 Stir in the ground chili and salt. The chutney will thicken as it cools.
7 Pour it into sterilized bottles.

Serving Suggestions

• Serve with any dish. This chutney will last indefinitely (just like jam) in airtight containers in the refrigerator.

Notes

• This is my family's favourite chutney. I make it in bulk every summer when I can buy mangoes in abundance. It lasts me for a whole year.

• See Glossary under **Sugar Syrup**.

Ingredients

1 cup semi-ripe mango, grated and squeezed dry of juice

1 tsp olive or sunflower oil

¼ tsp cumin seeds

¼ tsp mustard seeds

2 small dried red chilies

1¼ cups sugar

½ tsp ground chili

¼ tsp salt

Time

30 minutes

Yield

1 cup

Coconut Chutney

Ingredients

1 cup warm milk,
1%, 2% or 3%

1 cup fine, desiccated
unsweetened coconut

1 tsp sugar

½ tsp salt

½ cup fresh coriander leaves

1 fresh green chili pepper,
or to taste

1 tbsp lemon juice

Time
20 minutes

Yield
2 cups

Method

1 Combine the warm milk, coconut, sugar, and salt in a bowl. Let this stand for 15 minutes.

2 Put coriander leaves, chili pepper and lemon juice in the blender and blend to a smooth paste.

3 Add coconut mixture to the blender and blend for another 2 minutes.

Serving Suggestions

- Serve with *Chicken* or *Beef Kebabs (Malindi Mishkaki)* (p. 75), *Beef Cutlets Stir Fry* (p. 82), *Broiled or Fried Cassava (Mogho)* (p. 33).
- This chutney will last for 10 to 12 days in the refrigerator and can be frozen for up to three months.

Date & Tamarind Chutney

Method

1 Place the dates, tamarind pulp and water in a saucepan and simmer for 30 minutes. Let this cool. Alternatively, the tamarind can be soaked in hot water and left overnight.

2 Mash the pulp and strain it through a sieve to remove the tamarind fibres and pods.

3 Add a little more water to leftover pulp and mix thoroughly. Press through a sieve again.

4 Add jaggery or demerara sugar and boil until the jaggery has melted. Continue to boil for a few minutes. Add the vinegar, ground chili and salt.

5 Strain again. Divide the residual volume into 6 to 8 containers and freeze.

Serving Suggestions

• Serve with any chaat recipe (p. 31), or snacks such as samosas (p. 42), bhajias (p. 37–40), or added to various dishes to give them extra flavour.

• This chutney will last for up to two weeks in the refrigerator and can be frozen for up to a year.

Notes

• I make this chutney and freeze it so it is always on hand when I need it.

• See the Glossary under **Tamarind** and **Jaggery**.

Ingredients

2 cups dates, pitted

1 lb block tamarind pulp

8 cups water

1 cup jaggery, or demerara sugar

½ cup vinegar

2 tsp ground chili, or to taste

1 tsp salt

Time

40–50 minutes

Yield

6 cups

Accompaniments

Homemade Yogurt

Ingredients

4 cups milk,
1% or 2%

1 pkt Yogourmet™

Time

15 minutes,
plus overnight to set

Yield

4–5 servings

Method

1 Bring the milk to a boil and let it cool until slightly warm to touch.

2 Add Yogourmet™ and stir well.

3 Pour the mixture into 2 or 3 small glass bowls and cover.

4 Leave the bowls in a warm place overnight to set.

5 Refrigerate before serving.

Serving Suggestions

• This yogurt will keep in the refrigerator for up to two days.

Notes

• This yogurt can be used as a new starter by adding 2 tbsp of it to 4 cups of milk. Organic yogurt can also be used as a starter.

• Yogourmet™ can be purchased from health food stores.

• I like to make my own yogurt because I can control both the fat content of the milk and its final thickness or consistency.

• I leave my yogurt to set overnight in a cold oven with the oven light on.

• If you wish to make low fat yogurt, dissolve 1 cup of skim milk powder in 4 cups of skim milk. The addition of the powder gives the yogurt a thicker consistency.

Yogurt & Mint Chutney

Method
1 Process all of the ingredients to make a textured paste, similar in consistency to pesto. Add water to adjust the consistency.

Serving Suggestions
• This chutney will last for 10 to 12 days in the refrigerator.

Ingredients
½ tsp *Ginger Paste* (see p. 8)

2 green onions, chopped

¼ cup fresh mint leaves

½ cup fresh coriander leaves

2 tbsp yogurt

2 tsp lemon juice

¼ tsp salt

1 tsp sugar

Time
15 minutes

Yield
1 cup

Mango & Yogurt Chutney

Method
1 Place all of the ingredients in a blender and process until smooth.

Serving Suggestions
• This chutney can be served with any entree or snack. It will last for 8 to 10 days in the refrigerator and can be frozen for up to a year.

Ingredients
1 cup mango flesh

½ cup plain yogurt

½ cup desiccated coconut

1 tsp salt

½ tsp ground chili

Time
15 minutes

Yield
1½ cups

peach & mint Raita

Ingredients

1 × 14 oz can peaches

1 cup plain yogurt

2 tbsp fresh mint, chopped

¼ tsp salt

½ tsp ground cumin

Time

15 minutes

Yield

2 cups

Method

1 Drain the peaches and cut them into fine pieces. Save the juice.

2 Mix the fruit, yogurt, mint, salt and 2 tbsp of saved juice.

3 Sprinkle with ground cumin and serve cold.

Variations

• You can substitute mangoes for the peaches.

Serving Suggestions

• Serve with any spicy meat dish.

• This raita will keep in the refrigerator for 8 to 10 days.

Notes

• *Raitas* are essentially cooling chutneys of yogurt combined with a vegetable or fruit and are common accompaniments to spicy dishes—rather like the cool ocean is to the hot sand in Mombasa.

Mint & Coriander Raita

Method

1 Combine all of the ingredients in a bowl.

Serving Suggestions

- Serve with parothas, (see recipes on p. 140–141), fresh vegetables of your choice, or any spicy dish. This raita will keep in the refrigerator for 8 to 10 days.

Ingredients

1 cup yogurt or sour cream

¼ tsp chili paste, or to taste

¼ tsp ground cumin

¼ tsp paprika

¼ tbsp fresh mint, chopped

½ tbsp fresh coriander leaves, chopped

Time

10 minutes

Yield

1 cup

Cucumber Raita

Method

1 Squeeze the water from the cucumber.
2 Combine all of the ingredients and stir thoroughly.
3 Garnish with coriander leaves.

Variations

- Instead of cucumber, other vegetables can be used such as cauliflower, celery, carrots, broccoli, onion or radish.

Serving Suggestions

- Serve as a side dish with *Rotli* (p. 136) or with entrees. It can also be served as a vegetable dip.
- This raita will keep in the refrigerator for 8 to 10 days.

Ingredients

1 cup plain yogurt

1 cup cucumber, peeled and grated

salt to taste

¼ tsp ground cumin

¼ tsp black peppercorns, freshly ground

½ tsp chili pepper, chopped, or to taste

1 tbsp fresh coriander leaves, chopped

2 tsp fresh mint leaves, chopped

Time

15–20

Yield

2 cups

Accompaniments

Peach Salsa

Ingredients

1 × 14 oz can peaches,
sliced and chopped

3 green onions,
chopped

1 tbsp green bell pepper,
finely chopped

2 tbsp lime juice

½ tsp ground cumin

½ tsp zest of lime

2 tbsp fresh mint leaves,
chopped

salt, to taste

Time

20 minutes

Yield

2 cups

Method

1 Combine all of the ingredients in a bowl and add salt to taste.

Serving Suggestions

• A refreshing fruit salsa which pairs well with grilled chicken, grilled fish or with any other spicy dish.

Appetizers
Salads, Snacks & Bhajia

Avocado, Mango & Almond Salad

Mango & Bell Pepper Salad

Crunchy Vegetable Salad

Potato & Corn Salad

Kachumber

Spicy Bean Salad

Potato Patties (Aloo Tiki)

Fried Tortillas

Spicy Cashews

Paapdi Chaat

Broiled or Fried Cassava (Mogho)

Pav Bhaji

Vegetable Kebabs

Bread & Cheese Bhajia

Spinach Bhajia (Palak Pakora)

Onion Bhajia

Potato (Nylon) Bhajia

Chicken Samosas

avocado, mango & almond Salad

Ingredients

Salad

2 cups mixed salad greens

1 mango, ripe but firm, peeled and sliced

1 red bell pepper, julienned

1 green bell pepper, julienned

2 oranges, segmented

2 avocados

2 tsp lemon juice

½ cup green onions, chopped

½ cup slivered almonds, toasted

Dressing

¼ cup orange juice

1 tsp oil

½ tsp *Garlic Paste* (see p. 8)

2 tsp brown sugar or honey

½ tsp ground cumin

¼ tsp ground coriander

¼ tsp black peppercorns, freshly ground

½ tsp salt

Time

30 minutes

Yield

4 servings

Method

1 Arrange the salad greens in a large, shallow bowl. Arrange the mangoes, bell peppers, and oranges on top of the salad greens.

2 Peel and slice the avocado and coat with lemon juice (to maintain its colour) and arrange on top of the salad. Sprinkle with green onions.

3 Put all of the ingredients for the salad dressing in a jar and shake well.

4 Pour the dressing over the salad and garnish with the toasted almonds.

Notes

• To toast slivered almonds, put the almonds on a baking tray and bake in an oven preheated to 350°F. Toast for a few minutes until nuts are a very light, golden colour. Remove them from the oven and immediately transfer them to a cold plate to prevent burning.

• Tempt your taste buds with the sweetness of mango and oranges, the crunchiness of bell peppers, and the smooth, subtle flavour of avocado. Avocado trees grew well in Nairobi and fruit-laden trees could often be seen right by the roadside. The warm climate of the coast was more suitable for growing oranges and mangoes where one could pick them warm, ripe and ready for eating straight from the tree.

mango & Bell pepper Salad

Method

1 Peel the mango and slice it into thin strips.
2 Slice bell peppers into similar size strips as the mango.
3 Slice the green onions into 1 inch pieces.
4 Julienne the green chilies.
5 Whisk the ground cumin, salt, lemon juice, olive oil, garlic paste, chili flakes, and honey together in a bowl.
6 Add the mango, bell peppers, onions, green chilies, and fresh coriander leaves.
7 Toss gently and set aside for half an hour before serving so that the flavours can mingle.

Variations

• A cup of chopped cabbage can also be added if desired.

Serving Suggestions

• This is a refreshing salad that goes well with *Spicy Baked Chicken* (p. 48), *Mustard Chicken* (p. 49), *Chicken Tikka* (p. 52), *Chicken Kebabs* (p. 53), or *Beef Kebabs (Malindi Mishkaki)* (p. 75), etc.

Ingredients

1 large, semi-ripe mango
½ red bell pepper
½ green bell pepper
4 green onions
2 green chilies, or to taste
2 tsp fresh coriander leaves, chopped
½ tsp ground cumin
½ tsp salt
2 tsp lemon juice
2 tsp olive oil
1 tsp *Garlic Paste* (see p. 8)
2 tsp chili flakes
2 tbsp honey

Time

20 minutes

Yield

4–5 servings

appetizers

Crunchy Vegetable Salad

Ingredients

Salad
1 ¼ cup carrots

½ cup celery sticks

1 cup red bell peppers

1 cup zucchini

1 cup tart apple,
(e.g., Granny Smith)

¼ cup onion,
quartered and sliced

Dressing
1 tsp oil

½ tsp mustard powder

½ tsp black peppercorns,
freshly ground

2 tbsp white vinegar
or apple cider vinegar

¼ tsp salt

1 tsp sugar

½ tsp *Garlic Paste*
(see p. 8)

½ tsp ground coriander

Time
30 minutes

Yield
4–5 servings

Method

Salad
1 Julienne the carrots, celery, peppers, zucchini and apple.

Dressing
1 Put all the ingredients for the dressing into a jar and shake well to mix.

2 Put the salad into a serving bowl, add the dressing, and toss.

Appetizers

Potato & Corn Salad

Method

1 Wash and halve or quarter the potatoes, boil them until cooked, and drain.
2 Mix the corn, tomatoes, green onions and potatoes.
3 Add the dressing, salt and pepper, and toss.
4 Refrigerate for half an hour.

Serving Suggestions

- Serve with *Grilled Salmon* (p. 92).

Ingredients

¾ lb small new potatoes

1 × 11 oz can corn

12 cherry tomatoes, halved

4 green onions, chopped

½ cup low fat Italian dressing

salt and pepper, to taste

Time

50 minutes, including refrigeration

Yield

3−4 servings

Kachumber

Method

1 Cut the carrot, onion, tomato and bell pepper into quarters and slice thinly.
2 Put the vegetables in a bowl. Add the coriander, chili pepper, salt and vinegar or lemon juice and mix well.

Notes

- *Kachumber* is a simple, mixed vegetable relish or spicy salad that can be served with many dishes.

Ingredients

1 carrot

1 onion

1 tomato

¼ green bell pepper

1½ tsp fresh coriander leaves, chopped

1 chili pepper, red or green, chopped, or to taste

salt to taste

1 tbsp vinegar or lemon juice

Time

15 minutes

Yield

2 cups

Spicy Bean Salad

Ingredients

1 x 19 oz can mixed beans
(chick peas, kidney beans)

½ red onion,
chopped

½ each of a red, green
and yellow bell pepper,
chopped

½ cup celery,
chopped

1 tsp *Garlic Paste*
(see p. 8)

1 tsp hot pepper sauce,
or to taste

1 tbsp fresh coriander leaves,
chopped

2 tsp olive oil

1 tsp mustard seeds

1 tsp cumin seeds

5 fresh curry leaves,
chopped

½ cup tamarind sauce
or *Date & Tamarind Chutney*
(see p. 17)

salt and pepper,
to taste

juice of ½ lime or lemon

Method

1 Empty the can of beans into a colander and rinse under cold water.

2 In a large bowl, mix the beans, onion, bell peppers, celery, garlic paste, hot pepper sauce and fresh coriander leaves.

3 Heat the olive oil in a small saucepan with a lid. Add the mustard seeds, cumin seeds and curry leaves. Cover the saucepan.

4 When the seeds start to splutter and pop, pour the oil and the seeds over the salad.

5 Add the tamarind sauce (or the *Date & Tamarind Chutney*), salt and pepper and lemon or lime juice. Toss the salad and serve.

Serving Suggestions

• This salad goes well with barbeques.

Time

30 minutes

Yield

4–5 servings

Potato Patties (Aloo Tiki)

Method

1 In a large bowl, combine the potatoes, cumin, green chilies, coriander leaves, lemon juice, egg, garam masala, salt and chana flour.

2 Mould this mixture into golf balls, and flatten each ball to make a patty.

3 Dip the tikis into the egg and dust with bread crumbs. In a shallow-sided, nonstick frying pan, fry the tikis with a little oil until both sides are golden brown and crisp.

4 Remove the cooked tikis from the pan and place on paper towels to drain the excess oil.

Serving Suggestions

• Serve warm with *Date & Tamarind Chutney* (p. 17), or a hot sauce.

Notes

• Crisp and spicy potato fritters or patties, traditionally called *Aloo Tiki*. They make great little appetizers, and travel well for picnics and lunch boxes.

• See the Glossary for **Chana Flour**.

Ingredients

1 lb potatoes,
boiled and mashed
while still hot

1 tsp ground cumin

2 green chilies,
chopped or to taste

1 tbsp fresh coriander leaves,
chopped

1 tbsp lemon juice

1 small egg

½ tsp *Garam Masala*
(see p. 2)

½ tsp salt

1 tbsp chana flour

1 egg, beaten,
for dipping

bread crumbs,
for dusting

olive or sunflower oil,
for frying

Time

60 minutes

Yield

10 patties

Fried Tortillas

Appetizers

Ingredients

1 lb pkt tortillas

sunflower oil,
for frying

1 tsp salt

1 tsp ground chili

½ tsp citric acid powder

¼ cup sugar

Time
30 minutes

Yield
1 lb fried tortillas

Method

1 Mix the salt, ground chili, citric acid powder and sugar in a small bowl.

2 Cut the tortillas into 3 inch by 1 inch strips.

3 In a deep fryer or wok, fry small batches of tortillas in oil on medium heat until golden brown and crisp. Use a tray lined with paper towel to drain and then sprinkle with salt mixture, to taste.

4 The fried tortillas can be stored in an airtight container for several days.

Notes

• Although not typically East Indian, tortillas are readily available. Samosa pastry can be used instead. The salt mixture imparts a sweet and sour taste. Once fried, this snack is called *Paapdi* and is an ingredient in dishes like *Paapdi Chaat*. (p. 31). *Fried Tortillas* make a change from potato chips.

• See the Glossary under **Citric Acid**.

Spicy Cashews

Ingredients

2 cups cashew nuts

½ tsp ground chili

½ tsp salt

½ tsp black peppercorns,
freshly ground

2 tsp olive oil or butter

Time
45–60 minutes

Yield
2 cups

Method

1 Mix ground chili, salt, black pepper and melted butter or olive oil together.

2 Add cashews to the above mixture.

3 Bake on a tray at 250°F for 45 minutes or until nuts are crisp.

Variations

• You can substitute peanuts, almonds, or pistachios in place of cashews.

Notes

• See the Glossary under **Cashews**.

paapdi Chaat

Method

1 Mix the ground cumin, ground chili, and salt. Sprinkle half over the cooked potatoes and half over the chickpeas.

2 In a bowl, layer the chickpeas first, followed by a layer of potatoes and then the broken tortillas. Top with sev.

3 Sprinkle with onions, coriander leaves and nuts.

Variations

- Green lentils or moong beans, soaked overnight and cooked, can be used instead of chickpeas.

Serving Suggestions

- Serve as a starter or snack with *Apple & Mint Chutney* (p. 14), *Date & Tamarind Chutney* (p. 17), plain or *Homemade Yogurt* (p. 18), and hot sauce of your choice.

Notes

- **Sev** or sevian is a vermicelli, noodle-like product made from besan or chana flour which is fried with canola oil and seasoned with salt and often used as a topping in chaats. (For an explanation of the meaning of *Nylon*, see p. 40).

- *Chevdo* can be used instead of Sev. Chevdo is a spicy blend of flattened, puffed rice called *poha*, deep fried peanuts and tossed with a mix of spices (a masala). Often raisins are added, with toasted fennel seed, ground chili and turmeric. Chevdo is crisp, with a complex flavour that is both salty and sweet. Chevdo is available at Indian grocery stores.

- Tortilla chips may also be sold as *puri* chips and they are available in Indian grocery stores. (See p. 143 for *Puri*).

Ingredients

1 lb potatoes, cut into ½" cubes, boiled

1 × 19 oz can of chickpeas, drained, rinsed

1 tsp ground cumin

½ tsp ground chili

½ tsp salt

1½ cups *Fried Tortillas* (see p. 30)

½ cup nylon sev

¼ cup green onion, chopped

2 tbsp fresh coriander leaves, chopped

¼ cup cashews or peanuts, roasted

Time

30–40 minutes

Yield

4–6 servings

• *Chaat* is a word used across India and Pakistan to refer to small servings of savoury snacks, typically served roadside from small carts or stalls. While some people believe the best chaat in the world is to be found in Delhi, all regions in India have their own styles and would dispute that claim. Most chaat are based on fried dough with a variety of other ingredients, of which the most common include: yogurt, chopped onions and coriander, sev, and *Chaat Masala* (p. 3). These ingredients are combined and served on a small metal plate and sold from chaat carts throughout India. Traditionally, banana leaves were formed into a bowl and used as the container, but this is largely a thing of the past.

Beef Stir Fry with Broiled or Fried Cassava (Mogho)

Broiled or Fried Cassava (Mogho)

Method

1 Cut the cassava into ¾ inch strips; remove any fibrous "strings."

2 Boil the cassava in salted water until it is cooked but still firm. Take care not to overcook. Drain thoroughly and leave it to cool.

To Broil

1 Spread the boiled cassava in a single layer on a greased baking sheet. Lightly brush or spray the cassava with oil.

2 Broil until it is golden brown on both sides, turning once.

3 Sprinkle with the ground chili, salt and citric acid mix. Toss the cassava to coat it with spices.

To Fry

1 When cool, deep fry the cassava in hot oil until golden brown.

2 Drain on paper towels.

3 Sprinkle with the chili powder, salt, and citric acid mix.

Serving Suggestions

• Serve as a snack with *Date & Tamarind Chutney* (p. 17), or with other spicy chutneys of your choice.

Notes

• Fried cassava is enjoyed as a snack throughout East Africa, and it is served everywhere from restaurants to roadside stalls.

• See the Glossary for **Cassava**.

Ingredients

1 lb pkt frozen cassava

water for boiling

½ tsp salt

½ tsp red ground chili

½ tsp salt

½ tsp citric acid powder

2 tsp sunflower or olive oil, to broil

Time

30–40 minutes

Yield

2–3 servings

Pao Bhaji

Ingredients

1 large potato,
peeled and diced

½ cup frozen peas

1 cup zucchini,
peeled and diced

2 carrots,
peeled and diced

8 to 10 French beans,
washed and chopped
into small pieces

2 tsp olive or sunflower oil

2 tbsp butter

1½ cup fresh tomatoes,
finely chopped

1 tsp *Ginger Paste*
(see p. 8)

¼ tsp *Garam Masala*,
or to taste
(see p. 2)

¼ tsp turmeric

¼ tsp ground coriander

½ tsp ground chili

1 tsp sugar

salt to taste

1 tbsp lemon juice

2 tbsp fresh coriander leaves,
chopped and divided

8 to 10 whole wheat buns

½ cup sev

Time

30–40 minutes

Yield

8–10 buns

Method

1 Cook all 5 vegetables separately so they remain firm and are not mushy. Drain all of the vegetables, put them into one bowl and partially mash them so that small pieces of vegetable are still visible.

2 Heat the oil and butter in a nonstick pan. Add the tomatoes and stir until they soften.

3 Add the vegetable mash, ginger paste, garam masala, turmeric, coriander, chili and sugar and sauté over high heat, stirring all the time.

4 Stir in the salt and lemon juice and half of the coriander leaves.

Serving Suggestions

• Slice, toast and butter the buns. To serve "sandwich style," put the vegetable mixture on half the buns, and garnish with chopped coriander leaves and sev, and cover each with the remaining half of each bun. To serve as an "open sandwich," divide the vegetable mixture over all the bun halves, and garnish with chopped coriander leaves and sev.

Notes

• *Pav Bhaji* or *pao bahji* is a specialty Indian dish with origins in Mumbai and Gujarat. In Marathi, the word *pav* means "bread" and *bhaji* means "vegetable mix." The dish is cheap and filling and may be eaten for breakfast, lunch, or dinner. The origin of the dish is traced to the heyday of the textile industry in Mumbai. Mill workers, who did not have time for a full meal at lunch hour and preferring a lighter meal, but still one which was made up of some of the key elements of Indian cuisine, embraced *Pav Bhaji*. The carbohydrate component of rice or rotli was substituted by the *pav* and the curries were amalgamated into one spicy concoction, the *bhaji*.

Vegetable Kebabs

Method

1 Put the rice in a food processor and process for 4 pulses.

2 Add the potatoes, peas, cauliflower and spinach and process for one minute or until everything is finely chopped.

3 Transfer the mixture to a bowl and add the chopped onion, chana flour, salt, turmeric, chili paste, ground cumin, garlic and ginger pastes, coriander leaves and mint (if using). Knead by hand until thoroughly mixed.

4 Take 1 tbsp of the mixture and shape it into a ball. This mixture should make about 22 kebabs. As you make each ball, place it on a cookie tray.

5 Pour oil into a wok or deep fryer. When the oil is hot (375°F), put a few balls at a time into the oil and fry until golden brown. Do not overcrowd the fryer or wok. Do not stir until the kebabs are slightly fried. Stir gently until they are fried and crispy. Remove and drain on paper towels.

6 If you are using a deep fryer, then perhaps 10 to 15 kebabs can be fried together, depending on the size of the fryer.

Serving Suggestions

• Serve hot with any chutney of your choice, as an hors d'oeuvre, or as a snack.

Notes

• See the Glossary for **Turmeric**.

Ingredients

1½ cups cooked rice

1 cup potatoes, peeled and cubed

1 cup frozen peas, thawed

1 cup cauliflower florets

½ cup frozen spinach, thawed and chopped

¼ cup green onion, chopped

½ cup chana flour, sifted

½ tsp salt

¼ tsp turmeric

1½ tsp green *Chili Paste* (see p. 7)

½ tsp ground cumin

½ tsp *Garlic Paste* (see p. 8)

½ tsp *Ginger Paste* (see p. 8)

2 tbsp fresh coriander leaves, chopped

2 tbsp fresh mint leaves, chopped, optional

sunflower oil for frying

Time

60 minutes

Yield

about 22 Kebabs

Vegetable Kebabs

Bread & Cheese Bhajia

Method

1 Mix all of the batter ingredients together in a bowl to make a smooth batter.

2 Press together 1 piece of bread and 1 piece of cheese and dip them in the batter. Deep fry a few bhajia at a time until each one is golden in colour.

3 Drain on paper towel.

Serving Suggestions

- Serve with *Apple & Mint Chutney* (p. 14).

Notes

- *Bhajia* (also *bhujia*) are deep fried fritters, and are also called *pakoras*. The batter is generally based on besan or chana flour and they can contain vegetables (onion, aubergine, potato, spinach, cauliflower, and chilies, etc.), and sometimes fish. Crisply fried bhajia are usually served as appetizers or snacks.

- See the Glossary for **Ajowain**.

Ingredients

Batter

½ cup chana flour

½ cup water

¼ tsp salt

¼ tsp ground cumin

¼ tsp turmeric

¼ tsp crushed ginger

¼ tsp crushed garlic

¼ tsp ajowain seeds

½ tbsp fresh coriander leaves, chopped

Filling

14 squares of sliced bread, cut 1½" × 1½"

14 squares of cheddar cheese, cut 1" × 1" × ¼" thick

oil, for frying

Time

40 minutes

Yield

14 pieces

Appetizers

Spinach Bhajia (Palak Pakora)

Ingredients

50 fresh Spanish spinach leaves, washed

1 cup chana flour

½ tsp ground chili

½ tsp salt

¾ cup water

oil for deep frying

ground cumin

Chaat Masala, optional (see p. 3)

Time

40–50 minutes

Yield

50 pieces

Method

1 Mix the sieved chana flour, ground chili and salt with water to make a medium consistency batter.

2 Heat the oil in a wok or deep fryer. Dip each spinach leaf in the chana batter and fry a few leaves at a time until they are golden brown.

3 Remove the bhajia and drain on paper towel. Repeat for the remaining spinach leaves.

4 Place the spinach bhajia on a plate and sprinkle with ground cumin and *Chaat Masala*, and serve.

Notes

- *Chaat Masala* is available from Indian grocery stores or make your own using the recipe on p. 3.

Onion Bhajia

Method

1 In a bowl mix the chana flour and warm water to make a paste of medium consistency.
2 Add the onion, cumin, turmeric, salt, garlic and chili pastes, coriander leaves and baking powder, and mix well.
3 In a wok or a fryer, heat the oil and fry a few bhajias at a time, by dropping individual heaped teaspoons of the mixture into the oil on medium heat until each bhajia is golden brown.
4 Remove the bhajias from the oil and place on paper towels to drain the excess oil.

Serving Suggestions

• Serve hot as a snack or starter with *Date & Tamarind Chutney* (p. 17) and any hot sauce of your choice.

Ingredients

1½ cups chana flour, sieved

¾ cup warm water

3 cups sliced onion, firmly packed

1 tsp ground cumin

¼ tsp turmeric

¾ tsp salt, or to taste

1 tsp *Garlic Paste* (see p. 8)

1 tsp *Chili Paste* (see p. 7)

2 tbsp fresh coriander leaves, chopped

¼ tsp baking powder

sunflower oil for frying

Time

40 minutes

Yield

2–3 servings

Appetizers

Potato (Nylon) Bhajia

Appetizers

Ingredients

1½ lb potatoes, peeled and thinly sliced, rinsed and drained

1 tsp salt

½ tsp red ground chili

¼ tsp turmeric

½ tsp paprika

2 tbsp fresh coriander leaves, chopped

1 cup chana flour

sunflower oil for frying

Time

30 minutes

Yield

2–3 servings

Method

1 In a bowl combine all of the ingredients, except the chana flour, and mix well. This mixture will be moist from the water in the potatoes and the washed coriander leaves.

2 Add the chana flour gradually to the above mixture while mixing by hand. Add water as required. The flour should be fairly thick and just enough to lightly coat each potato piece.

3 Deep fry a few pieces of potato at a time, dropping each one into the fryer or wok.

4 Remove the cooked bhajias and drain excess oil on paper towel.

Serving Suggestions

• To make bhajia slightly crisp, refry them before serving. Serve with *Date & Tamarind Chutney* (p. 17).

Notes

• *Nylon Bhajia* make a delicious snack. In Nairobi, this dish is also called *Maru Bhajia*, named after a local restaurant owner.

• *Why Nylon?* When garments made of nylon fabric were first introduced in East Africa, they very rapidly came to be judged as the best available. Nylon clothing was sought after and subsequently it was widely distributed and readily available. The word "nylon" entered the vernacular as a term for anything considered to be of the best quality, and thus, *Maru Bhajia* became known as *Nylon Bhajia*, because they were judged by people to be the best bhajia in Nairobi.

Potato (Nylon) Bhajia & Onion Bhajia

Appetizers

Chicken Samosas

Ingredients

1 medium-size chicken,
roasted, skinned,
and deboned

1 tbsp olive oil

1 tbsp *Garlic Paste*
(see p. 8)

1 tbsp *Ginger Paste*
(see p. 8)

2 tsp *Chili Paste*,
or to taste
(see p. 7)

2 tsp ground cumin

1 tsp turmeric

1 tsp ground chili

1½ tsp salt

2 tbsp lemon juice

2 tsp *Garam Masala*
(see p. 2)

2 jalapeno peppers,
finely chopped

2 cups green onion,
finely chopped

1 cup onion,
finely chopped

2 tbsp fresh coriander leaves,
chopped

1 pkt TYJ™ spring roll pastry

4 tbsp all purpose flour

water to make the paste

Time
60–90 minutes

Yield
36 Samosas

Method

1 Chop the chicken meat into very fine pieces; you require 5 cups.

2 Heat the olive oil in a pan.

3 Add the garlic, ginger, and chili pastes, ground cumin, turmeric, ground chili, salt, lemon juice and cook for 2 to 3 minutes. Add the chicken and mix thoroughly. If the mixture is too dry add a little water.

4 Remove from the heat and add the garam masala and transfer to a tray.

5 When this chicken mixture has cooled, add the jalapenos, onions and coriander leaves, mix and set aside.

6 Mix the flour and enough water to make a paste of medium consistency.

7 To wrap the samosas, I use TYJ™ spring roll pastry for wrappers which is available frozen. Use the 9½ × 9½ inch size (30 sheets). Thaw the pastry at room temperature (never thaw in a microwave) and cut into 3 equal strips (Fig. 1) to make 90 wrapper-size sheets 3⅙ × 9½ inches (Fig. 2). Of these, cut 18 sheets into half making 36, 3⅙ × 4¾ inch strips (Fig. 3). Cut off the corners of the remaining sheets and discard (Fig. 4). Keep all of the pastry covered with a damp kitchen towel as they dry out quite quickly.

8 Because the pastry is very thin, use 2½ wrappers (2 long and 1 short to reinforce the pocket) per samosa and fold as shown (Figs. 5 & 6). Fill with about 1 tbsp of the prepared mixture and seal all the layers of the spring roll pastry using a small amount of the flour paste (Figs. 7–9).

9 Fry or bake. *Fry*: Deep fry the samosas on medium until golden brown. A deep fryer is recommended. *Bake*: Spray oil all over the samosas and bake at 350°F in the oven until golden.

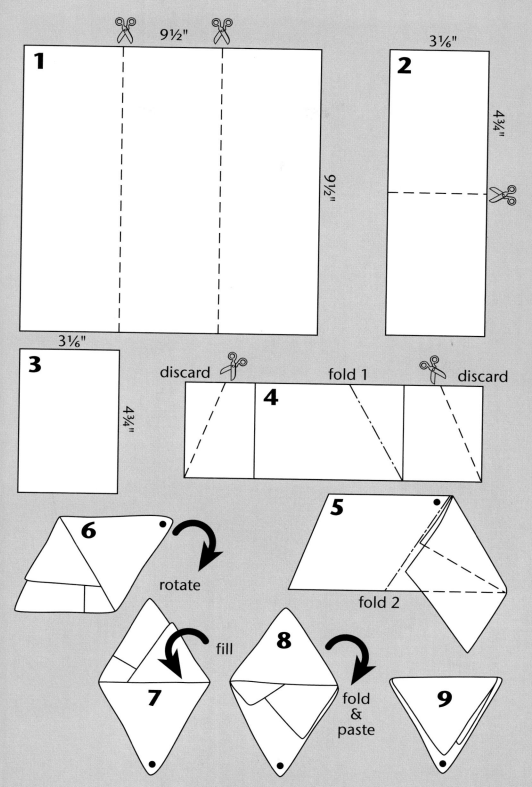

Chicken Samosas

Appetizers

Main Dishes
Chicken

Curried Chicken Submarines*

Hot 'n' Spicy Chicken Wings*

Spicy Baked Chicken

Mustard Chicken

Sweet & Sour Chicken

Chicken Tikka

Chicken Kebabs*

Chicken Drumsticks with Coriander & Chili Peppers

Chicken Thighs with Vegetables*

Chicken with Bell Peppers

Chicken with Bell Pepper Sauce

Chicken in Cardamom Sauce

Chicken in Tomato Sauce*

Chicken Masala

Chicken Moghulai Style

Exotic Chicken & Rice (Pilau)

Chicken Vindaloo

Pakistani Rice with Chicken

Bombay Biryani

Butter Chicken Moghulai Style

* = *Fast & Friendly* recipes which are quick and easy to prepare

Curried Chicken Submarines

Ingredients

1 lb chicken breast, boneless, skinless and thinly sliced

3 tbsp olive oil

1 tbsp tomato paste

¼ cup hot water

1 tsp *Garlic Paste* (see p.8)

1 tsp *Ginger Paste* (see p. 8)

1 tsp *Chili Paste* (see p. 7)

½ tsp paprika

1 tsp ground cumin

½ tsp salt, or to taste

1 tbsp fresh coriander leaves, chopped

6 crispy whole wheat submarine buns

Time

30 minutes
(*Fast & Friendly*)

Yield

6 servings

Method

1 Heat the olive oil in a wok.

2 Sauté the chicken until the water evaporates.

3 Mix the tomato paste and water, and add it to the chicken.

4 Stir in the garlic, ginger, and chili pastes, paprika, cumin, and salt.

5 Cook until the mixture is dry and the chicken is tender.

6 Stir in the freshly chopped coriander leaves.

7 Layer the mixture with long thin slices of cucumber between toasted submarine buns.

Serving Suggestions

• Serve with *Apple & Carrot Pickle* (p. 13), hot sauce and a salad of your choice.

main Dishes

Hot 'n' Spicy Chicken wings

Method

1 Mix all of the ingredients for the marinade.

2 Add the chicken wings and marinate for 2 hours.

3 Spread wings out on a lightly oiled cookie tray and lightly spray them with oil.

4 Broil both sides of wings until cooked.

5 To make the hot sauce, melt the butter/ghee in a saucepan. Add the coriander, black pepper, Louisiana sauce and cook for a couple of minutes until the sauce thickens.

6 Coat the chicken wings with the sauce and serve.

Serving Suggestions

• Serve hot as an appetizer with celery and carrot sticks, and ranch dip/dressing.

Notes

• See the Glossary for **Ghee**.

Ingredients

2 lb chicken wings, wash, split and pat dry with paper towels

Marinade
1 tsp red ground chili

1½ tsp *Garlic Paste* (see p. 8)

1½ tsp *Ginger Paste* (see p. 8)

1 tsp salt

Hot Sauce
2 tbsp melted butter or ghee

1 tbsp fresh coriander leaves, chopped

½ tsp black peppercorns, freshly ground

1½ cups Louisiana Hot Sauce™

Time

30–40 minutes, not including marination (*Fast & Friendly*)

Yield

4 servings

main Dishes

Spicy Baked Chicken

Ingredients

2 lb chicken pieces

Marinade

2 tsp tomato paste

1½ tsp *Ginger Paste* (see p. 8)

1½ tsp *Garlic Paste* (see p. 8)

2 tsp olive oil

½ tsp salt, or to taste

½ tsp ground chili

1 tbsp lemon juice

1 tbsp light soy sauce

½ tsp paprika

½ tsp green *Chili Paste*, optional (see p. 7)

½ tsp ground cumin

Time

50–60 minutes, not including marination

Yield

4 servings

Method

1 Skin and rinse the chicken pieces, and pat dry with paper towels. Make long diagonal slits in the meat.

2 Combine all the ingredients for marinade and marinate the chicken for a minimum of 3 hours or overnight in the refrigerator.

3 Spread the chicken pieces on a lightly oiled cookie tray and lightly coat the chicken with oil.

4 Broil the chicken pieces for a few minutes, turning once so they are light brown on both sides.

5 Cover chicken with foil and bake at 350°F for 20 to 25 minutes, or until the chicken is fully cooked. The chicken can also be barbequed.

Serving Suggestions

• Serve with *Spicy Potatoes* (p. 107), *Spicy Green Beans* (p. 120), *Naan* (p. 138), and your choice of salad. Kept cool after cooking, it's a tasty dish for picnics and potlucks.

mustard Chicken

Method

1 Marinate the chicken in black pepper, salt, garlic, ginger and chili pastes, and mustard powder. Set aside for 2 hours.

2 Brown chicken (a few pieces at a time) in hot oil in a wok.

3 Drain oil.

4 Return chicken to the wok, add tomato sauce and vinegar, and cook on low heat for 2 minutes.

5 Arrange the chicken pieces in an ovenproof serving dish and pour the remaining sauce from the wok over the chicken.

6 Bake in an oven preheated to 350°F for 15 to 20 minutes or until the chicken is tender. The sauce should be thick and sticking to the chicken.

Serving Suggestions

• Serve with a salad of your choice, *Spicy Potatoes* or *Fries* (p. 107), *Spicy Mushrooms, Baby Corn & Cauliflower* (p. 115), or *Spicy Green Beans* (p. 120), and *Naan* (p. 138).

Notes

• See notes on *Tomato Sauce* on p. 10.

Ingredients

2¼ lb chicken pieces, skinned and washed

Marinade

1 tsp black peppercorns, freshly ground

1 tsp salt

1 tsp *Garlic Paste* (see p. 8)

1 tsp *Ginger Paste* (see p. 8)

½ tsp *Chili Paste*, or to taste (see p. 7)

1 tsp mustard powder

2 tbsp tomato sauce

½ cup vinegar

olive oil, for browning

Time

50–60 minutes, not including marination

Yield

4–5 servings

main Dishes

Sweet & Sour Chicken

Ingredients

2 lb chicken breast,
boneless and skinless

Marinade
1 tsp *Garlic Paste*
(see p. 8)

1 tsp *Ginger Paste*
(see p. 8)

1 tbsp honey

1 tsp salt

1 tsp red chili pepper flakes

4 tsp olive oil

½ tsp turmeric,
optional

1 tsp paprika

Time

30–40 minutes,
not including marination

Yield

4 servings

Method

1 Slice each chicken breast in two, horizontally, to reduce the thickness of the meat.

2 Combine all the ingredients except the chicken in a bowl, then place chicken in the mixture to marinate for 2 hours or overnight.

3 Place the chicken in a lightly oiled ovenproof pan and bake at 400°F for 10 minutes. Then reduce heat to 350°F and bake for another 15 minutes, or until the chicken is well done.

Serving Suggestions

• Serve with *Avocado, Mango & Almond Salad* (p. 24) as a light lunch or with *Kashmiri Rice* (p. 135).

main Dishes

Sweet & Sour Chicken

Chicken Tikka

Ingredients

2 lb chicken breast,
boneless and skinless

Marinade
2 tbsp plain yogurt

2 tsp *Garlic Paste*
(see p. 8)

2 tsp *Ginger Paste*
(see p. 8)

1 tsp green *Chili Paste*
(see p. 7)

2 tbsp tomato paste

1 tsp salt,
or to taste

1 tbsp olive oil

½ tsp ground chili,
optional

bamboo skewers,
water soaked

PAM® cooking spray

Time
30–40 minutes,
not including marination

Yield
4–5 servings

Method

1 Cut the chicken into 1 inch cubes.

2 In a bowl, mix the yogurt, garlic, ginger, chili, and tomato pastes, salt, oil and ground chili (if used).

3 Add the chicken to the marinade. Mix thoroughly and refrigerate for about 4 hours.

4 Soak the bamboo skewers in water for at least 2 hours (skewers only need soaking if made of bamboo).

5 Thread 5 to 6 marinated chicken cubes onto each skewer. Place these side by side on a cookie tray and spray with cooking spray.

6 Broil 6 inches away from the broiler until the chicken is golden brown.

7 Turn the chicken and spray again with cooking spray and broil the other side.

8 If the meat is not cooked, wrap in foil and bake in the oven at 350°F for 10 to 15 minutes.

Serving Suggestions

• Serve hot with your choice of salad, *Date & Tamarind Chutney* (p. 17), any raita of your choice (p. 20–21), and *Naan* (p. 138).

Notes

• **Tikka** which is a Hindi word for "chunks of meat cooked on skewers," therefore similar to kebabs, is one of the most popular chicken dishes in the world. In Nairobi, *Chicken Tikka* was a favourite family snack when we went to the drive-in movie theatre.

• *Chicken Tikka* can also be barbequed.

• See notes on *Tomato Sauce* on p. 10.

main Dishes

Chicken Kebabs

Method

1 Combine the ground chicken, yogurt, garlic, ginger, and chili pastes, salt, cumin, egg, breadcrumbs and coriander leaves. Mix well.

2 Divide the mixture into golf ball sized spheres and shape into 18 to 20 thumb-sized kebabs.

3 Arrange these in a single layer on a lightly oiled tray, and spray the kebabs with oil.

4 Broil on high, 6 to 8 inches from the broiler, turning when required until both sides are broiled and cooked.

Variations

- You can substitute ground turkey for the ground chicken.

Serving Suggestions

- Serve with your choice of salad, chutneys, raita and *Naan* (p. 138).

Ingredients

1 lb ground chicken

1 tbsp yogurt

¾ tsp *Garlic Paste* (see p. 8)

¾ tsp *Ginger Paste* (see p. 8)

½ tsp *Chili Paste* (see p. 7)

½ tsp salt

½ tsp ground cumin

1 egg

½ cup bread crumbs

1 tbsp fresh coriander leaves, chopped

Time

30–40 minutes (*Fast & Friendly*)

Yield

2–3 servings

main Dishes

Chicken Drumsticks with Coriander & Chili Peppers

Ingredients

2 lb chicken drumsticks, skinned

½ cup fresh coriander leaves, firmly packed

2 fresh green chilies, or to taste

1 tsp *Garlic Paste* (see p. 8)

1 tsp *Ginger Paste* (see p. 8)

½ tsp *Garam Masala* (see p. 2)

2 tbsp lemon juice

1 tbsp olive oil

1 tsp salt

Time

60 minutes, not including marination

Yield

4 servings

Method

1 Make cuts through the flesh on both sides of the drumsticks about 1 inch apart and down to the bone.

2 In a blender, purée the coriander leaves, chilies, garlic and ginger pastes, garam masala, lemon juice, olive oil and salt. Add water if needed.

3 Marinate drumsticks in the masala purée. Cover and refrigerate for 2 hours or overnight.

4 Place the drumsticks on a baking tray. Bake uncovered in an oven preheated to 350°F for about 40 minutes, until they are well browned and cooked. Turn once after 20 minutes.

Serving Suggestions

• Serve with a salad of your choice and naan.

Notes

• Chicken requires marinating for a minimum of 2 hours or overnight.

Main Dishes

Chicken Thighs with Vegetables

Method

1 Remove the skin and any visible fat from the thighs.

2 Rinse the chicken and pat dry with paper towels.

3 In a nonstick frying pan, heat the olive oil to medium heat, add the garlic and ginger pastes and sauté for ½ minute.

4 Add the chicken and brown the thighs on both sides.

5 Add the salt and water and cook covered, on low heat, until chicken is tender. Stir in the tomato sauce, ground cumin and ground chili.

6 Cut each zucchini into 4 pieces lengthwise and slice each quarter piece into 1½ inch lengths.

7 Add the zucchini to the chicken and cook covered until the zucchini is tender. Add a little water if necessary, but the sauce should be thick and the zucchini will release water as it cooks.

Serving Suggestions

• Serve with any salad of your choice and *Naan* (p. 138).

Notes

• Vegetables other than zucchini can be used.

• See notes on *Tomato Sauce* on p. 10.

Ingredients

2 lb chicken thighs

4 tsp olive oil

2 tsp *Garlic Paste* (see p. 8)

2" piece fresh ginger root, slivered

1 tsp salt

1 cup water

½ cup tomato sauce

1 tsp coarsely ground cumin

½ tsp red ground chili

2 small zucchini

Time

60 minutes (*Fast & Friendly*)

Yield

4–5 servings

main Dishes

Chicken with Bell Peppers

Main Dishes

Ingredients

1 lb chicken breast, boneless and skinless

1½ tsp *Garlic Paste* (see p. 8)

1 tsp *Ginger Paste* (see p. 8)

½ tsp *Chili Paste* (see p. 7)

1 tsp ground cumin

½ tsp ground coriander

½ tsp turmeric

½ tsp paprika

¾ tsp salt

1 tsp black peppercorns, freshly ground

3 tbsp olive oil

1 tsp cumin seeds

1½ tbsp fried onion

1½ cups fresh tomato, finely chopped

1 green chili, chopped

½ each of a green, red and yellow bell pepper, sliced

¼ cup half-and-half cream (10% MF) or yogurt

½ tsp *Garam Masala* (see p. 2)

2 tbsp fresh coriander leaves, chopped

Method

1 Cut the chicken into 1 inch cubes.

2 Mix the garlic, ginger and chili pastes with the ground cumin, coriander, turmeric, paprika, black pepper and salt in a small bowl.

3 Heat the olive oil in a nonstick wok. Add the cumin seeds and sauté for ½ minute. Add the onion and give everything a good stir.

4 Stir in the spice mixture and sauté for a minute.

5 Add the fresh tomato and cook for another 5 minutes.

6 Add the chicken and cook until the meat is tender. Sprinkle hot water, a little at a time, if needed.

7 Add the green chili and bell peppers and cream and cook until the oil separates.

8 The gravy should be thick and stick to the chicken.

9 Sprinkle garam masala and coriander leaves on top before serving.

Serving Suggestions

• Serve with *Saffron Rice* (p. 133), and *Naan* (p. 138).

Time

30–40 minutes

Yield

2–3 servings

Chicken with Bell Pepper Sauce

Method

1 Marinate the chicken for 3 hours in a mixture of garlic, ginger, and chili pastes and yogurt.
2 Place marinated chicken in a pot. Add the water, salt and kashmiri masala paste.
3 Bring to a boil.
4 Reduce the heat to medium and cook until the chicken is tender, stirring occasionally.
5 Heat the olive oil in another pot and add the tomato paste and cumin, sauté for a couple of minutes.
6 Add the puréed bell pepper and cook for a few minutes, then add this mixture to the chicken.
7 Cook on low heat for 5 minutes and then add the pre-cooked potatoes and simmer for a couple of minutes, adding water if needed. The sauce should cover the chicken.
8 Serve garnished with freshly chopped coriander leaves.

Serving Suggestions

- Serve with *Naan* (p. 138), or any rice dish of your choosing.

Ingredients

1½ lb chicken pieces, skinned and washed

Marinade
1½ tsp *Garlic Paste* (see p. 8)
1½ tsp *Ginger Paste* (see p. 8)
½ tsp *Chili Paste* (see p. 7)
1½ cups plain yogurt

Sauce
2 cups water
1 tsp salt, or to taste
1 tbsp *Kashmiri Masala* (see p. 4)
1 tbsp olive oil
4 tbsp tomato paste
1½ tsp ground cumin
1 large red or green bell pepper, puréed
2 medium potatoes, each cut into 8 pieces, fried or roasted
1 tbsp fresh coriander leaves, chopped

Time

60–75 minutes, not including marination

Yield

4 servings

main Dishes

Chicken in Cardamom Sauce

Ingredients

2 lb chicken breast, boneless and skinless, cut into strips

3 tbsp olive oil

1½ tsp cardamom seeds, coarsely ground

1 tsp ground chili

½ tsp turmeric

1 tsp paprika

1 tbsp tomato paste

1 tsp salt

1 cup plain yogurt

1 tbsp fresh coriander leaves, chopped

Time

30 minutes
(*Fast & Friendly*)

Yield

4–5 servings

Method

1 Heat the olive oil, add the cardamom and sauté for one minute.

2 Add the chicken and sauté for five minutes.

3 Stir in the ground chili, turmeric, and paprika, tomato paste and salt, and cook until chicken is tender.

4 Stir in the yogurt, one tablespoon at a time, and simmer, stirring until all the yogurt has been added.

5 The mixture should be quite thick. If not, remove the chicken with a slotted spoon and reduce the gravy, and then replace the chicken.

6 Garnish with fresh, chopped coriander leaves just before serving.

Serving Suggestions

• Serve with *Naan* (p. 138) and any chutneys of your choice.

Main Dishes

Chicken in Tomato Sauce

Method

1 Wash the chicken and cut it into 2 inch strips.

2 Heat the olive oil in a frying pan and sauté chicken for 3 to 4 minutes.

3 Stir in the garlic and ginger pastes, ground chili, salt and black pepper. Sauté for 1 minute.

4 Stir in the tomato sauce and cook until chicken is tender. Add a little water if needed. The mixture should be fairly dry.

5 Sprinkle with freshly chopped coriander leaves and serve.

Variation

- Reduce tomato sauce to 1 tbsp and add 1 tbsp yogurt, or ½ tbsp coconut powder mixed with 1 tbsp water.

Serving Suggestions

- Serve hot with salad, rice or any vegetable.

- See notes on *Tomato Sauce* on p. 10.

Ingredients

1 lb chicken breast, boneless and skinless

2 tsp olive oil

¾ tsp *Garlic Paste* (see p. 8)

¾ tsp *Ginger Paste* (see p. 8)

½ tsp ground chili, or to taste

½ tsp salt, or to taste

¼ tsp black peppercorns, freshly ground

2 tbsp tomato sauce

½ tbsp fresh coriander leaves, chopped

Time

20–30 minutes
(*Fast & Friendly*)

Yield

2 servings

main Dishes

Chicken masala

Ingredients

2 lb chicken,
skinless, cut into small pieces

Marinade
½ tsp *Ginger Paste*
(see p. 8)
½ tsp *Garlic Paste*
(see p. 8)
½ tsp *Chili Paste*
(see p. 7)
½ tsp salt

Masala
5 tbsp olive oil
1 tbsp coarsely ground cumin
4 fresh tomatoes,
blended (about 2 cups)
6 tbsp canned tomato,
crushed
1 tsp paprika,
optional
2 tsp *Garlic Paste*
2 tsp *Ginger Paste*
½ tsp *Chili Paste*,
or to taste
1 tsp salt
1 tsp *Garam Masala*
(see p. 2)
1 tbsp lemon juice
1 cup fresh coriander leaves,
chopped, divided

Time
2 hours,
not including marination

Yield
4–5 servings

Method

1 Marinate the chicken in the garlic, ginger, and chili pastes and salt for 3 hours or overnight.

2 Arrange the chicken pieces in a single layer on a greased, foil-lined tray. Spray with oil, and broil until light brown on both sides, remove from the oven and set aside.

3 In a heavy-bottomed pan, heat the olive oil on medium.

4 Add the cumin and sauté for ½ a minute.

5 Add the fresh and canned tomatoes, paprika, garlic, ginger, and chili pastes, and salt, and cook for 10 minutes or until dry.

6 Add the broiled chicken, and ½ cup of water. Cook on low until chicken is done.

7 Stir in the garam masala, lemon juice and ½ of the coriander leaves.

8 Serve garnished with the rest of the coriander leaves.

Serving Suggestions
• Serve with *Naan*, *Rotli*, or *Parotha* (p. 136–142).

Notes
• At step 6, you can add 2 tsp of dried fenugreek leaves (*Kasoori Methi*) or 2 tbsp of fresh fenugreek leaves. The aroma of *Kasoori Methi* is more pungent, but either fresh or dried fenugreek enhances the delicious taste of this dish.

• **Fenugreek**, either fresh or dried, is usually available at Indian grocery stores.

• See Glossary under **Fenugreek**.

main Dishes

Chicken Moghulai Style

Method

1 Cut the chicken into bite-sized pieces.

2 Heat oil in a saucepan and add the chopped onion. Sauté the onions until they are lightly browned (If using previously fried onion, sauté for ½ a minute and be careful not to burn).

3 Mix the garlic, ginger, tomato sauce, and tomato paste in a bowl. Add the mixture to the fried onion and cook for 1 minute

4 Add the ground chili and cumin and salt.

5 Stir in the yogurt, a spoonful at a time.

6 Add the chicken and cook for 5 minutes.

7 Stir in the chicken bouillon dissolved in water, and simmer covered until chicken is cooked.

8 Add the coconut milk, garam masala and coriander leaves, and simmer uncovered for 5 minutes. The sauce should be quite thick and just covering the chicken.

Serving Suggestions

• Serve with *Plain Rice* (p. 132), and *Naan* (p. 138).

Notes

• The *Moghulai style* comes from northern India, including the Hindi belt and the states of Bihar, Uttar Pradesh, Haryana and Punjab, and Madhya Pradesh, throughout which there is a huge diversity of cuisine, including some which is rich in dairy products and grain and others, such as the Jain style, which are predominantly vegetarian. The region is home to the tandoori (clay oven) and dum-pukth (sealed clay pots on low heat) styles of cooking. Tandoori chicken and naan are both from this style of cooking. Regional favourites also include a variety of kebabs and biryani dishes.

• See notes on *Tomato Sauce* on p. 10.

Ingredients

2 lb chicken breast, boneless and skinless

2 tbsp olive oil

1 cup fresh onions, chopped
or
3 tbsp fried onion

2 tsp *Garlic Paste* (see p. 8)

2 tsp *Ginger Paste* (see p. 8)

1 cup tomato sauce

2 tsp tomato paste

½ tsp ground chili

2 tsp ground cumin

1 tsp salt, or to taste

1½ cups yogurt

2 chicken bouillon cubes

½ cup water

½ cup coconut milk

½ tsp *Garam Masala* (see p. 2)

2 tbsp fresh coriander leaves

Time

60 minutes

Yield

4–5 servings

main Dishes

Exotic Chicken & Rice (Pilau)

Ingredients

1½ lb chicken pieces, skinned and washed

2 cups basmati rice

2 tbsp olive oil

1 medium onion, chopped

1 to 3 whole green chilies, slit

1 tsp cumin seeds

½ tsp *Garam Masala* (see p. 2)

1½ tsp *Garlic Paste* (see p. 8)

1½ tsp *Ginger Paste* (see p. 8)

1 cup tomato, finely diced

½ cup yogurt

1 tbsp lemon juice

2½ tsp salt, divided

2 tbsp fresh coriander leaves, chopped and divided

For later use

6 pieces of potato, 2" × 2½" (fried or roasted)

1½ cups fried onion

or

6 cups fresh onions, sliced and oil for frying

⅛ tsp yellow food colouring, powdered

20 strands of saffron

Time

90 minutes

Yield

5–6 servings

Method

1 Wash and soak the basmati rice for 10 minutes.

2 In a large pot, heat the olive oil and add the onion. Sauté until it is a light golden brown.

3 Stir in the chilies, cumin seeds, garam masala, garlic and ginger pastes. Sauté for ½ minute.

4 Stir in the tomato, yogurt, lemon juice and 1 tsp salt.

5 Add the chicken and simmer until it is almost cooked.

6 Add enough water to make 4 cups of liquid in the mixture. When it starts to boil, add the rice, 1 tbsp coriander leaves, and 1½ tsp salt.

7 Cook partially covered over medium heat for about 5 minutes. Reduce heat to low and continue cooking for about 15 minutes or until most of the water has been absorbed. Simmer until the remaining water evaporates.

8 If you are using fresh onions, fry the onions in a separate pan until golden brown. Remove with a slotted spoon and spread on paper towels to remove excess oil. Set the onions aside for later use. Skip this step if using previously fried onions.

9 In ¼ cup of water, stir in the food colour and saffron, and then set aside.

10 In another ovenproof pot or casserole, make a layer with half of the cooked chicken and rice mixture (pilau). Top with ½ of the potatoes and sprinkle with ½ the fried onions and ½ the coloured water.

11 Add the balance of the pilau and potatoes and cover again with onions and colour. (The reason the pilau, potatoes, onions and the colour are divided is so that all components are equally infused with flavour and colour).

12 Cover the casserole and cook in a preheated oven (300°F) for 15 to 20 minutes.

13 Garnish with coriander leaves just before serving.

main Dishes

Serving Suggestions

- Serve hot with *Kachumber* (p. 27) and a raita of your choice or plain yogurt.

Notes

- A *pilau* or *pulao* dish is one in which rice is cooked in a well-seasoned broth with onions and tomatoes and usually poultry, game, shellfish or vegetables. Saffron imparts a special flavour to this particular recipe. The best results are achieved if fresh fried onion is used instead of commercially fried onion.

main Dishes

Chicken Vindaloo

Ingredients

1½ lb chicken pieces, skinned and washed

1½ tbsp desiccated coconut

1½ tsp ground coriander

1½ tsp ground cumin

¾ cup onions, chopped

1½ tsp *Garlic Paste* (see p. 8)

1½ tsp mustard seeds

4 dry, whole red chilies

1/4 cup white wine vinegar

4 tbsp canned tomatoes, crushed

2 tbsp olive oil

1 tsp salt, or to taste

1 tsp *Garam Masala* (see p. 2)

2 cups hot water

1 tbsp fresh coriander leaves, chopped

Time
60 minutes

Yield
3–4 servings

Method

1 Broil the desiccated coconut until it is lightly browned.

2 Allow the coconut to cool and then blend it together with the coriander, cumin, onions, garlic, mustard seeds, red chilies, white wine vinegar and crushed tomatoes into a paste.

3 Heat oil in a saucepan. Add the paste and cook until oil separates (about 5 minutes).

4 Add the chicken, salt, and garam masala. Cook until the chicken is tender.

5 Add 2 cups of hot water and simmer for 5 minutes.

6 Garnish with chopped coriander leaves.

Serving Suggestions

• Serve with chapattis or *Naan* (p. 138) and a rice dish of your choice.

Notes

• Originally, *vindaloo* was a Portuguese dish which was named because the main ingredients were "vinho" (wine/wine vinegar) and "alhos" (garlic). Over time, spices were added to the dish by the indigenous people of the former-Portuguese colony of Goa. In the west, vindaloo dishes tend be among the hotter and more spicy of curry dishes with the addition of more chilies, they are often prepared with diced potato, lemon for tartness, and black pepper for additional pungency.

• This is a fiery hot and very spicy Goan dish. However, you may make it with any meat and as hot or as mild as you desire by increasing or reducing the amount of chilies. This particular recipe is moderately spicy.

Main Dishes

Pakistani Rice with Chicken

Method

1 Cut the chicken breast into bite-sized cubes.

2 Rinse the rice and soak it for 10 to 15 minutes.

3 Cook the rice in 4½ cups of water and 1 tsp of salt for 15 minutes until the rice is nearly cooked

4 Drain the rice and set it aside.

5 Heat the butter in a pan, add the chicken and sauté until it is cooked. Sprinkle with water if needed.

6 Add the mixed vegetables, ½ tsp salt and cook until tender.

7 Add the green onion, bell and chili peppers and the beaten egg and stir until the egg is cooked.

8 Add the partially cooked rice, sprinkle with a little water and coriander leaves, and fold gently.

9 Bake in an oven preheated to 325°F for 20 minutes, or until the rice is fully cooked.

Serving Suggestions

- Serve with *Beef Shish Kebabs with Sauce* (p. 76). If you wish, you can omit the chicken from the above recipe when serving it with the Shish Kebabs.

Ingredients

½ lb chicken breast, boneless and skinless

1½ cups basmati rice

1½ tsp salt, divided

4 oz butter

1¼ cups mixed vegetables (e.g., peas and carrots)

6 to 8 green onions, chopped

½ green bell pepper, cubed

½ red bell pepper, cubed

1 egg, beaten

1 or 2 chili peppers, red or green, or to taste

¼ cup fresh coriander leaves

Time

40–50 minutes

Yield

5–6 servings

main Dishes

Bombay Biryani

Ingredients

2 lb frying chicken,
skinless, cut into pieces

Marinade

1 cup yogurt

1½ tsp *Garlic Paste*
(see p. 8)

1½ tsp *Ginger Paste*
(see p. 8)

1 tsp *Chili Paste*,
or to taste (see p. 7)

1 tsp salt

15 strands of saffron

Biryani

2 tbsp olive oil

1 cup fried onions
or 4 cups fresh onions,
thinly sliced

½ tsp cumin seeds

1 cup fresh tomatoes,
finely chopped

1 tsp ground cumin

2 tsp tomato paste

2 tbsp lemon juice

½ tsp *Special Garam Masala*
(see p. 2)

2 tbsp fresh coriander leaves,
chopped

¼ tsp yellow food
colouring powder,
mixed in ¼ cup water

½ cup warm olive oil
or ghee

Potatoes

2 large potatoes,
cut into 8 pieces

¼ tsp salt

¼ tsp paprika powder

2 tsp olive oil

- The chicken should be marinated for several hours or overnight before cooking.
- Ingredients are listed under the different steps, so read the recipe in its entirety to make sure you have everything you need before you start. At the final stage, the various components of the dish are layered in a casserole dish that is covered with a lid and baked in the oven.

Method

Chicken

1 Marinate the chicken in yogurt, garlic, ginger and chili pastes, salt, and saffron for 2 to 3 hours or overnight.

Potatoes

1 Peel the potatoes, cut them into quarters and coat with salt, paprika, and oil.

2 Bake or broil in a preheated oven at 500°F for 15 minutes or until golden brown and partly cooked—this is for colour only. The potatoes will finish cooking when the dish is combined and baked in the oven.

Rice

1 Wash and soak rice for 15 minutes

2 In a pot, boil water, salt, and lemon juice.

3 Add the rice and cook on medium heat for 10 minutes (so rice is partially cooked).

4 Drain the rice and set it aside.

To assemble the Biryani

1 Heat 2 tbsp of olive oil in an ovenproof pot large enough to hold all the chicken, potatoes and rice.

2 Add ¼ cup fried onions and sauté until brown again. (Note: Pre-fried onions lose their colour, so fry them again to maintain a golden brown colour). Be careful not to burn the onions. If using fresh onions, sauté on medium heat until golden

Main Dishes

noorbanu Nimji

Bombay Biryani

Ingredients

Rice

2½ cups basmati rice

8 cups water

2 tsp salt

1 tbsp lemon juice

Time

90–120 minutes,
not including marination

Yield

4–5 servings

in colour. You will need more oil for fresh onions to fry properly. You can reduce the amount of oil after the onions are fried.

3 If using fresh onions, remove about ¾ cup of the onions after frying with a slotted spoon, and drain it on paper towels so the onions become crisp. Set this aside for later use.

4 Leave 2 tbsp of oil in the pot. Add the cumin seeds, tomatoes, cumin powder, tomato paste, and lemon juice and sauté for 2 minutes.

5 Stir in the raw, marinated chicken and all of the marinade.

6 Remove from the heat. At this point the chicken is not cooked, but it will cook when everything is combined and put into the oven later.

7 Layer potatoes on top of the chicken, and sprinkle them with half of the remaining onions, the special garam masala and lastly the coriander leaves.

8 Cover the garnished potatoes with half of the rice. Sprinkle the rice with the rest of the fried onions, ¼ cup of warm olive oil or ghee, ¼ cup of water, and half of the food colouring.

9 Add the balance of the rice.

10 Sprinkle the rice with another ¼ cup of water, the remaining food colouring and ¼ cup warm oil or ghee. (The reason the rice, onions, oil and colour are divided is so that all of the rice becomes equally infused with flavour and colour)

11 Cover the pot and make sure the lid fits tightly.

12 Place the pot in a preheated oven at 450°F for 30 minutes.

13 Reduce heat to 350°F and bake for another 30 minutes.

14 Remove the pot from the oven and, using a spoon, check the mixture at the bottom of the pot. There should be very little liquid. If there seems to be more than a ½ cup of liquid, uncover the pot and return it to the stove on medium high heat to reduce the liquid. Also ensure the chicken is completely cooked.

Main Dishes

Serving Suggestions

• To serve the Biryani, make a bed of rice and cover it with the potatoes and chicken. Serve with *Cucumber Raita* (p. 21), plain yogurt and *Kachumber* (p. 27).

Notes

• *Biryani* originated in Persia and, at its simplest, was a rice and meat dish cooked together. Cooks to the Moghul emperors took the dish and transformed it into a delicacy by adding spices and other exotic Ingredients. There are many versions of this casserole-type dish containing meat or fish or vegetables and rice. The addition of saffron or turmeric gives biryani a characteristic flavour and aroma. A traditional biryani is time consuming to prepare but it is often made and served on festive occasions.

main Dishes

Butter Chicken Moghulai Style

Ingredients

x5 5½lb 1½ lb chicken breast, boneless and skinless

Marinade

x5   15   3 tbsp yogurt
x5   7   1½ tsp *Garlic Paste* (see p. 8)
   7   1½ tsp *Ginger Paste* (see p. 8)
   10   2 tsp tomato paste
x5   2½   ½ tsp *Chili Paste* (see p. 7)
   2½   ½ tsp paprika
   5   1 tsp ground cumin
   1¼   ¼ tsp ground chili
   1¼   ¼ tsp *Garam Masala* (see p. 2)
   pinch saffron
   3/4   ¾ tsp salt

Sauce

¼ cup onion, roughly chopped
two 2" × 1" pieces of bell pepper, red and green
¾ cup water, divided
¼ cup butter
1 cup tomato sauce
2 tsp dried fenugreek leaves
1¼ cups whipping cream or, to reduce fat content, 1 cup sour cream and 2 tbsp whipping cream

Time
45 minutes

Yield
4–5 servings

Method

1 Cut the chicken into 1 × 1 × ½ inch pieces.
2 In a large bowl, combine all of the marinade ingredients.
3 Add the cubed chicken and marinate 3 to 4 hours or overnight in the refrigerator.
4 Put the onion, green and red bell peppers, and ¼ cup water in a blender, purée and set aside.
5 Heat the butter in a saucepan.
6 Add the puréed onion/pepper mixture and sauté for 2 to 3 minutes.
7 Add the marinated chicken and any remaining marinade, and cook stirring for 5 minutes.
8 Add the tomato sauce and continue cooking until the chicken is tender.
9 Add the fenugreek leaves and more water as required.
10 Add the whipping cream or whipping cream/sour cream substitute.
11 There should be enough gravy to just cover the chicken. Add more fluid: water, milk, or cream as required.
12 Simmer until the mixture starts to boil and reduce the heat. Do not cover and do not over-boil.

Variations

• As an alternative to stovetop cooking, the chicken can be threaded on skewers and barbequed or broiled.

Serving Suggestions

• Serve with *Saffron Rice* (p. 133) and *Naan* (p. 138).

Notes

• See notes on *Tomato Sauce* on p. 10.

main Dishes

Butter Chicken Moghulai Style

main Dishes

Personal notes

Main Dishes
Beef & Lamb

Beef Turnovers

Beef Kebabs (Malindi Mishkaki)

Beef Shish Kebabs with Sauce

Beef Stir Fry (Mishkaki)

Barbequed Beef Ribs

Beef & Pigeon Peas with Rice (Bharazi Khavo)

Beef Cutlets Stir Fry

Beef Nihari

Lamb Chops

Lamb Masala

Lamb Rhogan Josh

Beef Turnovers

Ingredients

1 lb ground beef

½ cup hot water

½ tsp salt

1½ tsp *Garlic Paste* (see p. 8)

1 tsp *Ginger Paste* (see p. 8)

1¼ tsp *Chili Paste* (see p. 7)

1 tsp ground cumin

¼ tsp turmeric

2 tsp lemon juice

5 tbsp fresh coriander leaves

5 tbsp green onion, chopped

5 tbsp red banana pepper, chopped

2 eggs, beaten

salt and pepper to taste

5 large tortillas

1 tbsp butter

Time

30–40 minutes

Yield

5 Turnovers

Method

1 Place the ground beef and water in a pot and simmer, stirring to remove all lumps, until the beef is cooked.

2 Add salt, garlic, ginger and chili pastes, the ground cumin, turmeric, and lemon juice.

3 Cook until this mixture is quite dry and divide the mixture into 5 portions.

4 Add salt and pepper to the beaten eggs and set aside.

5 Butter one side of a tortilla and place it buttered-side down in a frying pan on medium-low heat.

6 Place one portion of the prepared meat on half of the tortilla. Sprinkle 1 tbsp of coriander leaves, 1 tbsp of green onion and 1 tbsp of banana peppers on top of the meat.

7 Drizzle 1 tbsp of egg on top and fold the tortilla to make a half-moon shape.

8 Cook the tortilla, pressing the turnover with a spatula so that the egg cooks and the tortilla is golden brown on the bottom.

9 Flip it over and cook the other side until it is also golden brown. If the tortilla begins to brown too quickly and the egg is not cooking, then lower the heat and cook more slowly.

10 When both sides are golden brown and the egg is cooked, flip the turnover out onto a plate.

11 Cut the turnover into 4 triangular quarter pieces by cutting it in half, and each half in half again.

12 Repeat steps 5 to 11 with the other 4 tortillas.

Variations

• Substitute ground chicken for the ground beef or a medley of cooked vegetables.

Serving Suggestions

• Serve as a starter or light lunch along with your choice of salad or vegetables.

main Dishes

Beef Kebabs (malindi mishkaki)

Method

1 Cut the beef into ¾ inch pieces.

2 Marinate in ground chili, olive oil, lemon juice and garlic paste for at least 4 hours or overnight.

3 Add the salt and toss.

4 Thread the beef onto skewers and barbeque.

Serving Suggestions

• Serve with hot sauce and tamarind chutney, a green salad and naan.

Notes

• This recipe was given to me many years ago by an old man in Malindi. He had a small coffee store with just a few tables and a few chairs but people used to line up for his mishkaki that he cooked on hot charcoal. We used to travel to Mombasa three times each year for family holidays and we always drove up to Malindi especially to eat mishkaki.

• Mombasa is a coastal town about 300 miles from Nairobi and Malindi is a smaller community a few miles outside Mombasa.

Ingredients

2 lb beef,
sirloin grilling steak

1 tbsp ground chili

2 tbsp olive oil

2 tbsp lemon juice

½ tsp *Garlic Paste*
(see p. 8)

1 tsp salt

Time

20–30 minutes,
plus marination time

Yield

4–5 servings

main Dishes

Beef Shish Kebabs with Sauce

Ingredients

1 lb lean ground beef

2 slices brown bread

½ cup grated onion

1½ tbsp coriander leaves, chopped and divided

½ tsp *Garlic Paste* (see p. 8)

1 tsp *Ginger Paste* (see p. 8)

½ tsp *Chili Paste* (see p. 7)

½ tsp salt

½ tsp ground chili, or to taste

1 tsp ground cumin

1 small egg

½ tsp *Garam Masala* (see p. 2)

Sauce

5 tbsp canned tomatoes, crushed

1 tsp tomato paste

1 tbsp Worcestershire sauce

½ tsp *Chili Paste*

1 tbsp light soy sauce

½ tsp *Garlic Paste*

½ tsp *Ginger Paste*

½ tsp salt

1 tbsp lemon juice

2 tbsp fresh coriander leaves

½ red and green bell pepper, cut into ½" slices

Method

To make the Kebabs

1 Remove the crusts and process the bread until it crumbles. Transfer the bread into a bowl and set it aside.

2 Put the onion and half of the coriander leaves in the food processor and process for 1 minute.

3 Add the ground beef, garlic, ginger and chili pastes, salt, the ground chili and cumin, egg and garam masala and process for another minute.

4 Put the beef mixture into a bowl with the bread crumbs.

5 Mix well by hand, and then divide into 24 balls.

To bake the Kebabs

1 Line an oven tray with foil, and spray with oil.

2 Thread one ball onto a skewer and shape the meat mixture into a thumb-sized kebab around the skewer. Then slide out the skewer. (The ground beef kebabs actually cook better off the skewer because there's nothing for the meat to stick to.)

3 Place the meat kebabs on the tray and broil at least 6 inches away from the heat for about 4 minutes each side, or until kebabs are thoroughly cooked.

Sauce

1 In a pot, mix all of the sauce ingredients except the red and green pepper and cook until thick. Add the peppers and ½ a cup of hot water and cook for a couple of minutes.

2 Add kebabs and juice from the pan and gently mix. Let it simmer on low heat for 2 to 3 minutes. Sprinkle with the remaining coriander leaves.

Time

40–50 minutes

Yield

2–3 servings

Serving Suggestions

• Serve with *Pakistani Rice with Chicken* (p. 65), or *Lemon Rice with Cashews* (p. 134), and *Naan* (p. 138).

Main Dishes

Barbequed Beef Ribs

Method

1 Combine all of the ingredients except the beef ribs.

2 Coat each rib with the marinade. Marinate overnight (8 hours) in the refrigerator in a covered container.

3 Barbeque the ribs according to your preference.

Serving Suggestions

- Serve with your choice of salad, chutneys, potatoes and vegetables.

Ingredients

1½ lb short beef ribs
½" thick

Marinade

1 tsp *Garlic Paste*
(see p. 8)

1 tsp *Ginger Paste*
(see p. 8)

1 tsp ground chili

1 tsp ground cumin

1 tsp ground coriander

2 tbsp lemon juice

1 tbsp white vinegar

¼ tsp black peppercorns, freshly ground

¾ tsp salt

2 tbsp oil

Time

30 minutes,
not including marination

Yield

3−4 servings

main Dishes

Beef Stir Fry (Mishkaki)

Main Dishes

Beef Stir Fry (Mishkaki)

Method

Mishkaki

1 Cut the beef into 1 inch cubes.

2 Marinate in the mishkaki marinade overnight.

3 Thread the beef onto skewers and barbeque.

4 Remove from the skewers and set aside.

Stir Fry

1 Heat the olive oil in a wok and stir fry the onion until transparent.

2 Add the bell peppers and sauté for another 2 minutes.

3 Stir in the salt, black pepper, garam masala, ground cumin, and chili, and mix well.

4 Add the mishkaki and mix well.

Variations

• You may substitute chicken in place of the beef.

Serving Suggestions

• Serve hot as a meal, with *Date & Tamarind Chutney* (p. 17), *Yogurt & Mint Chutney* (p. 19), *Mango & Bell Pepper Salad* (p. 25), *Fried or Broiled Cassava* (p. 33), or *Spicy Potatoes* (p. 107), and *Naan* (p. 138).

Ingredients

1½ lb beef,
sirloin grilling steak

Marinade

1½ tsp *Garlic Paste*
(see p. 8)

1½ tsp *Ginger Paste*
(see p. 8)

1 tbsp lemon juice

1 tbsp olive oil

½ tsp ground chili

¾ tsp salt

Stir Fry

2 tsp olive oil

¾ cup onion,
sliced lengthwise

1 cup red bell peppers,
sliced lengthwise

¼ tsp salt

¼ tsp black peppercorns,
freshly ground

¼ tsp *Garam Masala*
(see p. 2)

½ tsp ground cumin

¼ tsp ground chili,
or to taste

Time

30 minutes,
not including marination

Yield

3–4 servings

main Dishes

Beef & Pigeon Peas with Rice
(Bharazi Khaoo)

Ingredients

Beef & Pigeon Peas

1lb stewing beef
or a sirloin grilling steak
cut into ¾" cubes

1 tsp *Ginger Paste*
(see p. 8)

1 tsp salt,
divided

1 cup water

1 × 19 oz can pigeon peas,
drained

2 tbsp olive oil

½ cup onions,
finely chopped

½ cup fresh tomatoes,
finely chopped

1½ tsp *Garlic Paste*
(see p. 8)

¼ cup yogurt

1½ tsp ground cumin

½ tsp paprika

2 chili peppers,
preferably serranos

two pieces red bell pepper,
1 × 1¼" cut into ¼" slices

1 cup milk

2 tbsp coconut cream powder

1 tbsp lemon juice

½ tsp *Garam Masala*
(see p. 2)

1 tbsp fresh coriander leaves,
chopped

Method

Beef & Pigeon Peas

1 Place the beef, ginger paste, salt, and water in a pot and cook on low, until the meat is tender (about 1½ hours.) There should be ½ cup of beef stock remaining. If there is more, then continue simmering to reduce the volume. (A pressure cooker will reduce the cooking time.)

2 In another pot, heat the olive oil, add the onions and sauté until the onions are a light golden colour.

3 Add the tomatoes, garlic paste, yogurt, salt, cumin and paprika. Cook for 3 to 4 minutes or until the tomatoes are cooked.

4 Add the beef, pigeon peas, chili peppers and red bell peppers.

5 Mix the milk and coconut cream powder together and add this to the beef and pigeon peas, stirring as you go.

6 Continue cooking until the stew thickens.

7 Add the lemon juice, garam masala and coriander leaves.

main Dishes

Rice

1 Wash and soak rice for 10 minutes.
2 Heat olive oil in a pot. Add the onion and sauté until transparent.
3 Stir in the garlic paste, salt and turmeric, and sauté for a minute.
4 Add the water and coconut cream powder, and let the mixture boil for 2 to 3 minutes.
5 Add the rice and cook for 5 minutes.
6 Lower the heat to minimum and simmer until the rice is cooked and all the water has been absorbed.
7 Simmer until the rice is dry.

Serving Suggestions

• Top the rice with the beef and bharazi and serve with *Apple & Carrot Pickle* (p. 13) and *Kachumber* (p. 27).

Rice

1½ cups basmati rice

2 tsp olive oil

¼ cup onion, chopped

½ tsp *Garlic Paste* (see p. 8)

1¼ tsp salt

¼ tsp turmeric

3 cups water

½ tbsp coconut cream powder

Time

120 minutes, including rice

Yield

6–8 servings

main Dishes

Beef Cutlets Stir Fry

Ingredients

1 lb lean ground beef

2 slices whole wheat bread

1 small onion

1 tsp *Garlic Paste* (see p. 8)

1 tsp *Ginger Paste* (see p. 8)

½ tsp ground chili

1 small egg

1 tsp ground cumin

½ tsp black peppercorns, freshly ground

¼ tsp *Garam Masala* (see p. 2)

½ tsp salt, or to taste

2 tbsp fresh coriander leaves, chopped

Stir Fry

2 tsp olive oil

1 cup onion, sliced lengthwise

2 cups bell pepper, red, green and yellow mix

½ tsp salt

¼ tsp black peppercorns, freshly ground

¼ tsp ground chili

¼ tsp *Garam Masala*

2 tbsp fresh coriander leaves, chopped

Time

30–40 minutes

Yield

2–3 servings

Method

Beef Cutlets

1 Remove the crusts from the bread. Use a food processor to blend the crustless slices to crumbs. Set aside.

2 Add the onion and process for 1 minute.

3 Add ground beef, bread crumbs, garlic and ginger pastes, ground chili, egg, cumin, black pepper, garam masala, salt and coriander leaves and very briefly process again for ½ a minute until all the ingredients are just mixed. Alternatively, you can mix the ingredients by hand.

4 Divide the mix into 15 equal balls.

5 Flatten each ball to make a patty about 2½ inches wide.

6 Broil each patty for 3 to 5 minutes until they are browned on both sides. Set aside.

Stir Fry

1 In a wok heat the olive oil and sauté the onion until it is slightly soft.

2 Add the bell peppers and sauté for 2 to 3 minutes.

3 Stir in the salt, black pepper, ground chili, garam masala and the cutlets.

4 Fold everything until mixed well.

5 Sprinkle with coriander leaves.

Serving Suggestions

• Serve with *Naan* (p. 138) and your choice of salad.

Beef Nihari

Method

1 Cut the beef into large chunks.

2 Heat the butter in a pot that is oven safe.

3 Brown the beef in the butter.

4 Add the crushed tomatoes and cook for 2 minutes.

5 Add the yogurt and cook for another 2 minutes.

6 Add the garlic, ginger and chili pastes, ground cumin, turmeric, paprika, and fried onions.

7 Stir fry until the oil starts to separate.

8 Add hot water and place in an oven preheated to 325°F or cook on the stove top, on low heat, for 4 to 5 hours, until the meat is well cooked and tender.

9 Add the beef consommé, salt and hot water to make 5 to 6 cups of gravy in the mixture.

10 Mix the flour and water together and stir into the mixture to thicken the gravy.

11 Cook for 3 to 4 minutes.

12 Add the garam masala and coriander leaves.

Serving Suggestions

- Serve with *Naan* (p. 138), chilies, ginger, green peppers and fried onions on the side. Individuals can choose from these garnishes to satisfy their personal taste.

Notes

- Known as the breakfast curry, because *Nihari* is traditionally eaten in the early hours of the morning as a breakfast or brunch before a day of manual labour, this spicy stew made from beef or lamb and curry originated as a dish of the upper class Muslim community in Delhi. Subsequently it was introduced to wide popularity in Pakistan. In time, the dish passed to other classes as Muslim ascendency and power declined after the waning of Mughal power during the mid- to late-18th century, when many families from the Mughal nobility

Ingredients

1½ lb beef, sirloin tip

4 tbsp butter

3 tbsp canned tomatoes, crushed

1 tbsp plain yogurt

1 tsp *Garlic Paste* (see p. 8)

2 tsp *Ginger Paste* (see p. 8)

½ tsp *Chili Paste* (see p. 7)

1 tsp ground cumin

½ tsp turmeric

1 tsp paprika

2 tbsp fried onions

1 × 13 oz can beef consommé

1 tsp salt, or to taste

5 cups hot water

1½ tbsp whole wheat flour

¼ cup water

1 tsp *Special Garam Masala* (see p. 2)

2 tbsp fresh coriander leaves, chopped

Garnish

¼ cup chopped chilies

½ cup green bell peppers, chopped

½ cup fresh ginger, slivered

½ cup fried onion

Time

5–6 hours

Yield

4 servings

Main Dishes

became impoverished. Traditional *Nihari* recipes, of which there are myriad variations of spiciness and texture, all require 5 to 6 hours of cooking time in addition to the time required to prepare the ingredients. Preparation and cooking today usually takes less time, since more tender cuts of meat are used and chicken has been substituted for the beef or lamb. However, no connoisseur or aficionado of *Nihari* will ever accept the dish being made with anything other than tender beef.

Lamb Chops

Ingredients

2 lb lamb chops

Marinade
1½ tsp *Garlic Paste* (see p. 8)
1½ tsp *Ginger Paste* (see p. 8)
3 tbsp light soy sauce
2 tbsp sweet chili pepper sauce
1 tbsp lemon juice
½ tsp salt, or to taste
2 tbsp olive oil

Time

30–40 minutes, not including marination

Yield

4 servings

Method

1 Combine and whisk all of the ingredients for the marinade.

2 Coat the lamb chops with marinade and marinate for a minimum of 3 hours or overnight in the refrigerator.

3 Broil the chops on a baking tray or over a barbeque.

Serving Suggestions

• Serve with *Spicy Potatoes* (p. 107), and *Naan* (p. 138), and your choice of salad.

Main Dishes

Lamb Chops

main Dishes

Lamb Masala

Ingredients

2 lb boneless, lean lamb

½ cup vinegar

2 tbsp olive oil

1 cup onion, chopped

2 tsp *Garlic Paste* (see p. 8)

2 tsp *Ginger Paste* (see p. 8)

½ tsp green *Chili Paste* (see p. 7)

1 cup tomatoes, finely chopped

2 tsp tomato paste

½ tsp turmeric

2 tsp coarsely ground cumin

½ tsp *Garam Masala* (see p. 2)

2 tbsp fresh coriander leaves, finely chopped

Time

2 hours

Yield

4–5 servings

Method

1 Cut the lamb into 1 inch cubes. (Have your butcher do this for you by deboning a leg or shoulder and cutting it up as if for stewing.)

2 Marinate the lamb in a bowl of water and ½ cup vinegar for 20 minutes.

3 Drain the lamb and set it aside.

4 Heat the olive oil in a heavy-bottomed pan.

5 Add the onion and sauté until it turns transparent.

6 Reduce the heat and continue cooking until the onion turns golden brown.

7 Add the garlic, ginger, and chili pastes and sauté for a minute.

8 Add the tomatoes and cook for 5 minutes.

9 Add the lamb and cook covered on low heat until the meat is tender, adding water as required. Alternatively, it can be cooked covered in the oven at 350°F for 1½ hours or until tender. Check periodically, adding water if required.

10 When the lamb is cooked, add the tomato paste, turmeric and cumin and cook further on the stove until the oil starts to separate, which indicates that the curry is ready.

11 Garnish with the garam masala and coriander leaves.

12 If there is excess oil in the curry it can be removed before serving.

Variations

• Substitute grilling sirloin of beef for the lamb.

Serving Suggestions

• Serve with *Rotli* (p. 136), *Naan* (p. 138), or *Parotha*, (p. 140–142).

Lamb Rhogan Josh

Method

1 Mix the lamb with garlic, ginger, and chili pastes, vinegar and yogurt, and set it aside to marinate for 2 hours or overnight.

2 Heat the olive oil in a heavy-bottomed pan. Add the onion and sauté on high heat until the onions soften, then reduce the heat and sauté until golden brown.

3 Add the marinated lamb and cook for 5 minutes.

4 Stir in the ground cumin and coriander, tomato paste, ground chili, turmeric, and simmer covered for 1½ hours until the meat is tender. Alternatively, the dish can be placed in an oven preheated to 325°F and cooked for 1½ hours until meat is tender. Check the fluid level at intervals and add water as required. The cooking time depends on the quality of the meat.

5 Stir in the garam masala, salt, chopped coriander and mint leaves, and simmer for 5 minutes on the stovetop.

6 The gravy should be fairly thick.

Variations

- You can substitute beef (sirloin tip) for the lamb.

Serving Suggestions

- Serve hot with *Rotli* (p. 136), or *Naan* (p. 138).

Notes

- Originally a Kashmiri dish but equally at home in Punjab, an authentic *Rhogan Josh* will be made with lamb and, at its most elaborate, contain dozens of spices. Both Kashmiri and Punjabi versions are highly spiced and share a deep red colour derived from the liberal use of dried, red Kashmiri chilies and, more recently, in other parts of the world, tomatoes and fresh coriander leaves.

Ingredients

1½ lb lamb, cut into 1" cubes

Marinade

1½ tsp *Garlic Paste* (see p. 8)

1½ tsp *Ginger Paste* (see p. 8)

½ tsp green *Chili Paste* (see p. 7)

1½ tbsp vinegar

1 cup yogurt

Sauce

2 tbsp olive oil

2 cups onion, finely chopped

2 tsp ground cumin

1½ tsp ground coriander

2 tbsp tomato paste

½ tsp ground chili, or to taste

¼ tsp turmeric

1 tsp *Garam Masala* (see p. 2)

¾ tsp salt

2 tbsp fresh coriander leaves, chopped

1 tbsp fresh mint, chopped

Time

120 minutes, not including marination

Yield

4 servings

main Dishes

Lamb Rhogan Josh

Main Dishes

Main Dishes
Seafood

Tuna Cakes

Dry Tuna Curry

Grilled Salmon*

Spicy Basa with Spinach

Basa Curry

Basa in Orange Sauce*

Halibut in Rich Creamy Masala

Prawns & Halibut in Coconut Cream

Garlic & Pepper Prawns*

Prawns in Fresh Coriander Leaves

Kashmiri Prawns*

Prawns Vindaloo

* = *Fast & Friendly* recipes which are quick and easy to prepare

Tuna Cakes

Ingredients

2 × 6 oz cans tuna,
flaked

1 lb potatoes,
boiled and mashed

2 tbsp fresh coriander leaves,
chopped

¼ tsp *Chili Paste*,
or to taste (see p. 7)

1 tsp *Garlic Paste*
(see p. 8)

1 tsp ground cumin

½ tsp black peppercorns,
freshly ground

1 tsp salt

1 cup bread crumbs,
for coating

1 egg,
beaten

4 tbsp sunflower oil
(to fry all 12 cakes)

Time
20–30 minutes,
with pre-cooked potatoes

Yield
12 Cakes

Method

1 Drain and press the tuna with a wooden spoon to remove as much liquid as possible.

2 Mix the tuna, potatoes, coriander leaves, chili and garlic pastes, cumin, black pepper and salt.

3 Divide the mixture into 12 golf ball sized spheres and flatten these into small patties.

4 Dip the patties into the egg and then dust with bread crumbs.

5 Heat oil in a frying pan and fry the cakes until both sides are golden brown and crisp.

Serving Suggestions:

• Serve with a salad of your choice and *Apple & Mint Chutney* (p. 14), or *Date & Tamarind Chutney* (p. 17) for a light lunch.

main Dishes

Dry Tuna Curry

Method

1 In a small pan, heat the olive oil, add the onions and sauté until transparent.

2 Add the potatoes and sauté for 2 minutes.

3 Add the canned crushed tomatoes, ground cumin, turmeric, paprika, and salt to taste.

4 Simmer until the potatoes are cooked.

5 Sprinkle with extra water if needed.

6 Add the bell pepper, chili pepper, lemon juice, coriander leaves and tuna and cook for 2 minutes. (The mixture should be quite dry).

Serving Suggestions

• Serve as a meal with *Rotli* (p. 136), or *Naan* (p. 138).

Ingredients

1 × 6 oz can chunked tuna, drained

1 tbsp olive oil

½ cup onion, chopped

½ cup potatoes, peeled and chopped

1½ tbsp canned tomatoes, crushed

½ tsp ground cumin

¼ tsp turmeric

¼ tsp paprika

⅓ tsp salt, or to taste

1 × 2" piece red bell pepper, julienned

1 chili pepper, preferably serrano, divided into half and cut into 1" long pieces

2 tsp lemon juice

1 tbsp fresh coriander leaves, chopped

Time

30 minutes

Yield

2 servings

main Dishes

Grilled Salmon

Ingredients

2 × 5 oz salmon fillets

1 tbsp olive oil

1 tsp ground coriander

¼ tsp ground chili,
or to taste

1 tsp ground cumin

½ tsp mustard powder

½ tsp *Garlic Paste*
(see p. 8)

1 tbsp lemon juice

salt and pepper to taste

Time

40–50 minutes
(*Fast & Friendly*)

Yield

2 servings

Method

1 Mix the olive oil, ground coriander, chili and cumin, mustard powder, garlic paste, lemon juice, salt and pepper.

2 Brush the salmon fillets with the above mixture and leave to marinate for 30 minutes.

3 Broil the fish 4 to 5 minutes on each side, or until cooked.

Servings Suggestions

• Serve with *Spicy Potatoes* (p. 107), and your choice of salad.

Notes

• Instead of broiling, the salmon can be baked in an oven preheated to 400°F for 10 to 15 minutes.

main Dishes

Spicy Basa with Spinach

Method

1 Rinse and dry the fish on paper towels, and cut into 2 inch pieces.

2 Marinate the fish in salt and lemon juice for 10 minutes.

3 Brush a little olive oil on the fish and broil it on both sides for 3 to 4 minutes. Set aside.

4 Heat the balance of the olive oil in a wok.

5 Stir in the mustard seeds, cumin seeds, curry leaves and chilies.

6 As soon as the seeds start spluttering, stir in the tomato sauce, ground cumin, chili and coriander, turmeric, black pepper and garlic paste, and sauté until nearly dry.

7 Add the spinach, lemon juice, salt, sugar and ½ cup of water. Cook for 3 to 4 minutes.

8 Add the fish and all the juice from broiling, and cook until most of the liquid has evaporated and the fish is cooked. Do not stir the fish, if you stir the fish at this point, it will break. Gently push the fish around in the wok with a wooden spoon to prevent sticking.

9 Sprinkle with freshly chopped coriander leaves and serve.

Serving Suggestions:

• Serve hot with *Spicy Baked Fries* (p. 106), *Rotli* (p. 136), or *Naan* (p. 138). Daal and rice could also be served with this dish.

Notes

• See notes on *Tomato Sauce* on p. 10.

Ingredients

1 lb basa steaks or fillets, or any other white fish

¼ tsp salt

2 tsp lemon juice

2 tbsp olive oil, divided

½ tsp mustard seeds

½ tsp cumin seeds

6 curry leaves

3 dried red chilies

½ cup tomato sauce

1½ tsp ground cumin

¼ tsp ground chili

½ tsp ground coriander

½ tsp turmeric

¼ tsp black peppercorns, freshly ground

2 tsp *Garlic Paste* (see p. 8)

2 or 3 oz of a pkt frozen spinach, thawed

2 tbsp lemon juice

½ tsp salt

1 tsp sugar

½ cup water

2 tbsp fresh coriander leaves, chopped

Time

30 minutes

Yield

2–3 servings

main Dishes

Basa Curry

Ingredients

1 lb basa fillet,
½" to ¾" thick,
or any other white fish

½ tsp salt,
divided

2 tsp vinegar

4 tbsp canned tomatoes,
crushed

1 tsp *Garlic Paste*
(see p. 8)

½ tsp *Chili Paste*
(see p. 7)

¼ tsp turmeric

¼ tsp paprika

1 tsp ground cumin

1 tbsp fried onion

1 cup hot water

2 tbsp olive oil

½ tsp cumin seeds

½ tsp *Garam Masala*
(see p. 2)

1 tbsp fresh coriander leaves,
chopped

Time

20–30 minutes

Yield

2–3 servings

Method

1 Wash the fish, pat it dry and cut it into 2 inch pieces.

2 Sprinkle the fish with ¼ tsp salt and vinegar and marinate for 10 minutes.

3 In a bowl, mix the crushed, canned tomatoes with ¼ tsp salt, garlic and chili pastes, turmeric, paprika, cumin, and fried onion, and set aside.

4 Heat the olive oil in a saucepan. Add the cumin seeds and stir for ½ a minute.

5 Add the mixture from Step 3.

6 Sauté for 5 minutes, until the oil starts to separate.

7 Add the fish and cook for 2 minutes. Do not stir. Gently move fish with a wooden spoon to prevent it from sticking to the bottom of the pan.

8 Add 1 cup of water. Cook for 6 minutes, or until fish is cooked.

9 Sprinkle with garam masala and freshly chopped coriander leaves and serve.

Serving Suggestions

• Serve with *Cumin-scented Rice* (p. 133), *Rotli* (p. 136), or *Naan* (p. 138).

main Dishes

Basa in Orange Sauce

Method

1 Grate the zest from half an orange and set it aside. Peel and slice the orange. In a nonstick frying pan, arrange the slices as a bed for the fish.

2 Place the pieces of fish on the orange slices and sprinkle with salt, pepper and orange zest.

3 Cover and cook on low heat for about 6 minutes or until done.

4 Remove the fish from the pan and put on a serving dish.

5 Put the remaining ingredients from the pan together with a ¼ cup of water, the lemon juice and sugar into a blender. Blend and strain.

6 Return the sauce to the pan and bring it to a boil.

7 Pour the sauce over the fish.

8 Garnish with freshly chopped coriander leaves and serve.

Serving Suggestions

• Serve with *Spicy Baked Fries* (p. 106), *Spicy Green Beans* (p. 120), or *Lemon Rice with Cashews* (p. 134), and *Naan* (p. 138).

Notes

• If desired, you can substitute ½ cup of orange juice (pulp included) for the orange slices.

Ingredients

1 lb basa fillet,
or any other white fish,
cut into 4 to 8 pieces

½ orange,
zested and sliced

¼ tsp salt

¼ tsp black peppercorns,
freshly ground

1 tsp lemon juice

¼ cup water

½ tsp sugar

1 tsp fresh coriander leaves,
chopped

Time

30 minutes
(*Fast & Friendly*)

Yield

2 servings

main Dishes

Basa in orange Sauce

main Dishes

Halibut in Rich Creamy Masala

Method

1 Cut the fish into 2 inch pieces.
2 In a pan, add the olive oil and sauté the onion on medium heat until it is a light golden brown.
3 Stir in the garlic, ginger, chili and tomato pastes, cumin and coriander, salt, and tomato sauce and cook for 5 minutes.
4 Add the fish and cook covered for about 3 minutes.
5 Add the cream and lemon juice, stirring gently so that the fish does not break. Simmer for 2 minutes or until the fish is cooked.
6 Garnish with fresh, chopped coriander leaves and serve.

Variations

- To reduce the fat content, replace the whipping cream with 1 cup of skim evaporated milk mixed with 1 cup skim milk powder.
- You may use any white fish you like. If you select halibut, you may have to debone and skin the steaks before cutting them into pieces.

Serving Suggestions

- Serve with *Plain Rice* (p. 132), and *Naan* (p. 138).

Notes

- See notes on *Tomato Sauce* on p. 10.

Ingredients

2 lb halibut, thick, boneless fillets

1 tbsp olive oil

½ cup onions, finely chopped

1 tsp *Garlic Paste* (see p. 8)

1 tsp *Ginger Paste* (see p. 8)

½ tsp *Chili Paste* (see p. 7)

1 tsp tomato paste

2 tsp ground cumin

2 tsp ground coriander

1 tsp salt

1 cup tomato sauce

1 cup whipping cream

1 tbsp lemon juice

2 tbsp fresh coriander leaves, chopped

Time

20–30 minutes

Yield

3–4 servings

Main Dishes

Prawns & Halibut in Coconut Cream

Ingredients

½ lb prawns, peeled, cleaned, deveined

½ lb halibut, cut into 2" × 2" pieces, discard bones

Marinade

1 tbsp olive oil, divided

1 tsp *Garlic Paste* (see p. 8)

½ tsp *Chili Paste*, or to taste (see p. 7)

½ tsp salt

1 tbsp lemon juice

½ tsp ground cumin

½ red bell pepper, chopped

½ green bell pepper, chopped

1 × 14 oz can coconut milk

pinch turmeric

1 tbsp fresh coriander leaves, chopped

Time

40–60 minutes, excluding time required to clean prawns

Yield

3–4 servings

Method

1 To make the marinade, mix 1 tsp of olive oil, garlic, and chili paste, salt, lemon juice and cumin.

2 Divide the marinade evenly between the fish and prawns and let each sit for at least 30 minutes.

3 Spread the fish on a greased baking tray, spray with oil, and broil for 2 to 3 minutes on each side.

4 Heat 1 tsp of olive oil in a wok and sauté the shrimp for 2 minutes until they curl and turn pink. Remove the prawns from the wok and set aside.

5 In the same wok, heat the remaining 1 tsp oil and sauté the bell peppers. Remove these and set them aside.

6 Add coconut milk, turmeric and any remaining marinade or pan juice to the wok.

7 Simmer the fluids for 10 to 12 minutes or until sauce thickens.

8 Add the fish and cook for 2 to 3 minutes.

9 Add the shrimp and cook for 2 minutes.

10 Garnish with the freshly chopped coriander leaves and serve.

Serving Suggestions

• Serve with rice and your choice of pickles and *Coconut Chutney* (p. 16).

Notes

• A touch of the tropics—seafood in a spicy coconut sauce. This dish always reminds me of family picnics on the white sandy beaches of Mombasa. There we used freshly caught kingfish and prawns purchased from the fishermen as they dragged their catch out of the sea. While waiting for the fish to cook to perfection, we would drink the sweet, cool milk of *Madafus*—the young coconuts which were freshly picked from the palm trees and sold by hawkers on the beach.

Garlic & Pepper Prawns

Method

1 Melt the butter in a wok.
2 Add the remaining ingredients (except prawns) and sauté for 1 minute on high heat.
3 Add the prawns, reduce the heat to medium high and cook until prawns change colour to pink and curl.

Variation

- Add 2 tbsp of crushed tomatoes at Step 2.

Serving Suggestions

- Serve hot as a starter or as a light lunch with salad, vegetables of your choice and *Naan* (p. 138).

Ingredients

1 lb prawns, peeled, deveined, washed, and dried on paper towels

2 tsp butter

2 tsp *Garlic Paste* (see p. 8)

½ tsp black peppercorns, freshly ground

1 tbsp lemon juice

½ tsp ground chili, or to taste

¼ tsp salt, or to taste

Time

20–30 minutes, excluding time required to clean prawns
(*Fast & Friendly*)

Yield

2–3 servings

main Dishes

Prawns in Fresh Coriander Leaves

Ingredients

2 lb large prawns, uncooked

2 tbsp olive oil

2 tbsp water

2 tbsp lemon juice

1 cup fresh coriander leaves, firmly packed

6–8 fresh mint leaves

1 red or green chili pepper

2 tsp *Garlic Paste* (see p. 8)

1 tsp paprika

½ tsp salt

zest of ½ a lemon

Time

20–30 minutes, excluding time required to clean prawns

Yield

4–5 servings

Method

1 Peel, devein and clean prawns, leaving tail intact.
2 Rinse, drain and pat them dry on paper towels.
3 Blend the olive oil, water, lemon juice, coriander, mint, chili pepper, garlic, paprika and salt into a smooth paste. Add more water if needed.
4 In a wok, cook the above paste until the oil separates.
5 Add the prawns and lemon zest and stir gently until the prawns curl and turn pink.
6 The mixture should be quite dry.
7 Serve hot as a starter.

Serving Suggestions

• Can be served as a starter or with *Sweet Chillie Green Beans* (p. 119), *Dill Rice* (p. 133), and *Rotli* (p. 136), or *Naan* (p. 138), for a light lunch.

Notes

• If you like very hot and spicy prawns, you can use red chillie powder instead of paprika.

Main Dishes

Prawns in Fresh Coriander Leaves

Kashmiri prawns

Ingredients

1½ lb prawns,
peeled, deveined, washed,
and dried on paper towels

2 tsp butter

½ tsp *Garlic Paste*
(see p. 8)

½ cup onion,
sliced

4 tsp *Kashmiri Masala*,
(see p. 4)

1 cup yogurt

1 tbsp fresh coriander leaves,
chopped, divided

Time

20 minutes
(*Fast & Friendly*)

Yield

3–4 servings

Method

1 Sauté the prawns in butter and garlic until pink and curled and set aside.

2 In a pot add the onions, Kashmiri masala paste, yogurt and ½ of the coriander leaves and cook on medium heat until creamy.

3 Add the prawns and simmer for 2 minutes. The sauce should cover the prawns.

4 Garnish with the remaining coriander leaves and serve.

Serving Suggestions

• Serve with *Saffron Rice* (p. 133), and *Naan* (p. 138), or *Parotha* (p. 140–142).

Main Dishes

Prawns Vindaloo

Method

1 Broil the desiccated coconut until it is lightly browned.

2 Allow the coconut to cool and combine it with the ground coriander and cumin, onions, garlic paste, mustard seed, sugar, red chilies, and white wine vinegar and blend it all into a smooth paste.

3 Heat the olive oil in a saucepan. Add the paste and cook until oil separates, about 5 minutes.

4 Add the shrimp, ½ tsp of salt and garam masala. Cook until the shrimp is tender, about 3 minutes.

5 Add 1 cup of hot water and simmer for 2 minutes.

6 Garnish with freshly chopped coriander leaves and serve.

Serving Suggestions:

• Serve with *Rotli* (p. 136), or *Naan* (p. 138), and a rice dish for a full meal.

Notes

• Traditionally, this is a very spicy Goan dish, but you can control the heat of the dish by reducing the number of chilies. The current recipe yields a moderately spicy dish so you can also increase the number of chilies for more heat.

Ingredients

1 lb prawns, medium size, peeled, deveined, washed, and dried on paper towels

1 tbsp desiccated coconut

1 tsp ground coriander

1 tsp ground cumin

½ cup onions, chopped

1 tsp *Garlic Paste* (see p. 8)

1 tsp mustard seeds

½ tsp sugar

4 dry, whole red chilies

¼ cup white wine vinegar

2 tbsp olive oil

½ tsp salt, or to taste

½ tsp *Garam Masala* (see p. 2)

1 cup hot water

1 tbsp fresh coriander leaves, chopped

Time

30–40 minutes, excluding time required to clean prawns

Yield

2–3 servings

Main Dishes

Personal Notes

Main Dishes
Vegetables & Pulses (Daal)

Spicy Baked Fries

Spicy Potatoes

Spicy Cassava (Mogho)

Peas & Potato Stir Fry

Corn with Cumin-scented Butter

Corn on the Cob in Coconut Sauce

Spinach & Cottage Cheese Curry

Peas & Cheese (Matar Paneer)

Spinach & Corn with Cream (Palak Makai Malai)

Spicy Mushrooms, Baby Corn & Cauliflower

Cauliflower, Peas & Potato Curry

Peas & Zucchini Curry

Ghisoda (Ridge Gourd)

Sweet Chili Green Beans*

Spicy Green Beans

Spinach with Red Kidney Beans*

Red Kidney Beans with Cream

Chickpea & Potato Salad

Chana Daal Curry

Tuvar Daal with Peanuts & Tamarind Sauce

Dry Moong Daal Curry (Suki Mug Ni Daal)

* = Fast & Friendly recipes which are quick and easy to prepare

Spicy Baked Fries

Ingredients

1 lb fries,
frozen or fresh

2 tsp oil

¼ tsp ground cumin

½ tsp ground chili

½ tsp salt

Time

40 minutes

Yield

2–3 servings

Method

1 Preheat the oven to 400°F. If you are using fresh potatoes, parboil the fries and drain. Pat the fries dry with a paper towel.

2 Sprinkle the olive oil, ground cumin, ground chili, and salt over the fries and toss so the fries are well coated.

3 Spread the fries out on a baking tray and bake in the oven for 30 minutes, or until crisp.

Serving Suggestions

• Serve fries as an accompaniment to other dishes, or sprinkle with lemon juice and serve alone.

Notes

• These fries are baked in the oven so they need very little oil.

Spicy Potatoes

Method

1 Peel and cut potatoes into 1½ inch cubes.
2 Boil the potatoes in salt water until cooked. Drain.
3 Heat the olive oil in a saucepan and add mustard and cumin seeds, garlic, ginger, and chili pastes. Stir for ½ minute.
4 Add the ground cumin and coriander, turmeric, paprika, salt and black pepper, and stir for 1 minute. Add a little water if needed.
5 Add the bell peppers, and stir for 2 minutes.
6 Add the potatoes, lemon juice and coriander leaves and mix well.

Serving Suggestions

• Serve with any barbequed meats or as a savoury accompaniment to any other dish.

Ingredients

2 lb potatoes

2 tsp olive oil

½ tsp black mustard seeds

½ tsp cumin seeds

1 tsp *Garlic Paste*
(see p. 8)

1 tsp *Ginger Paste*
(see p. 8)

¼ tsp *Chili Paste*,
or to taste
(see p. 7)

½ tsp ground cumin

¼ tsp turmeric

½ tsp ground coriander

1 tsp paprika

¾ tsp salt

¼ tsp black peppercorns,
coarsely ground

½ cup green bell pepper,
cut into strips

½ cup red bell pepper,
cut into strips

1 tbsp lemon juice

1 tbsp fresh coriander leaves,
chopped

Time
30–40 minutes

Yield
6 servings

main Dishes

Spicy Cassava (Mogho)

Ingredients

2 lb frozen cassava,
thawed with central fibres
or strings removed
and the remainder cubed

½ cup tomatoes,
chopped

¾ tsp turmeric

2 tbsp olive oil

1 tsp cumin seeds

1 tsp mustard seeds

6 fresh curry leaves

1 or 2 dried red chilies,
to taste

1 tsp salt

1 tsp *Garlic Paste*
(see p. 8)

1 tsp *Chili Paste*
(see p. 7)

2 tbsp lemon juice

½ tsp sugar

2 tbsp fresh coriander leaves,
chopped

Time

45 minutes

Yield

4–5 servings

Method

1 Place the cassava in a large pot and add water to cover it by 2 inches.

2 Add the chopped tomatoes and turmeric to the pot and simmer until the cassava is soft and cooked.

3 In another small saucepan, heat the olive oil and add the cumin and mustard seeds, curry leaves and dried red chilies.

4 When the seeds start to pop, add the salt, garlic and chili pastes, and then transfer the contents of the small saucepan to the cooked cassava.

5 Cook the mixture for a further 5 minutes.

6 Add the lemon juice, sugar and coriander leaves, and serve.

Serving Suggestions

• Serve with potato chips and/or chevdo.

Notes

• In Nairobi, this dish is known as *Vagharelo Mogho*. The term vagharelo refers to the technique of sautéing the cumin and mustard seeds, curry leaves and dried red chilies in oil, as in Step 3 above.

Peas & Potato Stir Fry

Method

1 In a bowl, mix the green peas with ground cumin, turmeric, salt, sugar and lemon juice.
2 Heat the olive oil in a wok. Add the cumin seeds and chilies while stirring for about ½ minute.
3 Stir in the spiced peas and continue cooking. Add a little water if required.
4 Once the peas are cooked, add the boiled potatoes and sauté for 3 minutes.
5 Sprinkle with the freshly chopped coriander leaves and serve.

Serving Suggestions

• Serve hot with *Rotli* (p. 136), or *Naan* (p. 138).

Ingredients

2 cups green peas, frozen

½ tsp ground cumin

¼ tsp turmeric

½ tsp salt

¼ tsp sugar

1 tbsp lemon juice

2 tbsp olive oil

1 tsp cumin seeds

1 fresh green chili, chopped

2 cups potatoes, peeled, cubed and boiled

1 tbsp fresh coriander leaves, chopped

Time

20 minutes

Yield

4–5 servings

Corn with Cumin-scented Butter

Method

1 Boil corn for about 7 minutes, or it can be roasted on a BBQ.
2 Mix the butter, cumin, pepper, and salt together.
3 Serve the hot corn with cumin butter.

Notes

• Fresh corn dripping with butter is one of the joys of summer. This flavoured butter adds an extra special taste.

Ingredients

6 fresh cobs of corn

4 tbsp butter, softened

2 tsp ground cumin

2 tsp black peppercorns, freshly ground

¼ tsp salt

Time

15 minutes

Yield

6 servings

main Dishes

Corn on the Cob in Coconut Sauce

Ingredients

3 large cobs of corn

1 tsp salt

¼ cup onion, coarsely chopped

¼ cup fresh tomato, coarsely chopped

1 green chili pepper, or to taste

1 small piece, green bell pepper

1 small piece, red bell pepper

2 tsp olive oil

2 × 13 oz cans coconut milk

or

1¼ cups coconut milk powder and 2½ cups of the stock

2 tbsp lemon juice

2 tbsp fresh corriander leaves, chopped

Time

30 minutes

Yield

3–4 servings

Method

1 Peel and break each cob into 2 pieces, then place them in a saucepan with salt and enough water to cover the pieces.

2 Boil the corn for about 7 minutes, covered, until it is tender. Save ½ cup of stock if using coconut milk or 2½ cups of stock if using coconut powder.

3 When cool, cut the corn into 2 inch pieces. You can also do this before boiling.

4 Put the onion, tomato, chili, green and red bell pepper, and ½ cup of saved stock in a blender and purée.

5 Heat the olive oil in a nonstick pot and add the purée. Sauté for 5 minutes or until the water evaporates.

6 Add the coconut milk or coconut milk powder mixed with 2 cups of the stock and cook until mixture is thick like the consistency of cream soup. Add corn and cook uncovered for 3 minutes.

7 Add the lemon juice and freshly chopped coriander leaves, adjust the salt to taste, and serve.

Serving Suggestions

• Serve with *Coconut Rice* (p. 132), or by itself in bowls with extra sauce for dipping.

Notes

• Corn grew in abundance in Kenya, and I often made this dish which we called *Makai Paka* when young corn was in season. We made coconut milk from fresh coconuts. Scraping the flesh from the coconuts was a laborious task but thankfully we can now buy canned coconut milk or powder.

main Dishes

Spinach & Cottage Cheese Curry

Method

1 In a pot, heat the olive oil and add the mustard and cumin seeds, dried chilies, and sauté for about ½ minute.

2 Add the tomato, ground chili, coriander and cumin, turmeric, black pepper, and garlic paste. Sauté until the oil separates.

3 Add the thawed, drained spinach and cook for 2 minutes.

4 Stir in the lemon juice, salt, sugar, and hot water. Cook until spinach is tender.

5 Add cottage cheese and cook for 2 to 3 minutes.

6 Stir in the freshly chopped coriander leaves.

Serving Suggestions

- Serve with *Rotli* (p. 136), or *Naan* (p. 138).

Ingredients

2 tbsp olive oil

¼ tsp mustard seeds

¼ tsp cumin seeds

2 red dried chilies

½ cup crushed tomato

¼ tsp ground chili

½ tsp ground coriander

½ tsp ground cumin

½ tsp turmeric

¼ tsp black peppercorns, freshly ground

2 tsp *Garlic Paste* (see p. 8)

1 × 10 oz pkt frozen spinach, thawed

1 tbsp lemon juice

½ tsp salt

1 tsp sugar

½ cup hot water

1 cup cottage cheese

2 tbsp fresh coriander leaves, chopped

Time

20–25 minutes

Yield

3–4 servings

main Dishes

Peas & Cheese (Matar Paneer)

Ingredients

2¼ cups frozen green peas

2 tbsp olive oil

½ tsp mustard seeds

¼ tsp cumin seeds

3 curry leaves

1 or 2 dried red chilies

3 tbsp crushed tomato

1 tsp *Garlic Paste*
(see p. 8)

½ tbsp sweet chili sauce

¾ tsp ground cumin

¼ tsp turmeric

¾ tsp salt or to taste

¼ cup water

¼ lb paneer,
cut into cubes

1 tbsp fresh coriander leaves,
chopped

Time

30 minutes

Yield

4–6 servings

Method

1 Heat the olive oil in a pot and add the mustard and cumin seeds, curry leaves, and the dried red chilies.

2 When the seeds start to pop, add the tomato, garlic, sweet chili sauce, ground cumin, turmeric, and salt, and sauté for 2 minutes.

3 Add the water and peas and cook until peas are tender.

4 Add the paneer and cook for a further 2 minutes.

5 Add freshly chopped coriander leaves and serve.

Serving Suggestions

• Serve with *Rotli* (p. 136), or *Naan* (p. 138).

Notes

• Peas with cheese, or *Matar Paneer* is a tasty, healthy and nutritious dish.

• **Paneer**: Also called *panir* or *paner* is one of the few types of cheese indigenous to the Indian subcontinent. It is an unaged, acid-set (usually with lemon juice), unsalted, non-melting Farmer cheese which does not include rennet and is consequently completely vegetarian and a primary source of protein for Buddhists who adhere to vegetarian if not vegan diets. In preparing paneer, lemon juice is added to hot milk to separate curds from whey. The curds are then drained in muslin or cheesecloth and excess water is drained or pressed out. From this point, further preparation is dictated by ultimate use. In Moghulai cuisine, the paneer cloth is simply pressed under a heavy weight, often a stone slab, for several hours, after which the paneer is cut into cubes. Paneer is used in curries because it doesn't melt at normal cooking temperatures. It is very popular when wrapped in dough and deep

main Dishes

Peas & Cheese (matar Paneer)

Main Dishes

fried, as in a bhajia, or served with spinach (*Palak Paneer*) or peas (*Matar Paneer*). Pressing paneer for a shorter time (less than half an hour) produces a softer, fluffier cheese. Oriya and Bengali cuisine demand paneer-dough, produced by beating or kneading the paneer by hand into a dough-like consistency.

Spinach & Corn with Cream (palak makai malai)

Ingredients

1 pkt frozen spinach, thawed

1 tbsp olive oil

½ cup onion, chopped

1 tsp *Ginger Paste* (see p. 8)

½ tsp ground chili

¼ tsp turmeric

1 cup corn, frozen or canned

½ tsp salt

½ tsp *Garam Masala* (see p. 2)

1 tbsp lemon juice

½ cup whipping cream

Time
20–30 minutes

Yield
3–4 servings

Method

1 Gently squeeze the water out of the spinach and set the spinach aside.

2 In a pot, heat the olive oil and sauté the onion until it is transparent.

3 Add the ginger paste, ground chili, and turmeric, and sauté for 2 minutes.

4 Add the spinach and corn and cook until the spinach is tender.

5 Add the salt, garam masala, and lemon juice, and simmer until about ½ cup of liquid remains in the pot.

6 Stir in the whipping cream and continue simmering until the liquid thickens.

Serving Suggestions
• Serve hot with *Rotli* (p. 136), or *Naan* (p. 138), for a light lunch.

Spicy Mushrooms, Baby Corn & Cauliflower

Method

1 Heat the olive oil in a wok and stir in the cumin seeds and ginger.
2 Add the chopped onion and sauté until it becomes transparent.
3 Add the garlic paste, ground coriander, tomatoes, black pepper, chili flakes, sugar, and salt. Cook for 3 minutes.
4 Add all of the vegetables and yogurt. Simmer for a few minutes until all of the vegetables are cooked but still firm.
5 Stir in half of the coriander leaves.
6 Before serving, garnish the dish with the remaining coriander leaves.

Serving Suggestions

- Serve with *Rotli* (p. 136), or *Naan* (p. 138).

Ingredients

2 tbsp olive oil

½ tsp cumin seeds

1 piece ginger, finely chopped

1 cup onion, chopped

2 tsp *Garlic Paste* (see p. 8)

2 tsp ground coriander

2 fresh tomatoes, chopped

½ tsp black peppercorns, coarsely ground

1 tsp chili flakes

1 tsp sugar

salt to taste

1 cup mushrooms, halved

1 can baby corn, drained and rinsed

1 cup cauliflower florets, blanched

2 tbsp yogurt

2 tbsp fresh coriander leaves, chopped and divided

Time

15–20 minutes

Yield

4–5 servings

main Dishes

Cauliflower, Peas & Potato Curry

Ingredients

1 cup cauliflower, chopped

½ cup frozen peas

1 cup potatoes, cut into ¾" cubes

2 tsp olive oil

½ tsp mustard seeds

½ tsp cumin seeds

1 or 2 dried red chilies

1 tsp *Garlic Paste* (see p. 8)

½ tsp turmeric

1 tsp ground cumin

½ tsp ground coriander

½ tsp salt

1 cup fresh tomatoes, blended

1 tsp tomato paste

1 tbsp fresh coriander leaves, chopped

Time

20 minutes

Yield

2–3 servings

Method

1 Heat the olive oil in a saucepan. Add the mustard and cumin seeds and the red chilies.

2 When seeds start to pop, add the garlic paste, and stir for ½ minute.

3 Stir in the turmeric, ground cumin and coriander, salt, fresh tomatoes and tomato paste, and cook for 5 minutes.

4 Add the potatoes and peas, and simmer until potatoes are almost cooked, adding water as needed if vegetables become too dry.

5 Add the cauliflower and cook until the mixture is fairly dry, and potatoes are cooked.

6 Sprinkle with fresh, chopped coriander leaves and serve.

Serving Suggestions

• Serve with *Rotli* (p. 136), or *Naan* (p. 138).

Main Dishes

Peas & Zucchini Curry

Method

1 In a pot, heat the olive oil. Add the cumin and mustard seeds and the curry leaves, and cover for half a minute.

2 When the seeds start to pop, add the turmeric and salt.

3 At once, add the crushed tomatoes, garlic and chili pastes and the ground cumin.

4 Cook for 2 minutes, and then add all the vegetables and fenugreek leaves, if you are using them. Add hot water if needed.

5 Add the jaggery or demerara sugar and cook on low until the vegetables are cooked and the curry is fairly dry.

6 Add the freshly chopped coriander leaves and serve.

Serving Suggestions

• Serve with *Rotli* (p. 136).

Ingredients

1 cup zucchini, peeled and cut into small pieces

½ cup frozen peas

1 tbsp olive oil

¼ tsp cumin seeds

½ tsp mustard seeds

3 or 4 curry leaves, chopped

½ tsp turmeric

½ tsp salt

3 tbsp canned tomatoes, crushed

½ tsp *Garlic Paste* (see p. 8)

¼ tsp *Chili Paste* (see p. 7)

½ tsp ground cumin

1 tsp fresh fenugreek leaves, optional

1½ tsp jaggery or demerara sugar

1 tbsp fresh coriander leaves, chopped

Time

20 minutes

Yield

2 servings

main Dishes

Ghisoda (Ridge Gourd)

Ingredients

2½ cups ghisoda

2 tbsp olive oil

½ tsp mustard seed

½ tsp cumin seeds

2 dried red or green chilies

½ tsp *Garlic Paste* (see p. 8)

½ tsp *Ginger Paste* (see p. 8)

¼ tsp *Chili Paste* (see p. 7)

¼ tsp paprika

½ tsp turmeric

½ tsp salt

½ cup water

½ cup tomatoes, finely chopped

1 tsp tomato paste

2 tbsp fresh dill leaves, chopped, optional

Time

20–30 minutes

Yield

4 servings

Method

1 Peel the ridges off the ghisoda and wash.

2 Cut the ghisoda lengthwise into four and slice into ½ inch pieces. Do not rinse again.

3 Heat the olive oil, add the mustard and cumin seeds, and the dried or fresh chilies. Stir for ½ minute. Cover with a lid.

4 Stir in the ghisoda and sauté for 2 minutes.

5 In a small bowl, mix the garlic, ginger and chili pastes, paprika, turmeric, salt, and water. Add this mixture to the ghisoda. Cook for 2 minutes.

6 Stir in the tomatoes and tomato paste. Cook on medium-high heat until tomatoes are soft. Reduce the heat and cook on low until the ghisoda is tender.

7 Add the fresh dill leaves.

8 Simmer on low heat for a few more minutes to allow the flavours to mingle.

9 Adjust salt to taste.

Notes

• The Chinese name for Ghisoda is *Si Gua*.

• See the Glossary under **Ghisoda**.

Sweet Chili Green Beans

Method

1 Steam the green beans until tender. Drain.

2 In a nonstick wok, heat the olive oil.

3 Add the beans, salt, black pepper, garlic paste and ground cumin and sauté for 2 minutes.

4 Add the red bell pepper, sweet chili sauce and lemon juice and cook for 1 minute.

Serving Suggestions

- Serve hot with *Lamb Chops*, (p. 84), or *Basa in Orange Sauce*, (p. 95).

Ingredients

2 cups green beans, freshly cut

2 tbsp olive oil

¼ tsp salt

¼ tsp black peppercorns, freshly ground

½ tsp *Garlic Paste* (see p. 8)

½ tsp ground cumin

¼ cup red bell pepper, julienned

1 tbsp sweet chili sauce

1 tsp lemon juice

Time

15–20 minutes
(*Fast & Friendly*)

Yield

2–3 servings

main Dishes

Spicy Green Beans

Ingredients

1 lb green beans

pinch baking soda

½ tsp salt

2 tsp olive oil

½ tsp mustard seeds

½ tsp cumin seeds

1 clove of garlic, chopped

1" cube of ginger root, chopped

1 tsp dry chili flakes

½ cup coconut milk

1 tbsp fresh coriander leaves, chopped

2 tsp sesame seeds

2 tsp coconut flakes

Time

30 minutes

Yield

3–4 servings

Method

1 Top and tail the beans and cut them in half.

2 Boil the beans in water with baking soda and salt until cooked but still crispy. Drain.

3 In a wok, heat the olive oil. Add the mustard and cumin seeds.

4 As soon as the seeds start to splutter add the garlic, ginger and chili flakes.

5 Add the beans and stir for 3 minutes, adding a little water if necessary.

6 Add the coconut milk and cook, stirring until all the liquid evaporates.

7 Sprinkle with coriander leaves, sesame seeds and coconut flakes.

Serving Suggestions

• Serve as a side dish.

Spicy Green Beans

Spinach with Red Kidney Beans

Ingredients

1 × 10 oz pkt frozen spinach, thawed

1 × 19 oz can red kidney beans

2 tbsp olive oil

½ cup finely chopped onion

5 tbsps canned tomatoes, crushed

½ tsp *Garlic Paste* (see p. 8)

½ tsp *Ginger Paste* (see p. 8)

1 tsp ground cumin

½ tsp ground coriander

½ tsp ground chili, or to taste

1 tbsp water

½ tsp salt

Time

15 minutes
(**Fast & Friendly**)

Yield

4–5 servings

Method

1 Gently squeeze the water out of the spinach and set the spinach aside.

2 Drain and rinse the kidney beans.

3 Heat the olive oil in a pan. Add the onion and sauté until it is transparent.

4 Add the canned tomatoes and sauté until they are cooked.

5 Add the garlic and ginger pastes, the ground cumin, coriander, and chili, and salt and cook for 2 minutes.

6 Add the spinach and cook until the spinach is tender. Add water if more gravy is preferred. Stir in the kidney beans and cook for a few minutes. The mixture should be fairly dry.

Serving Suggestions

• Serve with pickles and chutneys of your choice (p. 14–17), and *Rotli* (p. 136), or *Naan* (p. 138).

main Dishes

Red Kidney Beans with Cream

Method

1 Drain and rinse kidney beans.
2 Heat the olive oil in a saucepan. Add the mustard and cumin seeds and the curry leaves. Cook until seeds start to splutter.
3 Add the crushed tomato, ground chili and coriander, turmeric, garam masala, lemon juice and salt, and sauté for 3 to 4 minutes.
4 Add the kidney beans.
5 Add the beaten yogurt gradually.
6 Add the cream and water and bring to a boil and cook for a few minutes.
7 Add ½ of the coriander leaves and mix.
8 Serve in a bowl and garnish with the remaining coriander leaves.

Serving Suggestions

• Serve with *Rotli* (p. 136), or *Naan* (p. 138).

Ingredients

1 × 26 oz can red kidney beans

1 tbsp olive oil

½ tsp mustard seeds

½ tsp cumin seeds

8 to 10 fresh curry leaves

½ cup canned tomatoes, crushed

½ tsp ground chili

1 tsp ground coriander

¼ tsp turmeric

¼ tsp *Garam Masala* (see p. 2)

1 tbsp lemon juice

salt to taste

½ cup yogurt, beaten smooth

2 tbsp whipping cream

½ cup water

1 tbsp fresh coriander leaves, chopped, divided

Time

20 minutes

Yield

4 servings

main Dishes

Chickpea & Potato Salad

Ingredients

1 x 19 oz can of chickpeas

1 large potato

1 medium tomato, diced

1 cup green onions, chopped

2 tbsp fresh coriander leaves, chopped

1 green chili, chopped

¼ tsp ground chili

½ tsp black peppercorns, freshly ground

½ tsp ground cumin

1 tbsp lemon juice

3 tbsp *Date & Tamarind Chutney* (see p. 17)

salt to taste

Time

25–30 minutes

Yield

3–4 servings

Method

1 Peel a large potato, cut it into cubes and boil in salted water until it is cooked.

2 Drain and rinse the chickpeas.

3 Place the potatoes and chickpeas in a large bowl.

4 Add the rest of the ingredients and mix well.

5 Serve cold.

Main Dishes

Chana Daal Curry

Method

1 Soak the daal in hot water for 1 hour, rinse and drain.
2 In a pan, heat the olive oil on medium.
3 Stir in the onion and sauté until it is golden brown.
4 In a small bowl, mix the garlic, ginger, tomato and chili pastes, the fresh tomatoes, the turmeric, ground cumin and coriander, and the salt.
5 Add the contents of the small bowl to the sautéed onion and cook for 5 minutes or until all the water evaporates.
6 Add the drained daal and cook for 3 to 4 minutes.
7 Add 2 cups of water and simmer until daal is tender (about ½ hour). Gravy should cover the daal.
8 Stir in half of the fresh coriander leaves, the garam masala, lemon juice and sugar.
9 Garnish with egg halves and the remaining coriander leaves.

Servings Suggestions

• Serve with *Plain Rice* (p. 132), or *Cumin-scented Rice* (p. 133), and *Rotli* (p. 136).

Notes

• **Chana daal** is a smaller and darker brown relative of the chickpea that is dull yellow in colour when dehusked and has a sweet, nutty flavour. It is used in both sweet and savoury dishes.

• See the Glossary under **Daal**.

Ingredients

1 cup chana daal

3 eggs, hardboiled, shelled and cut in half

1 tbsp olive oil

1/2 cup onion, chopped

1 tsp *Garlic Paste* (see p. 8)

1 tsp *Ginger Paste* (see p.8)

1 cup fresh tomatoes, chopped
or
½ cup canned tomatoes, crushed

2 tsp tomato paste

½ tsp *Chili Paste* (see p. 7)

½ tsp turmeric

1 tsp ground cumin

½ tsp ground coriander

1½ tsp salt, or to taste

2 cups water

1½ tbsp fresh coriander leaves, chopped, divided

½ tsp *Garam Masala* (see p. 2)

2 tsp lemon juice

1 tsp sugar

Time
60 minutes

Yield
4–6 servings

main Dishes

Tuvar Daal with Peanuts & Tamarind Sauce

Ingredients

¾ cup tuvar daal

¼ cup raw peanuts

1 tbsp desiccated coconut

5 cups water

1 tbsp olive oil

6 curry leaves

½ tsp mustard seeds

½ tsp cumin seeds

1 fresh chili,
stem removed and slit

½ cup onion,
chopped

½ cup fresh tomato,
chopped

½ tsp black peppercorns,
coarsely ground

2 tsp paprika

1 tsp ground cumin

½ tsp ground coriander

½ tsp turmeric

1 tsp *Garlic Paste*
(see p. 8)

1 tsp *Ginger Paste*
(see p. 8)

½ tsp *Chili Paste*,
or to taste (see p. 7)

1 tsp salt,
or to taste

½ cup water

½ cup long Chinese
eggplant, cubed

½ cup cauliflower florets

1 tbsp plain yogurt

½ tsp sugar

2 tbsp tamarind sauce

Method

1 Clean and wash the daal and soak it in hot water for one hour. Drain.

2 Put the daal, peanuts, coconut, and 5 cups of water in a large pot and cook for 1½ hours, until daal is well cooked. If using a pressure cooker, cook for 30 minutes and set aside.

3 Heat the olive oil in a pot big enough to hold the daal and the vegetables. Stir in the curry leaves, mustard and cumin seeds, and the fresh chili and sauté for ½ a minute.

4 Add the onion and sauté until it is transparent.

5 Stir in the tomatoes, black pepper, paprika, ground cumin and coriander, turmeric, the garlic, ginger, and chili pastes, and the salt and sauté until the tomatoes are soft and cooked.

6 Add ½ cup of water, the vegetables and the yogurt and cook for five minutes, or until vegetables are cooked.

7 Add the cooked daal, sugar, tamarind sauce, and garam masala, and cook until it's the consistency of a creamy soup.

8 Add the freshly chopped coriander leaves and serve.

Serving Suggestions

• Serve hot with *Plain Rice* (p. 132), or *Cumin-scented Rice* (p. 133).

Notes

• To make the tamarind sauce, take a 1½ inch cube of tamarind pulp, soak it in ½ cup of hot water and bring it to a boil. Simmer this for a few minutes and then leave it to cool. When cold, mash and press through a sieve. Add a little water to the remaining

Main Dishes

pulp, mixing thoroughly, and press through a sieve again. Retain the liquid and discard the remaining pulp.

- You may use *Date & Tamarind Chutney* (p. 17), or any other tamarind chutney you may find at Indian grocery stores, as substitutes for the tamarind sauce.

- **Tuvar daal** has a mild, nutty flavour and is often cooked as a side dish. Tuvar daal may also be called *tur, toor,* or *arhar.* Tuvar lentils are usually sold with an oily coating that should be rinsed off before cooking. Popular in southern and western India, Tuvar lentils have tan skins or jackets when whole but are usually sold skinned and split which reveals their yellow interiors.

¼ tsp *Garam Masala* (see p. 2)

2 tbsp fresh coriander leaves, chopped

Time
25–30 minutes

Yield
4–5 servings

main Dishes

Dry Moong Daal Curry
(Suki Mug ni Daal)

Ingredients

1 cup moong daal

½ cup onion, finely chopped

2 tbsp olive oil

½ cup tomato, finely chopped

1 tsp ground cumin

½ tsp turmeric

¼ tsp ground chili, or to taste

½ tsp salt

2 tsp tomato paste

1 cup water

1 tbsp lemon juice

1 tbsp fresh coriander leaves, chopped for garnish

Method

1 Soak the moong daal for ½ an hour in hot water, then drain.

2 Heat the olive oil in a pan.

3 Fry the onion until it is just transparent (before it starts to brown).

4 Stir in the tomatoes. Sauté for 1 minute.

5 Add the ground cumin, turmeric, chili, salt, tomato paste and the moong daal. Stir continuously on high heat for 2 minutes.

6 Reduce the heat and add the water. Bring to a boil, and then reduce to low heat. Cover and let simmer until the daal is cooked (15 minutes) and most of the water has evaporated.

7 Add lemon juice.

8 Garnish with freshly chopped coriander leaves.

Time

60 minutes, including soaking

Serving Suggestions

• Serve with *Rotli* (p. 136), or *Puri* (p. 143), and *Mango Juice* (p. 163).

Yield

4 servings

Notes

• **Moong daal** can be made from either split or split and skinned Mung beans (also known as whole green lentils, and green or golden gram). The flavour of each is quite different. Mung beans are whole beans and retain their green husk. Dehulled or washed mung beans can be used in a similar fashion to whole beans for making sweet soups. Stripped of their outer green skins, these yellow beans are flat, quick cooking and relatively easy to digest.

• The traditional name for this dish, *Suki Mug Ni Daal*, literally means dry moong curry.

Main Dishes

Dry Moong Daal Curry (Suki Mug ni Daal)

Personal notes

Starches
Rice & Bread

Plain Rice

Dill Rice

Cumin-scented Rice

Lemon Rice with Cashews

Kashmiri Rice

Rotli (Chapatti)

Naan

Healthy Breakfast Naan

Nutritious Spicy Parotha

Parotha Omelettes

Spinach Parotha

Puri

Makati Mimina

plain Rice

Ingredients

1½ cups basmati rice
2 tsp olive oil
3 cups water
1 tsp salt

Time

30 minutes stovetop,
20 minutes microwave,
soaking included

Yield

4–5 servings

Method

Stovetop

1 Wash and soak the rice in cold water for 10 to 15 minutes. Drain.

2 In a pot, put the water, salt, oil and drained rice, and bring it all to a boil.

3 Boil for 2 to 3 minutes, then reduce heat to low.

4 Simmer covered until all the water is absorbed. Check to see if the rice is cooked. If not, add a sprinkle of water.

5 Fluff rice with a fork and simmer until cooked. Each grain should separate easily.

Microwave

1 In a suitable microwave container put the water, rice, salt and oil. The cooked rice will at least double in size so be sure the container you use has sufficient volume to accommodate the expansion.

2 Cook uncovered in the microwave for 10 minutes.

3 Remove the container and stir, then cook for another 5 minutes.

4 Fluff the rice with a fork and cover, allowing it to stand for 2 to 3 minutes before serving.

Variations

• *Coconut Rice*: Add ½ tbsp coconut powder to the above recipe.

Serving Suggestions

• Serve with any curry dish or daal.

Dill Rice

Method
1 Wash and soak rice for 10 to 15 minutes.
2 In a heavy-bottomed saucepan, add the drained rice, water, oil, salt, dill and coriander.
3 Cook on medium heat until the rice is almost cooked.
4 Turn down heat and simmer until the rice is fully cooked and all the water has been absorbed.

Serving Suggestions
- Serve hot with any curry dish.

Ingredients
1½ cups basmati rice

3 cups water

1½ tsp olive oil
or 1½ tsp butter

1½ tsp salt,
or to taste

½ cup fresh dill leaves, chopped

¼ cup fresh coriander leaves, chopped

Time
40 minutes

Yield
4–5 servings

Cumin-scented Rice

Method
1 Wash and soak rice for 10 to 15 minutes.
2 In a saucepan, heat the olive oil, add the cumin seeds, and sauté for ½ minute. Add the water, salt, and drained rice. Bring it to a boil and cook for 2 to 3 minutes, then reduce heat.
3 Simmer until the rice is cooked and all the water has evaporated.
4 Check to see if rice is cooked. If not, you can add a little more water and continue cooking.
5 Turn off the heat and leave the pot on the stove for 2 to 3 minutes until the rice is dry.

Variations
- *Saffron Rice*: Omit the cumin and add 2 pinches of saffron after adding the rice to the salted water with olive oil.

Ingredients
1½ cups basmati rice

1½ tsp olive oil

½ tsp cumin seeds

2½ cups water

1 tsp salt

Time
40 minutes

Yield
4–5 servings

Starches

Ingredients

2 × 1" pieces cinnamon stick

2 cardamom pods

½ tsp cumin seeds

Variations

- *Lightly Spiced Rice*: Add these three ingredients (see left) to the olive oil.

Notes

- Cumin seeds give a wonderful flavour to plain rice. When I lived in Nairobi, this was one of my favourite ways of cooking rice.

Lemon Rice with Cashews

Ingredients

1½ cups basmati rice

1 tbsp olive oil

2 tbsp cashews, unroasted

½ tsp mustard seeds

½ tsp cumin seeds

10 fresh curry leaves, chopped

1 tbsp desiccated coconut

3 or 4 tbsp lemon juice

3 cups water

½ tsp turmeric

1 tsp salt

Time

40 minutes

Yield

4–5 servings

Method

1 Wash and soak the rice for 10 to 15 minutes.

2 In a heavy frying pan, heat the olive oil and add the cashews and sauté for 1 minute.

3 Add the mustard and cumin seeds and the curry leaves and sauté for ½ a minute.

4 Add the coconut and lemon juice, and set aside.

5 In another pot, add the drained rice, water, turmeric and salt. Bring this to a boil and keep it boiling for 3 minutes.

6 Lower the heat and simmer covered until the rice is cooked (20 to 25 minutes) and water has been absorbed.

7 Sprinkle the cashews and spice mixture over the rice and mix very gently.

8 Cover and simmer, or bake in an oven preheated to 300°F, for about 15 minutes.

Serving Suggestions

- Serve hot as a side dish.

Kashmiri Rice

Method

1 Wash and soak rice for 10 to 15 minutes.
2 In a heavy-bottomed pan, heat the oil and stir in the cumin seeds, cloves, cinnamon, and cardamom pods and sauté for ½ minute.
3 Add the milk, cream, sugar, salt and water.
4 Bring it to a boil and let simmer for 2 minutes.
5 Add the drained rice.
6 Cover and simmer on low until all of the liquid is evaporated and the rice is cooked.
7 Gently fold in the fruit and simmer on low for 2 more minutes.
8 Add the rose petals and serve.

Serving Suggestions

• Serve with any curry or as a side dish.

Notes

• What makes this dish particularly Kashmiri in style, is the inclusion of the milk and cream.

Ingredients

1 cup basmati rice

1 tbsp olive oil
or butter

¼ tsp cumin seeds

2 cloves

2 × 1" pieces cinnamon stick

2 cardamom pods

1 cup milk,
(1% or 2% MF)

½ cup whipping cream

½ tsp sugar

¾ tsp salt

½ cup water

½ cup canned fruit salad, drained

2 or 3 edible rose petals

Time

40 minutes

Yield

2–3 servings

Starches

Rotli (Chapatti)

Ingredients

2 cups whole wheat flour

2 or 3 tbsp sunflower oil

½ tsp salt

1 cup boiling water

Time

20–30 minutes

Yield

8 Rotli

Method

1 Using a wooden spoon, combine the flour, sunflower oil and salt and make a soft, pliable (but not sticky) dough with water.

2 Divide the dough into 8 equal portions and cover.

3 Roll each portion into a circle, 6 to 7 inches in diameter, on a lightly floured surface.

4 Bake on a hot griddle or in a nonstick skillet, placing the top side down first.

5 When little bubbles appear, turn the rotli over and continue cooking for 1 to 2 minutes.

6 Turn the rotli over again and continue cooking until both sides are browned. Pressing lightly with a spatula will cause the rotli to puff up.

7 Apply a little butter to the cooked rotli and stack together. This will keep the rotli soft.

8 Rotli can be wrapped in foil and frozen for future use. Reheat in an oven at 350°F or you can warm them up individually in a toaster oven.

Rotli (Chapatti)

Variation

- *Masala Rotli*: Knead the dough as above together with the following ingredients (see right) and cook as above, using 1 or 2 tsp of oil for each rotli when cooking.

Serving Suggestions

- Serve with any curry dish or with eggs for breakfast. Rotli can also be served with butter and jam, or sprinkled with sugar, or plain yogurt and *Apple & Carrot Pickle* (p. 13).

Notes

- The amount of water will vary with the brand or mixture of flour you use.

- *Rotli* or *roti*, generically speaking, means "bread" and is a term that may refer to many different kinds of bread. In Marathi, roti is often called *chapati* (also *chapatti* or *chapatee*). In Gujarati, the word is spelled rotli. Rotli and chapati are unleavened, round (5 to 6 inches in diameter) flatbread of northern India usually made with whole wheat flour and baked or browned on a very hot, dry griddle, tava or frying pan. Traditionally, each disc is finished off over an open flame for ten to fifteen seconds, causing the bread to puff up with steam, like a balloon. This final step is best achieved using a heated grill or broiler, or an open gas flame. Rotli or chapati are then brushed with ghee and served immediately.

  Many people eat Indian food with their hands so small pieces of rotli are used like a scoop or pusher (edible utensil) to carry the food, especially daal or vegetable dishes, from the dish to the mouth. Rotli are usually served at every meal, including breakfast! I usually make a batch of rotli and freeze them so I always have some on hand for unexpected guests or for those days when I don't have time to make them from scratch.

Ingredients

½ tsp turmeric

½ tsp ground cumin

1 tsp *Garlic Paste* (see p. 8)

1 tsp *Chili Paste* (see p. 7)

½ tsp ajowain

1 tbsp coriander leaves, freshly chopped

Starches

naan

Ingredients

2¼ cups flour,
all purpose, whole wheat,
or a mixture of the two

1 tbsp instant yeast (quick rise)

½ tsp sugar

1 tsp salt

3 tbsp sunflower oil
or melted butter

½ tsp ajowain,
optional

½ cup (approximately)
of warm milk (1% or 2% MF)

Time
60–70 minutes

Yield
10 Naan

Method

1 Mix all of the ingredients with sufficient warm milk to make a soft dough.

2 Cover the dough and let it rest in a warm place for 30 minutes or until dough doubles in size.

3 Divide the dough into 10 balls and flatten each slightly. If dough is slightly sticky, it helps to put a bit of oil on your hands when working with it.

4 Roll each ball into a 6 × 4 × ¼ inch thick oval shape. Dust your rolling board with flour to prevent sticking. Let each naan rest for 10 minutes on a lightly oiled tray.

5 Bake each naan on a hot frying pan or on a griddle, top side first.

6 When bubbles start to appear, turn the naan over and cook the other side until golden brown spots appear underneath. Alternatively, you can finish the cooking of the second side under a broiler.

7 Turn the naan again and cook until golden brown spots appear on the top side, and the naan is well cooked.

8 As each naan is cooked, put it on a plate and keep the plate covered until you have finished cooking the whole batch.

Serving Suggestions

• Serve with any curry or on its own with butter and chai (tea).

Notes

• **Ajowain** makes *Naan* more flavourful. See the Glossary under **Bishop's Weed**.

• *Naan* is a flat white or whole wheat flour bread from northwest India that is lightly leavened by natural yeast starter from airborne yeasts and baked in a tandoor oven. A flattened round of dough is placed on a cloth puff that is used to slap the naan directly onto the side of a special high-heat oven. In less than a minute, the naan puffs slightly, browns on the side touching the oven wall and takes on a light smokey flavour. The bread is then speared on a skewer and removed from the oven to be served hot, after lightly brushing it with butter or ghee.

Healthy Breakfast naan

Method

1 Mix all the dry ingredients together.
2 Add the sunflower oil and sufficient warm water to make a soft dough.
3 Cover the dough and set it aside to rise (about 30 minutes) or until it doubles in size.
4 Divide the dough into 10 balls. Flatten each slightly and roll them into circles 5 inches in diameter.
5 Place each on an oiled baking tray. Spray each lightly with oil. Cover and leave to rest for 20 minutes.
6 Remove the cover and cook on the middle rack of an oven preheated to 425°F.
7 Bake the naans for 7 minutes. Turn them over and bake for a further 3 minutes. They should be a light golden brown on both sides.

Serving Suggestions

• Serve for breakfast with butter and jam.

Ingredients

2½ cups whole wheat flour

½ cup seven grain cereal

½ cup sultanas, cranberries, sunflower seeds – mixed

2 tbsp sugar

1 tsp salt

4 tsp instant yeast (quick rise)

½ tsp ground cardamom

¼ tsp ground nutmeg

4 tbsp sunflower oil or butter

warm water

Time

60–70 minutes

Yield

10 Naan

Starches

nutritious Spicy parotha

Ingredients

3 cups whole wheat flour

¾ cup chana flour

½ cup olive oil

¼ cup ground flax seeds

1½ tsp *Garlic Paste* (se p. 8)

½ tsp turmeric

1 tsp ground cumin

2 tsp *Chili Paste*, red or green, or to taste (see p. 7)

2 tsp salt

¼ cup fresh coriander leaves, finely chopped

warm water to make dough

Time

60 minutes

Yield

15 Parotha

Method

1 Mix the whole wheat and chana flour.

2 Add the oil and mix well.

3 Add the rest of the ingredients, except for the water, and mix well.

4 Knead into a pliable dough with the warm water.

5 Cover the dough and let it rest for 15 minutes.

6 Divide the dough into 15 balls.

7 Flatten each ball into a small patty.

8 Rub a couple of drops of oil into the middle of the patty. Then sprinkle the oil with a little flour.

9 Draw the dough into the centre, resealing it over the oil and flour. Turn the pattie over onto a board for rolling.

10 Roll it into a circle about 7 inches in diameter.

11 Heat a griddle or heavy-bottomed nonstick frying pan on high heat.

12 Cook the parotha one at a time, placing them top side down, onto the griddle.

13 When little bubbles appear on the parotha, turn it over and cook for 1 to 2 minutes.

14 Flip the parotha over so it is again, top side down, to ensure both sides are cooked.

15 Stack the parothas together as you cook them. This will keep them soft.

16 Once cool, the parothas can be wrapped in foil and stored in the freezer. They can be reheated in the oven or individually in a toaster oven.

Serving Suggestions

• Serve for breakfast with plain yogurt and chutney or fried eggs, an omelette, or with any curry dish.

Starches

parotha Omelettes

Method

1 Combine the eggs, salt, coriander leaves, ground cumin, garlic and chili pastes, onion, tomato and flour.
2 In a nonstick frying pan, heat sufficient olive or vegetable oil to cook one parotha. Place a parotha in the pan and pour ⅙ of the egg mixture onto the parotha and spread it out towards the edges.
3 Cook for 2 minutes on medium heat. If the egg mixture begins to run off the parotha, use a spoon to contain the egg mixture on the parotha.
4 As the egg mixture consolidates, turn the parotha over and cook the other side until the egg mixture is fully cooked.
5 Slide the parotha onto a plate, egg side up and repeat steps 2 to 4 with the remaining parothas and the egg mixture.

Serving Suggestions

• Serve hot for breakfast with *Apple & Carrot Pickle* (p. 13).

Ingredients

6 Parothas,
either plain or spicy,
or *Masala Rotli*
(see p. 137)

3 eggs, beaten

½ tsp salt,
or to taste

1 tbsp fresh coriander leaves,
chopped

1 tsp ground cumin

½ tsp *Garlic Paste*
(see p. 8)

½ tsp *Chili Paste*
(see p. 7)

1 cup onion,
finely chopped

½ cup fresh tomato,
finely chopped

1 ½ tsp all purpose flour

olive, sunflower or corn oil

Time

30 minutes,
with previously
prepared Parotha

Yield

6 Omelettes

Starches

Spinach parotha

Ingredients

1 × 10 oz pkt frozen spinach, thawed, chopped

3½ cups whole wheat flour

6 tbsp sunflower oil

1 tsp salt

3 tbsp yogurt

1 tsp ground cumin

1 tsp *Garlic Paste* (see p. 8)

1 tsp *Chili Paste*, or to taste (see p. 7)

2 tbsp fresh coriander leaves, chopped

2 tbsp cooked rice or 2 slices brown bread, soaked in water with excess water squeezed out

sufficient water to make dough

sunflower oil for frying

Time

75–90 minutes

Yield

13 Parotha

Method

1 Gently squeeze out some water from the spinach.

2 Purée the spinach in a food processor.

3 Add the flour, oil, salt, yogurt, ground cumin, garlic and chili pastes, chopped coriander and boiled rice or bread to the food processor and blend into a soft dough. Add water only if needed.

4 Divide the dough into 13 balls.

5 Roll each ball into a small patty and spread 2 drops of oil on each. Sprinkle flour over the oil. Fold edges of each patty to the middle and pinch to seal so that the oil and flour stay inside the ball.

6 Flatten each patty and roll them into a circle about 6 to 7 inches in diameter with the folded side facing down.

7 Place each parotha, topside first, onto a hot griddle. When bubbles start to appear on the top, turn the parotha over. Drizzle 1 teaspoon of oil on each side when cooking.

8 Cook the parotha on the bottom side and flip it over again.

9 Press parotha with a spatula so it cooks evenly and to prompt it to puff up. Remove the parotha onto a tray lined with paper towel.

10 Repeat steps 5 to 9 with the rest of the patties.

11 Serve hot or stack on each other and store, wrapped in foil for future use. Parothas can also be frozen.

Serving Suggestions

- Serve with curry, yogurt, and chutney of your choice.

Starches

puri

Method

1 Rub the flour, salt and oil together until the mixture resembles fine crumbs.

2 Add water and knead lightly to make a dough.

3 Divide into 20 to 24 equal-sized balls and cover with a damp cloth.

4 On a lightly oiled surface, roll each of these balls into a circle about 4 to 5 inches in diameter.

5 Deep fry in hot oil, top side first.

6 Tap each of the puri lightly with a slotted spoon and gently push it down into the oil. The puri should puff up within seconds.

7 Turn the puri over and continue frying until golden brown.

Variation

- *Masala Puri*: To the above ingredients, include the following additional items, (see right).

Serving Suggestions

- Serve hot with honey, butter and jam, yogurt or vegetable curry, or *Dry Moong Daal Curry (Suki Mug Ni Daal)* (p. 128), and *Mango Juice* (p. 163).

Notes

- By using oil rather than flour to roll out the puris, you avoid the problem of excess flour burning in the oil when frying.

Ingredients

1 cup whole wheat flour

1 cup all purpose flour

½ tsp salt

2 tbsp sunflower oil

¾ cup (approximately), warm water

sunflower or corn oil, for frying

Time

60 minutes

Yield

20–24 Puri

Ingredients

¼ tsp turmeric

2 tsp fresh coriander leaves, chopped

½ tsp ground cumin

½ tsp *Ginger Paste*, (see p. 8)

½ tsp *Garlic Paste*, (see p. 8)

½ tsp *Chili Paste*, (see p. 7)

Starches

- *Puri*, (also *poori*, *pooree*, or *apuri*), is a light, thin, round and flat unleavened bread made from whole wheat or atta (whole grain durum wheat) flour, water, salt and ghee or other fat, to create a dough almost identical to that for chapati. The dough is usually deep fried in fat or oil, puffs up during frying, and is eaten immediately. Pieces of puri are usually torn off and used to scoop up morsels of rice, daal, or vegetables too small to pick up with one's fingers. Popular in northern India, puri are usually served at special or ceremonial functions and they sometimes play a part in rituals when various vegetarian foods are offered in prayer.

Puri

Starches

makati mimina

Method

1 Pour the hot water into a food processor.
2 Add the coconut cream and process until smooth. Add the desiccated coconut.
3 Add the rice flour and process for 2 minutes.
4 Pour the batter into a bowl and add the cardamom and cold water.
5 Add the yeast and sugar and mix until the sugar dissolves. Cover and set aside for 4 to 6 hours. The batter will be of liquid consistency.
6 In an ovenproof 10 inch nonstick frying pan, on high heat, heat 1 tbsp of oil. Pour half (about 3 to 4 cups) of the batter into the pan.
7 Immediately turn heat down to 2½ on the dial, and cook covered for 10 minutes. Sprinkle with 1 tsp of poppy seeds and cook for another 10 minutes or until the batter is set and has a spongy texture.
8 Broil under a preheated broiler on high for 2 to 3 minutes or until light golden brown.
9 Allow to cool for a few minutes and then turn it out onto a plate. Flip onto another plate so that the top (poppy seed side) is uppermost.
10 Repeat steps 6 to 9 with the remaining half of the mixture.

Ingredients

2¼ cups hot water

5 oz block pure creamed coconut

2 tbsp desiccated coconut

1 × 14 oz pkt of rice flour (gluten free)

1 tsp cardamom, coarsely crushed

2¼ cups cold water

1¼ tsp instant yeast (quick rise)

2 cups sugar

2 tbsp vegetable oil, divided

2 tsp poppy seeds, divided

Time

5–7 hours

Yield

2 Makati

Notes

• If you have 2 large burners and 2 large frying pans, you can make both halves of the makati batter at the same time. The best results are achieved when your frying pan has straight sides, perpendicular to the base. Ensure the yeast is not stale dated. Quick rise, instant yeast is sprinkled into the mix as opposed to dissolved in water. Cut the block of pure creamed coconut milk lengthwise to ensure inclusion of both the body and topping of the product.

makati mimina

- In Kiswahili (the language spoken in Kenya, Tanzania and Uganda), *makati* means bread. *Makati Mimina* is a traditional rice flour bread made using yeast, which is pan-fried and browned under a grill or broiler and very popular on the east coast of Africa.

Starches

Personal notes

_____

_____

_____

_____

_____

_____

_____

_____

_____

_____

_____

_____

_____

_____

_____

_____

_____

_____

_____

_____

_____

_____

_____

_____

_____

Starches

Desserts
Sweets & Drinks

Fruit Salad with Mango Cream

Fruit Salad Chaat

Kulfi

Kashmiri Faludo

Sweet Potato or Yam Kheer

Plain Burfi (Fudge)

Almond Burfi

Mango Burfi

Sev Paak

Chai with Masala

Mango Juice

Hot Ginger Drink

Tamarind Drink

Mango Lassi

Pistachio Lassi

Fruit Salad with Mango Cream

Ingredients

1 cup canned mango pulp

¾ cup whipping cream, whipped

5 cups any fresh or canned (drained) fruit combination, (e.g., mango, kiwi, raspberries, strawberries, grapes, melon, mandarin oranges, pineapple)

Garnish

1 tbsp chopped almonds

1 tbsp chopped pistachios

Time

15–20 minutes

Yield

6–8 servings

Method

1 Mix the chopped fruit, mango pulp and whipped cream together in a bowl.

2 Garnish with chopped almonds and pistachios. Serve chilled.

Variations

- Use two cups of vanilla ice cream and three small cups of tapioca pudding in place of the mango pulp.

Fruit Salad Chaat

Method

1 Mix all of the fruit in a bowl.
2 Warm the orange and lemon juice and mix in the green chili.
3 When cold, add to the fruit and toss.
4 Sprinkle with the chaat masala.

Serving Suggestions

• Serve with ice cream or *Kulfi* (p. 152) of your choice.

Note

• *Chaat Masala* is available at Indian grocery stores or you can make your own using the recipe on p. 3. Fresh fruit sprinkled with spices is very popular in India.

Ingredients

1 × 19 oz can pineapple chunks, drained

1 red apple, peeled, cored and cut into pieces the same size as the pineapple chunks

1 cup seedless grapes, halved

1 × 10 oz can mandarin oranges

½ cup orange juice

1 tsp lemon juice

1 green chili, seeded and chopped

½ tsp *Chaat Masala* (see p. 3)

Time

15–20 minutes

Yield

6–8 servings

Kulfi

Ingredients

1 × 14 oz can condensed milk

1 × 13 oz can evaporated milk

1 cup whipping cream, whipped

½ tsp ground cardamom

2 tbsp almonds, chopped

2 tbsp pistachios, chopped

pinch saffron

Time

20 – 30 minutes

Yield

20 × 2" squares

Method

1 Using an electric mixer, mix the condensed and evaporated milk until they are frothy.

2 Fold in the whipping cream and cardamom to the above mixture.

3 Pour the mixture into an 8 inch square container that can be used for freezing, and garnish with almonds, pistachios, and saffron and place in the freezer overnight.

4 Cut into the desired number and size of pieces and serve.

Variations

- *Mango Kulfi*: Add 1½ cups of canned mango pulp when adding whipped cream. Use a 10 × 8 inch container and omit the nuts.
- *Pistachio Kulfi*: Add a couple drops of green food colouring so that the mixture is pale green in colour. Add ½ cup chopped pistachios when adding whipped cream. Garnish with chopped pistachios.

Notes

- *Kulfi* is a popular South Asian ice cream made with boiled milk, traditionally from water buffalo. Produced in many flavours, the most popular of which are pistachio, mango, cardamom and saffron, the milk is boiled to half its original volume, sugar is added and the mixture is boiled for another ten minutes. Then the flavourings or dried fruit are added. The mixture is put into moulds and frozen. Kulfi is either eaten plain or can be garnished with ground cardamom, saffron, or pistachio nuts. A contemporary alternative employs canned condensed milk and whipping cream as time-saving alternatives to boiling and reducing the milk.

Kashmiri Faludo

Method

1 Dissolve the agar agar in hot water and microwave on high for 1 minute. Stir in 3 tbsp of grenadine and return to the microwave for 1 minute. When this liquid cools to room temperature, refrigerate it for about 15 minutes or until it sets. When set, it can be grated into fine slivers and set aside.

2 Soak the tukmaria in 2 cups of water for 15 minutes. The tukmaria will double in size. Drain the water and any debris that has floated to the top. Add more water and soak the tukmaria again until the tukmaria settles to the bottom, drain water again. Strain the tukmaria through a fine strainer and set it aside in a clean container.

3 In a 10 oz glass add 1½ tbsp of grenadine, 1 tbsp of the tukmaria and 1½ tbsp of the grated agar agar. Add two scoops of vanilla ice cream and fill the glass with milk. Add ½ tbsp of grenadine on top of the ice cream.

4 Garnish with chopped pistachios and serve with a dessert spoon and straw.

Notes

- **Agar agar** is derived from a number of species of red algae or seaweed, marketed in blocks, powder, or brittle strands. When dissolved in boiling water and cooled, agar agar becomes gelatinous and is used as a setting or thickening agent for soups and sauces. Gelatin can be substituted for agar agar, but agar agar has stronger setting properties which means you need to use less of it and, unlike gelatin, agar agar will set at room temperature.

- **Tukmaria** (also *takmaria, sabja, subja* or *falooda, faludo*), are the seeds of several varieties of the herb Basil. When soaked, these seeds become gelatinous and are used in Asian drinks and deserts.

Ingredients

2 tsp agar agar powder

1 cup hot water

1 tsp tukmaria (faludo)

18 tbsp grenadine, divided

2 cups vanilla ice cream

4 cups 2% milk, chilled

or

sherbet (see below)

¼ cup pistachios, chopped as a garnish

Time

30 minutes

Yield

4 servings

Ingredients

Shertbet

2 cups 2% milk

1 cup canned, evapourated milk

2 tbsp condensed milk

½ cup strawberry ice cream

½ tsp vanilla essence

4 drops rose essence

dash red or pink food colouring

Desserts

Kashmiri Faludo and mango Lassi

Sweet Potato or Yam Kheer

Method

1 In a saucepan, cook the sweet potatoes or yams in 1 cup water until they are well cooked but still firm.

2 While the sweet potatoes or yams are cooking, soak the bread (crusts removed) in ½ cup hot water. Leave for 3 minutes so that the bread absorbs the water. Mash the bread with a fork and set aside.

3 Stir the half-and-half cream, sugar, bread and cardamom into the sweet potatoe mixture. Cook until the mixture is thick and creamy.

4 Stir in the almonds and serve either hot or cold.

Notes

• When this dish is ready the sweet potatoes should be soft but still chunky.

• *Kheer* is a traditional Indian and Pakistani dish, like rice pudding, made by boiling rice with milk and sugar or jaggery/gur, flavoured with cardamom and pistachio and garnished with fried cashews and raisins. It is served at most festive occasions such as weddings, birthdays, and religious festivals. Traditionally made with rice, it can also be made with vermicelli (*sev, seviya, sevain*).

Ingredients

1½ cups sweet potatoes or yam, peeled and finely diced

1 cup water

2 cups half-and-half cereal cream (10% MF)

2 slices white bread

½ cup hot water

¼ cup sugar

¼ tsp cardamom seeds, coarsely ground

1 tbsp almonds, chopped

Time
30–40 minutes

Yield
4–5 servings

Plain Burfi (Fudge)

Ingredients

1 cup whipping cream

1½ cups sugar

4 oz butter

½ tsp cardamom seeds, crushed

¼ tsp nutmeg, grated

4 cups powdered skim milk

Garnish

2 tbsp almonds, chopped

2 tbsp pistachios, chopped

pinch saffron

Time

30 minutes

Yield

16 × 2" squares

Method

1 In a microwave-safe container, combine the cream, sugar, butter, cardamom and nutmeg.

2 Microwave on high power for 5 minutes.

3 Remove from the microwave and stir.

4 Return to the microwave, and cook on high power for a further 5 minutes.

5 Remove the mixture, add the powdered skim milk, stir and then microwave the mixture for 2 more minutes.

6 Remove from the microwave and mix thoroughly.

7 Transfer the mixture to a lightly greased 8 inch square pan and press it down with the back of a spoon.

8 While still warm, garnish with almonds, pistachios and saffron.

9 When the burfi has cooled completely, you can cut it into the desired number and size of pieces.

Variation

- *Chocolate Burfi*: Proceed as above, but instead of garnishing the burfi melt 4 oz of good milk chocolate and pour over the burfi. To melt chocolate, either use a double boiler or improvise by putting the chocolate into a Pyrex bowl or jug and place that into a pan of water and then slowly bring that water to a boil in order to melt the chocolate. Take care not to burn chocolate when melting it.

Notes

- *Burfi* (or *barfi*) is a traditional Indian and Pakistani dessert made from condensed milk, which is cooked until it solidifies, not unlike fudge. Burfi, is often flavoured with cashews, mango, pistachios and spices.

Desserts

Almond Burfi

Method

1 Powder the almonds in a food processor, and set aside.
2 In a pan, bring the sugar and cream to a boil. The desired consistency should be like one string sugar syrup or tar.
3 Add the almonds and cook on low heat until the mixture starts to leave the side of the pan slightly (approximately 2 minutes).
4 Transfer it to an 8 inch square greased cake pan.
5 Press the burfi down using the back of a spoon and garnish with chopped pistachios. Use the back of the spoon to press the nuts into the burfi, sufficiently so that they stick.
6 When the burfi has cooled completely, you can cut it into the desired number and size of pieces.

Variations

• *Pistachio Burfi*: Instead of blanched almonds, use unsalted pistachios and a few drops of green food colouring for a pale green coloured burfi.
• *Cashew Burfi*: Replace the ground almonds with cashews.

Notes

• *Burfi* or fudge is a popular Indian confection often served at birthday and wedding celebrations. It is also served at cultural and religious festivals such as Holi and Diwali when it is traditional to exchange gifts of confectionary with family and friends. I often serve burfi to guests with tea and a selection of other sweet or savoury snacks.

Ingredients

2 cups blanched almonds

1 cup sugar

1 cup half-and-half cereal cream (10% MF)

½ tsp cardamom seeds, coarsely ground

¼ cup unsalted pistachios, finely chopped for garnish

Time

30 minutes

Yield

16 × 2" squares

Desserts

Chocolate, Plain and Pistachio Burfi

Desserts

mango Burfi

Method

1 Put the mango pulp together with ½ cup of the sugar in a pan and cook over medium heat until it is reduced in volume by half. Be careful not to let it burn.

2 Stir in the remaining ¼ cup of sugar and the ricotta cheese.

3 Gradually, add the milk powder, cardamom and saffron while stirring and cook for 4 to 7 minutes or until the mixture starts to slightly pull away from the edges of the pot.

4 Pour into an 8 inch square greased cake pan.

5 Garnish the burfi while still warm with chopped pistachios.

6 When the burfi has cooled completely, you can cut it into the desired number and size of pieces.

Notes

- Unsalted pistachios are usually available at Indian or Middle Eastern grocery stores.

Ingredients

1¼ cups mango pulp

¾ cup sugar, divided

1¼ cups ricotta cheese

4 cups powdered skim milk

½ tsp ground cardamom

6 to 8 strands saffron

¼ cup unsalted pistachios, finely chopped for garnish

Time

30 minutes

Yield

16 × 2" squares

Sev paak

Ingredients

1 tbsp gum arabic (gund)

1 cup sunflower oil,
for frying gund

7 oz toasted sev

5½ oz unsalted butter

2 tbsp desiccated coconut

2 tbsp powdered skim milk

5½ oz almond flakes

1 × 10 oz can condensed milk

½ tsp cardamom,
coarsely ground

½ tsp ground nutmeg

¼ tsp saffron threads

¼ cup pistachios,
finely chopped as a garnish

Time
20–30 minutes

Yield
24 × 2" squares

Method

Step 1

1 In a small saucepan or a wok, heat the oil on medium and fry the gund. When the gund pops, remove it with a slotted spoon and set it aside. Discard leftover oil.

2 Break the sev into small pieces.

Step 2

1 Melt the butter in a clean saucepan.

2 Add the sev and sauté on low heat for 2 minutes.

3 Stir in the coconut and sauté for a further 2 minutes.

4 Stir in the powdered milk and sauté for another 2 minutes.

5 Stir in the almonds, cardamom, nutmeg, and saffron.

6 Stir in the condensed milk. Cook on very low heat and stir the mixture continuously for about 2 minutes, until all of the ingredients are well mixed. Finally, add the fried gund and mix well.

7 The mixture should leave the sides of the saucepan. If the mixture has not consolidated, add a little more condensed milk. The mixture should be moist.

8 Transfer the mixture to a 12 × 8 inch pan and press it down with the back of a spoon.

9 Garnish with pistachios while it is still warm and press them down with the back of a spoon, so they stick.

10 Let the *Sev Paak* cool for 10 minutes and then cut it into squares. Allow it to cool completely before removing the squares from the pan.

Notes

- **Gum Arabic** (*Gund*): Also know as *Acacia, Guar,* and *Xantham gum*, gum arabic is a natural fluid exuded by various African trees of the genus *Acacia,*

(*A. senegal* and *A. seyal*). It is a colourless, tasteless and odourless substance used in commercial food preparation to thicken, emulsify, and stabilize foods including candy, ice cream, and sweet syrups.

- Many varieties of sev are much thinner than the usual vermicelli noodles which are made from wheat flour as opposed to those made from rice flour and predominantly used in Asian cooking. Because there are several commercial ingredients called sev, make sure you buy the long, thin, toasted sev which often comes from Pakistan.

- For further details about sev, see the recipe for *Paapdi Chaat* on p. 31.

Chai with masala

Method

1 Boil the water, masala and teabags for 5 minutes. Add milk and sugar and boil for another 3 to 5 minutes. Strain and serve hot.

Notes

- This exotic blend of tea with roasted, ground spices may be served at tea time, after dinner and on special occasions. It is especially comforting on cold winter days!

Ingredients

3 cups water

1 tsp *Chai Masala* (see p. 5)

4 tea bags (e.g., orange pekoe)

3 cups milk

sugar to taste

Time

15 minutes

Yield

4 servings

Sev Paak

Mango Juice

Method

1 Bring the milk to a boil, add the sugar or jaggery and stir the milk until the sugar is dissolved. Let it cool down and strain.

2 Mix all of the ingredients and keep in the refrigerator until you are ready to serve.

Serving Suggestions

- Traditionally, *Mango Juice* is served in small bowls and eaten with *Dry Moong Daal Curry* (*Suki Mug Ni Daal*) (p. 128), and *Rotli* (p. 136), or *Puri* (p. 143).

Ingredients

1 × 24 oz can mango pulp

1 tbsp jaggery
or demerara sugar

2 cups milk

pinch saffron

½ tsp ground ginger, optional

Time

15 minutes

Yield

5–6 servings

Mango Juice

Hot Ginger Drink

Ingredients

2 tsp ground ginger
or 2 × 1" cubes of fresh
ginger, grated
6 cups water
3 tbsp lemon juice
5 tsp sugar,
or to taste

Time

30 minutes

Yield

4 servings

Method

1 Boil the water, and then add the ginger, lemon juice and sugar.
2 Simmer, covered, for a further 20 minutes on low heat.
3 Strain and serve hot.

Notes

• This is good for digestion or if you have a cold.

Tamarind Drink

Ingredients

4 oz tamarind pulp
4 cups water
¼ tsp ground cumin
¼ cup sugar
½ tsp salt
crushed ice

Time

30 minutes,
after soaking

Yield

4 servings

Method

1 Put 4 cups of hot water into a pot, add the tamarind and soak it for 2 to 3 hours; then bring to a boil.
2 Simmer the tamarind for a few minutes and then leave it to cool.
3 When the liquid is cold, strain it by mashing and pressing the tamarind through a sieve.
4 Add a little more water to the remaining pulp, mixing thoroughly, and press it through the sieve again.
5 Discard the remaining pulp.
6 Stir the sugar, salt, and cumin into the tamarind juice and serve over crushed ice.

Notes

• This is an ideal drink on a hot summer day.

mango lassi

Method

1 In a blender, combine the buttermilk, mango pulp, ground cardamom, saffron, and sugar and blend well.
2 Serve in a tall glass with crushed ice or ice cubes, and sprinkle with cardamom powder if desired.

Variation

• Instead of ground cardamom try ground ginger.

Notes

• *Lassi* is a traditional beverage, flavoured with spices, fruit, or other ingredients, made by blending yogurt and water until frothy and enjoyed chilled, as either a sweet or salty hot-weather refreshment. Sweet lassi is a recent invention, with more sugar, rosewater and/or lemon, mango, strawberry, or other fruit juice. Lassi are also served as coolers for spicy foods.

Ingredients

1 cup buttermilk

½ cup mango pulp

⅛ tsp ground cardamom, optional

½ pinch saffron

1 tsp sugar

½ cup ice cubes

Time

10 minutes

Yield

1 serving

pistachio lassi

Method

1 In a blender, combine the pistachios and buttermilk. Blend until pistachios are broken into pieces.
2 Add the sugar, cardamom and ice.
3 Blend for another ½ minute. When the liquid is light and frothy, it is ready to serve in a cold, frosted glass.

Ingredients

1½ cups buttermilk

5 or 6 unsalted pistachios

1½ tsp sugar, or to taste

¼ tsp ground cardamom, optional

1 cup crushed ice

Time

5 minutes

Yield

1 serving

Desserts

Personal Notes

Glossary

Agar Agar: See recipe on p. 153.

Ajowain: See **Bishop's Weed** below.

Asafoetida: See recipe on p. 3.

Bishop's Weed: (*Ajamo* in Gujarati): Native to southern India, also known as *Ajowan* or *Ajowain*, *Indian Thyme*, *Seeds of Bishop's Weed*, and *Carom*, it is the seed-like fruit of this annual or perennial plant (*Trachyspermum ammi*) that is typically marketed as **Ajowain** and is usually found in ground or seed form. Ajowain smells and tastes like thyme or caraway, only stronger, and is often confused with *Lovage* seed. A small amount of raw ajowain goes a long way and too much will completely dominate the food. In Indian cooking, it is almost always used dry-roasted or fried in ghee and used in vegetable dishes and flat breads like *ajowain ka paratha*.

Cardamom (*Elaychi*): Cardamom is a perennial rhizomatous Indian herb (*Elettaria cardamomum*) with capsular greenish fruits about the size of a cranberry, each of which contains 17 to 20 aromatic seeds that are used as a spice or condiment in curries, cakes, pickles and general cooking. Cardamom can be purchased in the pod (often sold bleached) as seeds or ground. Ground cardamom is more convenient but does not provide the same full flavour since seeds begin to lose their essential oils as soon as they are ground. Best stored in pod form, seeds can be removed from the pod and ground, or the whole pod can be ground using a mortar and pestle or a coffee grinder. Be frugal with cardamom as a little goes a long way. When using cardamom, follow the recipe as stated, using either whole pods or crushed roasted seeds. 10 pods = ½ to 1 teaspoon of ground cardamom, depending on the size of the pods: small, green cardamom pods (*Nani Elaychi*) or large, black/brown pods (*Moti Elaychi*).

Cashew (*Kajoo*): The edible seed of the evergreen cashew tree, (*Anacardium occidentale*) native to Brazil, is a kidney- or boxing glove-shaped drupe that is situated at the bottom of the cashew apple, a pseudo fruit that grows out of the peduncle. Cashews are nuts only in the culinary sense (in the botanical sense they are seeds), and have a sweet, buttery flavour. Their high fat content (48%) requires that they be stored tightly wrapped in the refrigerator to retard the onset of rancidity. They are usually available dry or oil roasted, with or without salt. Commercial production is centred in India which handles 90% of world trade in the commodity.

Cassava (*Mhogo* in Kiswahili): Also known as *Manioc* or *Yuca*, and *Mhogo*, *Muhogo*, or *Hogo* in East Africa, cassava (*Manihot esculenta*) is a shrubby, perennial tropical plant native to central and South America where it is widely grown for its large, tuberous, starchy roots that range from 6 to 12 inches in length and 2 to 3 inches in diameter. The roots are peeled and boiled as a vegetable not unlike sweet potatoes or potatoes. It is often deep fried after boiling or steaming. Cassava starch is also the source of tapioca. It can be stored fresh, unskinned, for up to four days but is also available commercially prepared and frozen.

Cayenne Pepper: Named for the city of Cayenne in French Guiana, cayenne pepper is an orange-red to dark red condiment consisting of the ground ripe fruit of several cultivated varieties (*Capsicum baccatum*; *C. frutescens*) of chili peppers. The fruits are generally dried and ground or pulped and baked into cakes that may be ground and sifted to make the powder. Cayenne is rated at 40,000 to 90,000 Scoville Units.

Chana Daal: See recipe on p. 125.

Chana Flour: Also known as *besan*, *gram* or *Bengal gram* (not to be confused with **Graham Flour**), chana is a pale yellow flour, and a staple in Indian cuisine, made from splitting and grinding chana daal, which is a major source of protein in a predominantly vegetarian culture. Flour made from chana daal is typically confused with chickpea flour. In an airtight container, chana flour can be stored in the refrigerator for up to six months. Best results are obtained by sieving chana before use to remove any lumps or impurities. Vegetables deep-fried in chana flour batter are known as *pakoras* (fritters). When onions are so fried they are known as *onion bhajias* or *pakoras*.

Chickpea Flour: See **Chana Flour**.

Chili (*Marchu*): Also known as chile, chilli, or hot peppers, chilies (*Marcha*) range in length from a quarter inch to over 12 inches, and in diameter from as thin as a pencil to others which are round and globular. There are more than 200 varieties of chilies (broken down into two groupings: bell, or sweet, and hot). They range in colour from yellow to green (essentially unripe fruit) to red and black. As a general rule, the smaller the chili, the hotter it will be; proportionally, a small chili contains more seeds and veins which contain the compound, capsaicin, which gives chilies their fiery nature. Milder, larger varieties are often referred to as bell peppers. Neither cooking nor freezing reduces the intensity of the capsaicin; only the removal of the seeds and veins will reduce the heat of any variety. The heat of chili peppers is measured in Scoville Units (SHU) with bell peppers ranking 0 SHU, jalapeños 3,000 to 6,000 SHU and habañeros 300,000 SHU. They are used to make a variety of products including paste, powder, dried flakes, Tabasco sauce, and cayenne and paprika. Chile powder is a spice made from dried ground ancho chilies with small amounts of cayenne for heat. Chili powder is composed of dried, ground chili peppers, cumin, garlic and oregano, and used in the dish *Chili Con Carne* popular in Mexico and the American southwest. Fresh chilies will keep for several days in the salad drawer of a refrigerator and it is always best to use rubber gloves when preparing or handling them before cooking. In northern India, bell peppers are commonly called *Simla Marchu/Marcha* (red chilies: *Lal Marchu/Marcha*; green chilies: *Lila Marchu/Marcha*). To make your own chili paste, see p. 7. If you like to freeze chilies or chili paste, purchase them at the end of the growing season when they are hottest. When frying or sautéing whole chilies in a recipe, make a slit so that the hot oil does not cause them to pop or splutter.

Cinnamon (*Thajh*): True cinnamon is the dried, aromatic inner bark of the evergreen tropical Asian shrub or tree, *Cinnamomum zeylanicum, C. loureirii,* or *C. verum*). The thin (1/50 inch) inner bark is removed in the rainy season, when it is more pliable, from suckers that grow up from the roots. The outer, woody portion is removed. As it dries, the yard long strips of bark curl up into rolls or quills; each quill comprises strips from numerous shoots, packed together. These quills are cut up into short 2 to 4 inch lengths and sold as cinnamon sticks or ground into a powder. True Ceylon/Sri Lankan cinnamon [as opposed to **Cassia** (*C. cassia; C. aromaticum*) which is often sold as cinnamon in North America] have many thin and softer layers and can easily be ground up in a coffee grinder.

Citric Acid: An organic, colourless, translucent, crystalline (white powder), and relatively strong water-soluble but non-toxic acid, which occurs in relatively large quantities in citrus fruits—lemon, lime, orange, pineapple, and gooseberry—as well as in other fruits, vegetables, and in animal tissues and fluids, either as the free acid or as a citrate ion. Commercially, it is principally derived by fermentation of carbohydrates or from citrus fruit juices. It is a natural preservative used in cooking to produce a sour, acidic, or tart taste and to complement fruit flavours in carbonated beverages, beverage powders, fruit-flavoured drinks, jams and jellies, candy, sherbets, water ices and wine. It may be purchased in powder form and may be called sour or citrus salt. It can be added to recipes as a substitute wherever fresh lemon juice is called for.

Clove (*Laving*): A clove is the dried, unopened flowerbud of the evergreen tree (*Syzygium aromaticum*), native to the Moluccas. The folded petals of each bud are enclosed by four toothlike lobes of the calyx, and are picked by hand and dried and used whole or ground as a spice for flavouring pickles, ketchup and sauces. Historically, cloves have been used in Indian cuisine throughout the country. In northern India, cloves are used extensively in sauces and side dishes, mostly ground up along with other spices. In southern India, cloves are used extensively in *Biryani* where it is normally added whole to enhance the presentation and flavour of the rice. For convenience, I tend to grind my own cloves and use them in that form, or substitute some garam masala that includes clove. Either approach means you can avoid having to pick whole cloves out of the cooked dish.

Coconut (*Nariyal*): Coconut is the large, brown hard-shelled seed of the coconut palm (*Cocos nucifera*) containing white flesh and a partially fluid-filled central cavity. A coconut has several layers: a smooth, deep tan outer covering (usually removed by the time they get into supermarkets); a hard, dark brown, hairy husk with three indented eyes at one end; a thin brown skin; the creamy white coconut meat and, at the centre, a thin, opaque coconut juice. This juice can be used as a beverage but should not be confused with coconut milk. Grated fresh coconut flesh can be tightly covered and refrigerated for up to four days or frozen for up to six months. Commercially available coconut comes in cans or plastic bags, either sweetened or unsweetened, shredded or flaked and dried, moist or frozen. Sometimes it is available toasted. Unopened canned coconut will last 18 months; unopened plastic bags, six months. Coconut milk or coconut cream are sometimes called for in recipes, particularly curries. Coconut milk is made by combining equal parts water with freshly shredded flesh, powdered or desiccated coconut that is simmered until foamy, and the liquid strained through a cheesecloth. The process can be repeated to make a second more dilute batch, of coconut milk. Coconut cream is made in the same manner but with only a quarter of the amount of water. Milk can be substituted for water to make even thicker cream. The coconut flesh is discarded after making milk or cream. Both coconut milk and coconut cream are also available canned. Be careful not to confuse sweetened cream of coconut, used mainly for desserts and mixed drinks, with unsweetened coconut milk or cream. Use the unsweetened kind for savoury dishes.

The health benefits of coconut, especially coconut oil, have received some considerable attention recently. The specific components of coconut that are increasingly believed to have physiologically beneficial effects are found in the fat part of both whole and desiccated coconut, and especially in the extracted coconut oil. Coconut oil contains Lauric and Capric acid, two fatty acids that have been recognized for their antiviral, antibacterial, and antiprotozoal functions. Recently published research suggests that natural coconut oil in the diet can lead to a normalization of body lipids (cholesterol), protect the liver against damage caused by alcohol, and improve the immune system's anti-inflamatory response.

Coriander (*Kothmeer*; *Dhania*): An aromatic, annual Eurasian herb in the parsley family (*Coriandrum sativum*) is cultivated for its edible fruits, leafy shoots, and roots. Fresh, young coriander leaves (known as **Cilantro** or **Chinese Parsley** in North America, and *Kothmeer* in the Indian subcontinent) of this herb are used whole or chopped in salads and various dishes such as daal and curries as a flavouring and garnish. Choose leaves with an even, dark green colour and no sign of wilting. As heat diminishes their flavour quickly, coriander leaves are often used raw and are added to the dish right before serving. In some Indian dishes, huge amounts of coriander leaves are cooked till they dissolve into sauce and their flavour mellows. Coriander leaves can be stored for a few days in airtight containers in the refrigerator after chopping off the roots. However, they do not keep well and should be purchased fresh and used promptly as they lose their aroma if frozen or dried. The seedlike fruit (*Dhania*) impart a warm, nutty, spicy citrus orange/lemon flavour and are used whole or ground as flavouring and seasoning in curries and soups and for pickling and special drinks. Best purchased whole and ground as needed, the seeds can be dry roasted in a pan before grinding to enhance their flavour. Whole coriander seeds should be used within six months but can be kept in an airtight container away from sunlight and heat for up to a year. Coriander leaves and seeds are not interchangeable in recipes. Split, roasted coriander seeds are called **Dhania Daal** and are eaten as a snack and used in various masalas, like *Paan Masala*. Paan is actually a type of edible leaf used to wrap the masala for ease of eating.

Cumin (*Jiru*): An annual mediterranean herb (*Cuminum cyminum*), in the parsley family, the seedlike fruit of which is used for seasoning in curry and chili powder as well meat sauces, rice, bread, pickles, and soups. The aromatic, nutty-flavoured seeds come in three colours; amber, white and black, with amber being the most commonplace. White cumin is interchangeable with amber but black cumin has a more complex and peppery flavour. All types are available either ground or in seed form and, like most seeds, herbs and spices, will keep better as seeds to be ground fresh as needed. The seeds can be stored in a cool, dark place for up to six months.

Curry Leaves (*Mitho Limbo*): Leaves from the subtropical curry tree (*Chalcas koenigii, Murraya koenigii* or *Bergera koenigii*) are best picked fresh and when the leaves are young or about 1 inch in length. They are dark green in colour, oval of shape, and have a pungent smell much like the leaves of a citrus tree. Typically they are sautéed in oil then cooked with the dish. Before serving, the leaves are removed, much like bay leaves are used in cooking. Sold fresh or dried, fresh leaves have much the better nutty flavour. To store fresh leaves, remove them from the twigs, wash and dry the leaves on paper towels. Then gently rub the leaves with a small amount of warm oil so that the leaves are lightly coated. Store in an airtight, sealed container in the freezer, they will retain both their colour and flavour for a considerable period of time.

Daal: A Hindi word for sixty varieties of dried pulses including peas, beans and lentils that have been skinned and split. Also known as *dal, dhal* and *dhall*, common varieties of daal include **Chana** (yellow split peas or split chickpea lentils), **Moong** (whole green lentils), **Masur/Masoor** (red/orange lentils), **Toovar** (tan/brown lentils) and **Urad** (black gram/lentils). They form the basis of a cooked dish called daal that is usually served at every traditional Indian meal as it is a good source of protein. Daal made with lentils or other pulses is cooked in water and seasoned with a variety of spices, tomatoes and onions. Occasionally, impurities or adulterants, such as tiny stones or sticks, will show up in a package of daal, so it is always a good idea to spread the daal on a tray and pick out any impurities before using.

Dhania Daal: See recipe on p. 6.

Dill (*Sura*): An annual or biennial aromatic herb of the parsley family (*Anethum graveolens*) native to Eurasia, with the leaves or seeds, or oil derived from each, commercially harvested. India is the primary producer of dill seed for culinary purposes where it is used in pickling and to flavour salads, vegetables, meats, sauces, and soups. The leaves and seeds are marketed both fresh and dried, and in whole or ground forms. As with other leafy herbs, dill loses its fragrance during heating so it is usually added towards the end of the cooking time. Heating or slightly roasting dill seeds will bring out their flavour which is stronger and more pungent than that of the leaves.

Fennel (*Variari*): A Eurasian annual or biennial aromatic herb of the carrot and parsley family (*Foeniculum vulgare*) which is grown for the bulb, stems, foliage, and seeds. The celery-like base and stems can be eaten raw in salads, as a garnish or as a last-minute flavour enhancer; alternatively, they can be cooked in a variety of manners such as braising, sautéing or in soups. The oval, greenish-brown fruit or seeds are dried and used in bread, pickles, liqueurs, and meat sauces and other dishes. Similar in aroma and flavour to anise and star anise, fennel can be distinguished by its warm, sweet character. Seeds are available whole or ground and can be stored in a cool, dark place for up to six months. For cooking, green seeds are optimal and the pollen is the most potent form of the plant, though exceedingly expensive. Fennel seeds may also be used as an ingredient in *Paan Masala*, traditionally served after meals in India to cleanse the breath. Fennel is an essential ingredient in the Bengali spice mixture, *Panch Phoron* or *Poran*, where fennel is known as *mouri*.

Fenugreek (*Methi*): A clover-like annual Eurasian plant (*Trigonella foenumgraecum*), fenugreek is used as both an herb (leaves) and a spice (seeds). The young, aromatic celery-like leaves and sprouts can be cooked and are usually added towards the end of the cooking process. Dried fenugreek leaves (well known from the Kasur region, hence called *Kasoori Methi*) are often encountered in northern Indian cuisine such as *Khakhra*, a type of bread. The yellow and rhombic-shaped seeds are mildly bitter, yet slightly sweet, and have been described as having an aroma similar to burnt sugar or maple syrup. Widely used whole or ground in southern Indian cuisine, fenugreek is used sparingly as an ingredient in curry powders and pastes, chutneys and pickles, spice blends and tea. Fenugreek seeds can be stored in a cool, dark place for up to six months.

Garlic (*Lasan*): A hardy, perennial Asiatic plant (*Allium sativum*) of the lily family and a cousin to leeks, chives, onions and shallots. The garlic bulb breaks up into separable cloves, each encased in its own parchment-like membrane. Three major types are generally available: white-skinned, strongly flavoured American garlic; mauve-skinned and milder Mexican and Italian garlic; and white-skinned elephant garlic, which is the mildest type and, being related to the leek, is not a true garlic. Best used fresh, garlic should be purchased as firm, plump bulbs with dry skins. Fresh garlic can be stored in an open container, away from other foods, in a cool, dark place. Properly stored, unbroken bulbs can be kept up to eight weeks, though they will begin to dry out towards the end of that time. Once a bulb is broken, individual cloves should last between 3 to 10 days. Garlic is usually peeled before use in recipes, and there are some simple techniques to make this laborious task a little easier. Crushing, chopping, pressing or puréeing garlic will release more of its essential oils and produce a sharper more assertive flavour than slicing alone or leaving cloves whole. Garlic is readily available as flakes, powder, paste or garlic salt. Making and freezing your own paste is simple. See the recipe on p. 8.

Ghee: Ghee is a clarified, semifluid butter used in Indian cooking. It can be made by slowly melting any unsalted butter (traditionally made from water buffalo milk) so that the milk solids (which sink to the bottom of the pan) separate from the golden liquid on the surface. This form of clarified butter is simmered until all of the moisture evaporates and the milk solids begin to brown, giving the resulting ghee a nutty, caramel-like flavour and aroma. This extra step gives ghee a longer shelf life and a much higher smoke (about 375°C). Tightly wrapped ghee can be refrigerated for up to six months and frozen up to a year. It can also be stored for extended periods (longer than butter) provided it is kept in an airtight container to prevent oxidation and that it remains moisture-free. At room temperature, ghee will be semi-liquid and the best quality has a rich, golden colour.

Ghisoda: Ghisoda belongs to a small genus (*Luffa acutangla*; *L. aegyptiaca*; *L. operculata*) of tropical, Old World gourds or vines, grown chiefly for their ornamental fruits. Picked young, before maturity, the fruit can be cooked and eaten as a vegetable, which is called *Si Gua* in China and in Asian markets. *L. acutangula* is also known as a **Ridge Gourd** and goes by many different names in India. The dried, fibrous cucumber or club-like skeletons (the xylem) are sold as bath or kitchen sponges or loofahs.

Ginger (*Adhu*): A perennial plant (*Zingiber officinale*) from tropical and subtropical Asia, grown for its pungent, aromatic rhizome, which is sold fresh, dried, powdered, cooked and candied, preserved or pickled. The name is believed to have been derived from the Pali language, an Indo-Iranian descendant of the Sanskrit word meaning "horn-root." Ginger root has a tan skin and flesh which ranges in colour from a pale greenish yellow to ivory. The flavour is peppery and slightly sweet and the aroma is pungent and spicy. Ginger is best used fresh and appears in a variety of forms—chopped, puréed, grated or slivered—in Indian cuisine. Fresh ginger is usually sold in two forms—young and mature. Young ginger or spring ginger has pale, thin skin and sometimes requires no peeling. Mature ginger has a thicker, tougher skin that requires careful peeling to preserve the delicate, most desirable flesh just under the surface. Fresh, unpeeled ginger can be tightly wrapped and stored in a refrigerator for up to three weeks or frozen for up to six months. Crystallized or candied ginger has been cooked in sugar syrup and coated with coarse sugar. Preserved ginger has been cooked in a sugar-salt mixture, and sweet red candied ginger has been preserved in red sugar syrup. Pickled ginger has been preserved in sweet vinegar. To make your own paste, see p. 8.

Graham Flour: Not to be confused with Gram flour, Graham flour is a type of whole wheat flour that is made by grinding the whole grain (bran, germ and endosperm) wheat kernel in two separate stages. The endosperm is ground to produce fine white flour and the bran and germ are ground coarsely. The two components are then recombined creating coarse-textured flour that bakes and keeps quite well. It is named after Sylvester Graham (1794–1851) an American Presbyterian minister and early advocate of dietary reform.

Gram Flour: See **Chana Flour**.

Gum Arabic (*Gund*): See recipe on p. 160.

Gur: See **Jaggery**.

Jaggery or **Cane Sugar**: Jaggery or *Gur* as it is known in northern India is unrefined sugar either made from the sap of various palm trees or from sugar cane juice. Technically jaggery refers solely to sugarcane sugar. Sugar made from date palms is the real *Gur* and is both more prized and less available outside of the areas in which it is made. Hence, outside of these areas sugarcane jaggery is sometimes called *Gol* or *Gur* to increase its market value. Jaggery comes in several forms of which the most common is a solid, cakelike block. Jaggery has a sweet, winey fragrence and flavour that lends distinction to every food it embellishes. If you cannot find true jaggery or gur, you can substitute real demerara sugar instead, which is a partly refined, golden brown sugar, and not coloured with molasses.

Mango (*Karee*): The edible fruit of the tropical, evergreen tree (*Mangifera indica*) which has a smooth green rind that turns yellow with red highlights when the fruit is ripe. The flesh is sweet, juicy and yellow-orange in colour and surrounds a large, single fibrous seed or stone. Mangos are in season from May through September, though imported fruit can be found in stores, sporadically, at other times of year. Because the mango seed is so large, the larger the fruit, the better the fruit-to-seed ratio. Ripe mangos can be stored in a plastic bag in the refrigerator for up to five days, and under-ripe fruit can be ripened in a paper bag at room temperature. Mangos are available fresh, canned and in a variety of other processed states, including nectar, purée, or pulp, all of which are usually fresh or frozen. Dried mango is available in chunks and strips. Green, unripe mangos are also used to make the Indian seasoning, mango powder (*amchur*) which is derived by pulverizing sun-dried, unripe mangoes into a fine powder. The powder has a tart, acidic, fruity flavour which adds character to meat, vegetable, and curried dishes as well as fruit chaats. It is also used as a tenderizer for poultry, game, and fish. India currently produces 75% of the world's commercial crop of mangos.

Masala: A general term, meaning "spices," used throughout India for a spice blend with numerous variations. It can refer to a simple combination of two or three spices or to a complex blend of ten or more. The most widely used blend is called Garam (which means "warm") Masala, the variations of which are countless, depending on the cook and the dish being seasoned. Masalas used in this book include *Garam Masala*, *Kashmiri Masala*, *Chaat Masala*, *Paan Masala* and *Rangola Masala*. You can make most of these masala mixes yourself. Toasting the whole-seed spices lightly will enhance the flavour. Kept in airtight containers, in a cool, dark place, they will last for up to six months.

Moong Daal: See recipe on p. 128.

Mung Beans: See recipe for **Moong Daal** on p. 128.

Mustard (*Rai*): Primarily three Eurasian plants (*Brassica nigra*; *Brassica juncea*; *Brassica* or *Sinapsis alba*), which are black, brown, and white (or yellow) mustard respectively, all of which are cultivated for their pungent seeds and edible leaves. Mustard is available either as whole seeds, as a dry powder made from the seeds with the seed coats removed, or as commercially prepared paste, containing water, vinegar, white wine, and other spices and ingredients. Mustard seeds can be stored up to a year in a dry, dark place and powdered mustard will keep for about six months. The seeds are commonly used in Indian cuisine, in curries for example, and are usually roasted in hot oil or ghee that causes the seeds to pop and release their characteristic nutty flavour. Mustard seeds contain a significant amount of oil, and mustard oil is often used as cooking oil in India. I use brown mustard seeds in most of my recipes.

Nutmeg (*Jayfal*): An evergreen tree (*Myristica fragrans*) native to the East Indies and cultivated for its spicy seeds which are used as a spice when grated or ground. The golden-yellow, mature fruits resemble apricots. As they gradually mature and lose moisture, the husk (pericarp) splits when completely ripe, exposing the shiny brown seed which is the commercial nutmeg. This seed is actually surrounded by a fibrous, lacy aril (seed covering) that separates the seed from the outer husk. When dried and ground, the aril becomes the spice we know as **Mace** (*Javantri*). The egg-shaped nutmeg seed is greyish-brown and about 1 inch long. Nutmeg is sold whole or ground and nutmeg ground fresh with a nutmeg grater is always superior to that commercially ground and packaged. In Indian cuisine, nutmeg is used almost exclusively in sweets but appears in small quantities in some masalas.

Paneer: See recipe on p. 112.

Paprika: A mild powdered seasoning made from sweet red peppers (*Capsicum annuum*) with nonpungent flesh, grown for its long red fruit. The seeds are removed from the mature fruit that is dried and ground to prepare the condiment commonly referred to as paprika. The flavour of paprika can vary from mild to pungent and hot and the colour can range from orange-red to deep crimson. Paprika can be stored in a cool, dark place for up to six months. In India, paprika comes from a pepper known as *Deghi Mirchi* that is widely grown but wherever it is grown, it takes on a slightly different flavour arising from local soil and climatic conditions.

Pistachio (*Pista*): The drupaceous, nut-like, semi-dry fruit of a deciduous tree (*Pistacia vera*) native to central and western Asia. The nutlike fruit of the tree have edible, oily green or yellow kernels. The fruit is borne on one-year-old wood in clusters, similar to grapes, and mature in the fall. The hull (exocarp and mesocarp) easily sloughs off the hard, tan-coloured shell (endocarp) which has already split, a sign of full maturity, exposing the pale green kernel or nut. Pistachios are usually available raw or roasted, salted or not. There used to be a practice of dying pistachio nuts either red or green (with vegetable dye), or blanching them until white, to eliminate blemishes on the shells from harvesting. The nuts have a pleasing, mild, resinous flavour and are used extensively as food and for their yellowish green colouring in confections.

Pistachio nuts turn naturally red if they are marinated in a salt and lemon or citrus salts marinade before roasting.

Poppy Seed (*Khaskhas*): Poppy seed, also called Maw seed, are derived from the opium poppy (*Papaveraceae somniferum*), and yet are not themselves narcotic. The annual, biennial or perennial plant is probably a native of Asia Minor. Poppy seeds are small in size (less than 1/16 of an inch; it would take 900,000 seeds to equal 1 lb), bluish-grey, near white to beige, or brown in colour and have a crunchy texture and nutty flavour. They are used in baking, as a filling or topping for myriad breads, cakes, and pastries, in salad dressings, and in a variety of cooked dishes. Poppy seeds can be purchased whole or ground for flour. The fat content of poppy seeds is high and poppy seed oil is produced on a commercial basis. Given their high fat content, poppy seeds are prone to rancidity although they can be stored for up to six months, so long as they are refrigerated in airtight containers. The natural flavour of poppy seeds is enhanced with roasting. I use the near-white to beige coloured poppy seeds in the *Makati Mimina* recipe.

Rice (*Chokha*) is an annual, herbaceous cereal grass (*Oryza sativa; O. glaberrima*) with more than 7,000 varieties, which are cultivated extensively in warm climates for their edible grain. Most rice is eaten steamed or boiled but it can be dried and ground into flour or processed into a breakfast cereal. Hulling or dehusking rice removes the chaff and produces what is known as brown rice where the grains retain the high-fibre outer germ or bran layer. Further processing, or milling, removes the bran layer and produces what we know as white or polished rice. However, milling rice removes much of the oil, vitamins and nutrients contained in the bran layer. Further processing is often undertaken to restore nutrient value to white rice that is then designated as converted rice. Brown rice is more nutritious but because of the oil in the bran layer, rancidity is an issue, and it will spoil more quickly than white rice with a shelf life of only about six months although refrigeration will extend this period considerably. Rice varieties are also classified as long, medium and short grain. Long grain rice has a lower starch content and produces drier, fluffier rice when cooked. Shorter grain rice has a higher starch content and produces stickier rice when cooked. Medium-grained varieties tend to have cooking qualities similar to short-grained varieties. One particular long-grained variety, widely used in Indian cooking, is the aromatic basmati variety that works well for many Indian savoury dishes. There are many kinds of rice which are labelled as basmati and not all are equal in quality. The two I use most frequently are *Lal Kila* and *817* brands. Other Indian varieties include long and medium grained Patna, and short-grained Masoori. Wash the rice gently in several changes of water then leave to soak for 15 minutes prior to cooking. It is economical to buy in 11 lb (5 kg) bags. White rice can be stored in an airtight container in a cool, dark place almost indefinitely. Rice that has been aged for 2 to 3 years and stored in a cool place is better than the new crop.

Saffron (*Kasar*): A corm-producing, fall-flowering perennial plant (*Crocus sativus*) native to the Old World, having purple or white flowers with orange stigmas, from which saffron is produced when the stigmas are picked and dried. *C. sativus* was developed from *C. cartwrightianus* after subjecting the latter to extensive artificial selection by growers who desired elongated stamens. Saffron has a strong orange-yellow to red-orange colour and is a pungent, aromatic spice primarily used, exceedingly sparingly because of its expense (for four decades, it has been the world's most expensive spice), to colour or flavour food. Each flower only provides three stigmas and it takes more than 4,000 flowers to produce 1 oz of the dye/powder. Saffron is marketed in powder form and as threads (whole stigmas). Powdered saffron loses its flavour more readily and is more easily subject to adulteration, being cut with other substances of a similar colour, such as marigold, to keep the price down. A good measure of the herb's potency and freshness is its odour. If saffron does not have a noticeable, pungent smell (metallic honey with grassy or hay-like notes), with a hay-like and somewhat bitter flavour, then it is probably past its best. The more vivid and darker red the colour, generally speaking, the better the quality as well. If you purchase threads, these should be crushed just before using. A vivid crimson colouring, slight moisture, elasticity, recent harvest date, and lack of broken-off threads are all traits of fresh saffron. Both kinds of saffron can be stored in an airtight container in a cool, dark place for up to six months. The herb can also be frozen and, properly stored, may last up to two years.

Serrano: A type of chili pepper, originating in the mountainous regions of the Mexican states of Puebla and Hidalgo. Unripe serranos are green while colour at maturity varies from yellow to red, orange, and brown. Serrano peppers grow to between 1 to 2 inches in length and a half an inch in diameter, are quite fleshy and thus do not dry well. Their heat rating lies between 10,000 and 20,000 Scoville Units.

Star Anise (*Anasphal*): Also known as *Star Aniseed* or *Chinese Star Anise*, are the dark brown pods or pericarp and anise-scented fruit of the eastern Asian, evergreen tree (*Illicium verum*) which has purple-red flowers and star-like clusters of fruit. Each fruit has a pea-sized seed in each of its eight segments. The fruits are harvested just before ripening. In Asian cuisine, star anise is a commonly used spice and flavouring in tea. It can be found whole in Indian and Asian markets and some supermarkets and is one of the ingredients in Chinese *Five-spice Powder*.

Sugar Syrup (*Chasni*): Also called simple syrup, different consistencies of sugar syrup are required for different desserts. Sugar syrup is a solution of sugar and water that is cooked over a low heat until clear, then boiled for a minute or so. It can be made in various densities depending on the ratio of sugar to water: 3 parts water to 1 part sugar will produce a thin syrup; 2 parts water to 1 part sugar, a medium syrup; and equal parts water and sugar, a thick syrup. The strength or viscosity of the syrup can also be measured in strings or tar. Check the viscosity by placing a drop between your thumb and forefinger. Press your fingers together and separate; if the syrup forms a string (tar), it is called one string or tar. If two or more strings form, the syrup will be thicker. Sugar syrup can also be tested with a candy thermometer or by placing a drop onto a plate. Lighter strength syrup will spread or flow while heavier syrup will not flow as far.

Tamarind (*Amli*): The fruit of the Asian evergreen tree (*Tamarindus indica*) sometimes known as *Indian Date*, has pale yellow flowers and pods about 5 inches in length which contain small seeds embedded in an edible, sour-sweet pulp that, when dried, becomes extremely sour. Tamarind pulp concentrate is used as a popular souring agent in Indian cuisine, in much the same way that lemon juice is used in the west. It is used to season chutneys, curry dishes, and pickled fish. It is also used to make sweet syrup flavouring for soft drinks. It can be purchased in jars of concentrated pulp with seeds, as canned paste or as whole pods that have been dried and pressed into bricks, or ground into powder.

Tukmaria: See recipe on p. 153.

Turmeric (*Haldhar*): A widely cultivated tropical, perennial plant (*Curcuma domestica*, or *C. longa*), which belongs to the ginger family, and is native to south Asia, is the source of turmeric, which is derived from the powdered tuberous rhizome of the plant. Turmeric root is actually a fleshy, oblong tuber, 2 to 3 inches in length and close to 1 inch in diameter. As a spice, turmeric can be yellow-orange, orange-red or reddish-brown in colour and has a decidedly fragrant, musky odour and a pungent, bitter, peppery biting taste reminiscent of ginger. Turmeric is very popular in Indian cuisine and is almost always used in curry preparations. It is also used to flavour and colour curry powder, butter, cheese, relishes, pickles, and prepared mustard. It is also used as a substitute for saffron.

Research activity into polyphenol curcumin, the active ingredient in turmeric is exploding. Due to its antioxidant, anti-inflamatory properties and its ability to stimulate and increase the immune system response, curcumin is currently being investigated for its potential role in the treatment of a wide range of medical conditions. These include: Alzheimer's, leukemia, breast and colon cancer, diabetes, liver disease, gallstones, osteo and rheumatoid arthritis, psoriasis, salmonella, and a number of STDs including chlamydia and gonorrhea.

Tuvar Daal: See recipe on p. 126.

Yellow Food Colouring: This is available in powdered form from Indian grocery stores. Yellow food colouring, commonly used in baking, can be used instead of the powder. To obtain an orange colour, mix a few drops of yellow and red colouring together.

personal notes

Sample Menus

Menu 1
Onion Bhajia
Chicken Kebabs
Naan
Chicken with Bell Pepper Sauce
Cumin-scented Rice
Sweet Potato *or* Yam Kheer
Chai with Masala
Paan Masala

Menu 2
Vegetable Kebabs
Red Kidney Beans with Cream
Rotli *or* Naan
Chicken Biryani
Kachumber
Mango Lassi
Fruit Salad with Mango Cream
Paan Masala

Menu 3
Hot 'n' Spicy Chicken Wings
Lamb *or* Beef Masala
Rotli *or* Naan
Prawns & Halibut in Coconut Sauce
Coconut Rice
Kulfi
Chai with Masala
Paan Masala

Menu 4
Malindi Mishkaki
Mango & Bell Pepper Salad
or
Kachumber
Spicy Potatoes
Naan
Exotic Chicken & Rice (Pilau)
Cucumber Raita
Date & Tamarind Chutney
Kashmiri Faludo
Hot Ginger Drink
or
Chai with Masala
Paan Masala

Menu 5
Chicken Samosas
Chick Peas & Potato Salad
Spinach & Corn with Cream
(Palak Makkai Malai)
Rotli *or* Naan
Bombay Biryani
Fruit Salad with Mango Cream
Chai with Masala
Paan Masala

Vegetarian Menu 1
Onion *or* Nylon Bhajias
Coconut Chutney
Date & Tamarind Chutney
Dry Moong Daal Curry
Peas & Zucchini Curry
Rotli *or* Puri
Daal with Peanuts & Tamarind Sauce
Sev Paak
Chai with Masala
Paan Masala

Vegetarian Menu 2
Nylon *or* Palak Bhajia
Date & Tamarind Chutney
Rotli *or* Naan
Matar Paneer
Ghisoda
Chana Daal Curry
Plain Rice
Kulfi
Chai with Masala
Paan Masala

Vegetarian Menu 3
Onion *or* Pav Bhajia
Date & Tamarind Chutney *or* Tamarind Sauce
Sweet Mango Chutney
Moong Daal Curry
Puri *or* Rotli
Mango Juice
Kashmiri Rice *or* Peas & Potato Stir Fry
Chai with Masala
Paan Masala

index

Index

index

about the author

A S THE FIFTH-BORN CHILD OF ISMAILI MUSLIM PARENTS—who had immigrated to Nairobi, Kenya from northwestern India in the late 1920s—Noorbanu Nimji, together with her two older sisters, was encouraged to take an active role in cooking and food preparation from a very young age.

Moving to a different country on another continent brought significant changes to daily life for this young family. The relocation meant having to get used to the local cuisine and dealing with issues of availability and quality of various ingredients and produce that had, until then, been staples of a northern Indian (Gujarati) diet. Living in East Africa meant once-familiar recipes had to be adapted and cooking with unfamiliar foodstuffs had to be learned. Thus, Noorbanu grew up learning Gujarati recipes that had necessarily been modified by the Kenyan environment of her early life.

In 1971 when foreign nationals were being ousted from several East African countries, Noorbanu and her husband, together with their own young family, made the decision to depart to the United Kingdom and, shortly thereafter, the Nimji family eventually settled in Canada. Another country, another continent and yet another reason to have to adapt recipes, in light of the produce then available in grocery stores in Calgary in the early 1970s.

Given this life history, it is appropriate that this third volume of *A Spicy Touch* be subtitled *A Fusion of East African and Indian Cuisine*. This is a subtitle to which "for the North American Palate," could easily have been added. The recipes presented in this volume represent the "state of the art" of Noorbanu's fusion of culinary influences—Indian, East African, and North American—this after thirty years of living in Canada and more than sixty years of consistent service in front of a hot stove.

Noorbanu Nimji is the author of two previous volumes of *A Spicy Touch* that, collectively, have sold more than 200,000 copies. Both are out of print but a compilation of the best recipes from both volumes will be published in 2008.

Noorbanu continues to make Calgary her home and, more often than not, can be found at home in her kitchen.

A Spicy Touch
A Fusion of East African & Indian Cuisine

A Spicy Touch III: A Fusion of East African & Indian Cuisine, presents 134 recipes, of which two dozen offer variations, and 90 are completely vegetarian. All recipes are presented with English names although, where appropriate, traditional names for ingredients and particular dishes are provided in Gujarati (the language of Gujarat in northwestern India) and/ or Kiswahili (the official Bantu language of Kenya, Tanzania and Uganda). The book is organized in six sections: BASICS (Masalas, Pastes & Sauces); ACCOMPANIMENTS (Pickles, Chutneys, Raitas & Salsa); APPETIZERS (Salads, Snacks & Bhajia); MAIN DISHES (Chicken, Beef & Lamb, Seafood, Vegetables & Pulses); STARCHES (Rice & Bread); DESSERTS (Sweets & Drinks). Recipes presented at the front of the book provide stock ingredients for many subsequent dishes. Preparing them and having them on hand will make the further preparation of this cuisine far less complex and more manageable in terms of time.

A detailed glossary and background notes specific to any unusual ingredients used in a particular recipe will help you understand what you require and then look for on the shelves of your neighbourhood grocery store.

In *A Spicy Touch III*, Noorbanu Nimji presents her recipes in a logical sequence designed to support anyone—who feels comfortable in a domestic kitchen environment—achieve competency in the preparation, cooking, and presentation of this flavourful, colourful, and healthy cuisine. With what this book can teach you, you can master the spicy touch!

About the Book

Order Form

Send *A Spicy Touch, Volume III* to a Friend!

A Spicy Touch, Volume III: A Fusion of East African & Indian Cuisine
is $19.95 per book plus $4.50 (total order) shipping and handling.

A Spicy Touch, Volume III .... × $19.95 = $ _____

Shipping & Handling .... = $ 4.50 _____

Subtotal .... = $ _____

In Canada, add 6% GST .... (Subtotal × .06) = $ _____

Total Enclosed .... = $ _____

US and International orders payable in US Funds. Price subject to change.

NAME: _____

ADDRESS: _____

CITY: _____ PROVINCE/STATE: _____

COUNTRY: _____ POSTAL/ZIP CODE: _____

PHONE: _____

E--MAIL: _____

Please make cheque or money order payable to:

A Spicy Touch Publishing (Canada) Ltd.
1629 – 12th Avenue SW
Calgary, Alberta, Canada T3C 0R3

To order by phone or online:
Phone: (403) 263 • 4101 / *Fax:* (403) 245 • 8302
E-mail: **noorbanu@aspicytouch.com**
Website: **www.aspicytouch.com**
or via: **www.amazon.com**

Please allow 2 – 3 weeks for delivery.

Contents

Tables

Figures

Foreword

In its Center on Urban and Metropolitan Policy, the Brookings Institution has established a vital research center and repository of information on American metropolitan development, and the center's director, Bruce Katz, has brought new perspectives and original ideas to the forefront of urban policymaking. The center not only focuses on how central cities can work toward renewed prosperity but also examines cities within the larger context of regional growth. Downtown is no longer the single locus of a metropolitan area—regions have sprawled and become increasingly decentralized. More and more, urban policy discussions address the effects of that decentralization.

Suburban sprawl certainly is not a new topic, but defining and measuring sprawl within the rapidly developing metropolitan environment certainly is a current concern. Robert Lang, director of the Metropolitan Institute at Virginia Tech, has conducted intriguing research on an emerging metropolitan form that furthers the Brookings Institution's innovative contributions to urban policy. Lang looks back at Joel Garreau's 1991 publication, *Edge City: Life on the New Frontier,* and determines that more is happening in suburbia than we thought. Garreau's book proved so influential that his edge city continues to be one of the major categories by which suburban and exurban development are described. To this literature Lang adds a new development category that he labels "edgeless cities"—free-form clusters of office space that have silently sprung up along highways and interchanges. It is astonishing that they typically contain more commercial office space than do established downtowns and that often they dwarf edge cities in total size. No longer is there just the push-pull of the downtown versus the edge city—now there is a new contender that has gobbled up much of the undeveloped space in between: the edgeless city.

The edgeless city concept was first introduced in the Brookings Institution's Survey Series in October 2000. Almost immediately, newspapers such as the *Washington Post,* the *Atlanta Constitution-Journal,* and *USA Today* picked it up, knowing that the category was indeed "new" news in the realm of regional politics and planning. Lang's research also generated discussion among academics, policymakers, and business leaders. The topic of edgeless cities has been featured at conferences held by the Lincoln Institute of Land Policy and the Urban Land Institute, and it has been written about in publications such as *Planning* magazine. Now, in this book, Lang provides an in-depth look at how edgeless cities evolved and how they have changed the metropolitan landscape.

Many have recognized that the edgeless city concept is a useful addendum to the urban policy literature that shapes how we live and work. The Brookings Institution is glad to have been part of the process and to add it to our effort to chronicle metropolitan evolution.

STROBE TALBOTT
President, Brookings Institution

Washington, D.C.
December 2002

Preface

Let me start out by stating my bias: I like cities. I have lived in cities my entire adult life and only recently moved to an older inner suburb. I would like to think that somehow suburban office areas were in the process of maturing into higher-density, more livable, and more urbane places. I support development practices and policies that help edge cities achieve a sense of place. However, as a social scientist I am compelled to deal with reality, as best as it can be understood. And from my read of the evidence that follows, I find that suburbia may be heading in the opposite direction.

At the same time I believe that much of metropolitan America has been misunderstood. Many dismiss the nation's built environment, especially the suburbs, as crass, corporate, and alienating. Whole careers have been built out of trashing what are admittedly easy targets. But despite my pro-urban bias, I see no reason to join the chorus. The suburbs need to be understood on their own terms. For better or worse, America is now a suburban nation.

The study reported in this book is part of a research program that I initiated while I was director of urban and metropolitan research at the Fannie Mae Foundation that looked at everything from how to measure sprawl better to identifying major differences in metropolitan development patterns. It is my hope that this new basic research on the nature of metropolitan growth patterns will inform the public policy debate on smart growth.

At the beginning of the 1990s, when the state of New Jersey was developing its master plan, I was a doctoral student at Rutgers University. As a research associate at the university's Center for Urban Policy Research, I began looking at where the state's office development had occurred during the booming 1980s. I sought to understand the geography of office development by addressing such issues as where offices were being built, how they were arrayed, and whether they were densely packed or scattered. The point was to see how the office economy fit into the New Jersey State Plan, which emphasized the redevelopment of urban centers as a way to curb sprawl and preserve open space.

What I found surprised me. I was expecting to see a reasonably well ordered polycentrism. This was, after all, New Jersey, which the book *Edge City* had depicted as the new "standard" polycentric region. Instead I found an often post-polycentric urban form. Most of the state's office clusters were *much* smaller than the 5 million square feet that would qualify them as an "edge city" as I defined it. In fact, New Jersey did not have a single edge city as defined by Garreau—or urban village as defined by Leinberger—which requires 5 million square feet of office space and an accompanying 600,000 square feet of retail space. No such combination existed in all of the Garden State. Three places had more than 5 million square feet of office space in a more or less contiguous area; however, the closest regional mall was miles away.

Recognizing that New Jersey might simply be an exception, I began to look around the country. I found that there were indeed edge cities in many locations, but I also found that, as in New Jersey, there was also a lot of what I originally called "office sprawl" competing with these places. After numerous conversations with consultants, field observations, and analyses of office data, I decided to construct a new preliminary model that accounted for all of the non-CBD office space outside edge cities. I termed this space "edgeless cities."

To a large extent this book reflects both my personal and professional experience of metropolitan America. I visited every one of the thirteen metropolitan areas included in the survey at least twice within the past several years. I drove their beltways, stayed in their hotels, and toured their office parks. I gathered extensive field notes. Most of these regions contain major universities with urban planning departments, and I spent hours on the phone interviewing faculty members about their respective regions. I also talked with regional planning agencies and pored over regional planning reports. Finally, I attended conferences and meetings with commercial real estate developers. A good portion of what is reported in the following data analysis reflects my own informed impressions and observations.

As with any large study, many people helped, and I want to acknowledge their efforts. Several people made key contributions to the development of this work. First among them is Frank Popper, who was the sounding board for much of the analytic thinking behind this book. Together we spent countless hours comparing our observations and speculating on how metropolitan areas were evolving.

Many of the faculty at Rutgers University also read all or parts of this work and offered valuable feedback, including Robert Gutman, David Popenoe, John Leggett, Robert Burchell, Michael Greenberg, James Hughes, and Robert Fishman (now at the University of Michigan).

I also acknowledge Bill Fulton, who gave very careful reads to two drafts of this book. His comments were very useful and helped shape subsequent rewrites. Anthony Downs of the Brookings Institution also reviewed the book; I appreciate the valuable insights and comments that he provided.

This book incorporates the work of two research partners. Myron Orfield and his staff at the Metropolitan Area Research Corporation (MARC) produced the office space maps that appear in chapter 7. I especially thank Tom Luce, who managed the project for MARC, and Aaron Timbo, who ran the GIS maps. George Galster led the academic team (including Royce Hanson, Hal Wolman, Stephen Coleman, and Jason Freihage) that conceptualized and measured housing sprawl in the thirteen metropolitan areas examined in the study. I thank them for using the first test of their sprawl indicator on the same regions that form the basis of my study.

Another important partner has been the Brookings Institution Center on Urban and Metropolitan Policy, which has helped at several key stages in this project. The center's staff has provided tremendous technical assistance in organizing and editing the data. I especially thank Dao Nguyen, Ben Margolis, Jennifer Bradley, and Jennifer Vey.

The Brookings Institution, the Lincoln Institute of Land Policy, and the Fannie Mae Foundation have been the main sources of funding for this research. I very much valued the support of these organizations, in particular the encouragement of Roz Greenstein at Lincoln, Bruce Katz and Amy Liu at Brookings, and Jim Carr at the Fannie Mae Foundation.

Graduate students in the University of Maryland–College Park's urban planning department did the really heavy lifting—data entry. One student in particular, Don McClauslin, did much of the work. His attention to detail and quality control work is very much appreciated. I also thank Heather Mahaley, a graduate student at Rutgers, who helped with the literature review by finding some rather obscure articles and writing up summaries.

As this project evolved, I had several chances to present preliminary findings to mostly academic audiences. I received especially good feedback from talks at New York University, Princeton University, and the University of Pennsylvania, and I thank the students and faculty who participated.

Most of this book was written during two extended stays in Blacksburg, Virginia. I picked this lovely college town on the recommendation of Ted Koebel of Virginia Tech. Ted not only generously offered his department's facilities, he found me a great bed and breakfast to stay in—the Clay Corner Inn—where I found a quiet place to write. I thank Ted for his help. I also thank Jennifer LeFurgy of the Metropolitan Institute at Virginia Tech for helping with the final edits on the book.

Finally, and most important, I want to thank my wife, Karen Danielsen, who supported my efforts despite two long absences. She read and edited early drafts of this work. In addition, Karen provided some of the NRI data for the study, and she also found the main office data source, which made this whole project possible.

Edgeless Cities

CHAPTER 1

Introduction

The bulletin is this: Edge Cities mean that density is back.

—JOEL GARREAU (1991)

That much-quoted line from Joel Garreau's compelling and influential book *Edge City* often is cited with a sigh of relief by those who hope that suburbia is finally growing up and starting to behave itself. Many people in the smart growth movement—which seeks among other goals to build higher-density, mixed-use suburbs—are especially invested in the idea that maturing edge cities represent a hopeful future. Given this author's sympathies with the smart growth movement,[1] he is not especially happy to deliver the latest bulletin: the long-standing presence of "edgeless cities" means that sprawl is back—or, more accurately, that it never went away.

Edgeless cities, a form of sprawling office development that does not have the density or cohesiveness of edge cities, account for two-thirds of the office space found outside downtowns. Among the nation's largest office markets, edgeless cities have nearly twice the space of edge cities. And they are everywhere—no major metropolitan area is without them. Edgeless cities are not mixed-use, pedestrian-friendly areas, nor are they easily accessed by public transit. They are not even easy to locate, because they are scattered in a way that is almost impossible to chart. Edgeless cities spread almost imperceptibly throughout metropolitan areas, filling out central cities, occupying much of the space between more concentrated suburban business districts, and ringing the metropolitan area's

---

1. See Danielsen and Lang (1998); Danielsen, Lang, and Fulton (1999); Lang (2000a).

1

built-up periphery. It is telling that the 1999 movie *Office Space*, which was filmed in an edgeless landscape outside Dallas, makes no direct mention of the environment, although the director turns his satiric attention to just about everything else in suburbia, including traffic jams, formula restaurants, and cheaply constructed condos.

In contrast, edge cities are easy to find. Their buildings rise over the horizontal suburban landscape like the Emerald City over Oz. Garreau got in his car and drove to these places. He stood at their center, surveyed the scene, and declared the new city found. On the way to the new city, he passed through miles of uncharted suburbia. At the exit ramps along the nation's beltways, unnoted, were the other new cities. But Garreau is a reporter, not a social scientist. It is his job to report the notable—not the mundane.

A good example of an edgeless city is central New Jersey, especially the area around Princeton. The town of Princeton is a traditional center that features an old main street, Nassau Street, running alongside the university. But outside the city, things are not so tidy. Princeton as a business center is less a center than a region, more accurately called greater Princeton. Much of the region's office development spills north from the city for miles along route 1 toward New Brunswick, while some reaches south to Trenton. More offices lie along routes 27 and 206. Development also spreads east toward the New Jersey Turnpike, and office parks line many county and other minor roads. And Princeton's edgeless city is not isolated. Office development in neighboring Monmouth, Middlesex, Somerset, and Hunterdon counties fits the same pattern. There are a few older cities and some newer suburban office concentrations, but the vast majority of office space in central New Jersey (or greater Princeton) is edgeless. In total, central New Jersey edgeless cities stretch over a thousand square miles of metropolitan area.

Measuring edgeless cities has been a conceptual challenge requiring several trials involving various errors. The form of edgeless cities can be described in various ways—as illimitable, indefinite, undiscovered, imperceptible, elusive. The term "edgeless city" captures the fact that most suburban office areas lack a physical edge. Edgeless cities thus are cities in *function*, in that they contain office employment, but not in *form*, because they are scattered, unlike traditional and even some suburban office development. In contrast to some larger edge cities that combine large-scale office with major retail development, most edgeless cities contain isolated office buildings or small clusters of buildings of varying densities over vast swaths of metropolitan space.

Many social critics disparage edge cities as sprawling, alienating, corporate versions of real cities.[2] But if those critics do not like edge cities, they are absolutely going to hate edgeless cities, which are not even cohesive enough to pretend to be cities. Critics focus on edge cities in part because they can at least identify them. By contrast, edgeless cities are stealthy—they come in under the radar. The new urbanists snidely describe "edge cities" as "a term which implies urbanism but is in fact only the statistical *agglomeration* of housing, subdivisions, shopping centers, and business parks."[3] For new urbanists, "an Edge City is equivalent but not equal to a city." Consider that edgeless cities fit the new urbanist description of edge cities—minus "agglomeration"—and you get an idea of how low such critics' regard for edgeless cities must be.

Garreau's book sparked considerable controversy. It had its fans and its detractors, yet all but a few took Garreau at his word: that for bad or good, edge cities represented the suburban future.[4] Garreau had it right—or at least partly right. Edge cities represent one suburban future, but only one. This book reports on the other new metropolis to have emerged in the past few decades. It covers an alternative suburban future, the post-polycentric version.[5]

The study on which this book is based explores America's metropolitan form by examining the growth and spatial structure of non-downtown office space. Using rental office space data from 1979 to 1999, it shows how the nation's largest metropolitan areas arrived at their current commercial geography.[6] It looks at the evolving spatial structure of rental office space in thirteen of the nation's largest markets, which together contain more than 2.6 billion square feet of office space and 26,000 buildings. The markets are found throughout the United States: six are in the Northeast and Midwest, and seven are in the South and the West. The metropolitan areas studied are Atlanta, Boston,

2. For example, see Soja (1997).

3. CNU (1999), emphasis added.

4. Fans included Delany (1993) and Kenneth Jackson, "The View from the Periphery," *New York Times*, September 22, 1991, sec. 7, pp. 1, 11; detractors included Beauregard (1995), Clarke (1992), and Sharpe and Wallach (1992). For a skeptic, see Abbott (1991).

5. Descriptions of post-polycentric urban form have an extensive literature. For example, see Lessinger (1962), Lewis (1983, 1995), Lynch (1961), Pressman (1985), and Webber (1967).

6. Even though the data end with the last quarter of 1999, new construction fell off dramatically after that, leaving many markets unchanged during the next two years (ULI 2002).

Chicago, Dallas, Detroit, Denver, Houston, Los Angeles, Miami, New York City, Philadelphia, San Francisco, and Washington, D.C.[7]

The study's major finding is that most metropolitan rental office space exists in either high-density downtowns or low-density edgeless cities. The medium-density office environments of edge cities and secondary downtowns, which account for eighty-one places in the study, constitute just one-quarter of metropolitan space. In addition, edgeless cities have more total space than the downtown in eleven of the thirteen metropolitan areas studied. Only New York City and Chicago, the two largest downtowns in the United States, surpass their region's edgeless cities in rental office space.

This book's main thesis is *not* that edgeless cities are especially new; the data show that they have been around for decades. It is that as both advocates and critics focused on edge cities, edgeless cities were overlooked. In the rush to find a new form of cohesiveness in the suburbs, most observers missed the chaos. That chaos is revealed by simply looking at the geography of office data. Most non-downtown office space falls outside large clusters, often appearing in smaller clusters, corridors, and scattered locations. Most important, exploring what drives the chaos may improve our comprehension of the new metropolis, which, despite being several decades old, is new to our understanding.

The study reported in this book is not intended to be an exhaustive multivariate statistical analysis, although the findings are partly data derived. The book is not an exercise in GIS (geographic information systems) technology, even though some preliminary office data maps are presented. Rather, the data, illustrations, maps, and photos shown help reframe current thinking on the metropolis. The typologies developed here are not definitive; follow-up research will refine them.[8] And although the study was national in scope, only thirteen metropolitan areas are included. Future work will greatly expand that number, adding many more modest-sized regions.

The book is less about offering new models than it is about challenging old ones. The term "edgeless city" may not stick. The label was picked in part to take the *edge* off the edge city concept and in the process open a new debate on metropolitan growth trends. The main

7. For purposes of this study, Washington, D.C., is treated as part of the Northeast/Midwest.

8. As a follow-up to this book, the author expects to work with the Metropolitan Area Research Corporation (now ameregis) on a series of projects that refine the categories through more sophisticated mapping and statistical analysis.

contribution is thus conceptual. Just as Myron Orfield's 1997 book *Metropolitics* distinguished two kinds of suburbs—those with high and low fiscal capacity—this study distinguishes two types of suburban office development: bounded and edgeless. And, like Orfield's work, this book has numerous implications beyond the data. One is that in many ways edgeless cities raise an even bigger challenge than edge cities for those who seek to build a less sprawling suburbia.

The Marked and the Unmarked

The subject of this book falls in a category that some cognitive sociologists refer to as "the unmarked." Whereas "marked" subjects have some exceptional quality that attracts study, the unmarked often go undocumented.[9] In some behavioral studies, for example, gay individuals such as those who live in the Castro neighborhood of San Francisco and participate in gay rights parades are the marked, and their behavior and lifestyle sometimes is taken as representative of that of all gays. Yet there are studies that show that a large portion of the gay community attempts to fit into the straight world.[10] By virtue of their more conventional lifestyle, these people, the unmarked, do not generate much media or research interest, but any comprehensive characterization of the gay world would have to include them.

Edgeless cities are the unmarked phenomena of the new metropolis. They are mundane, they are ubiquitous, and most people intuitively know what they are. But no national empirical study has characterized them. However, edgeless cities need to be understood; the public policy stakes surrounding smart growth alone warrant their study. And when they are described in a way that a general audience can understand, they can attract attention. A preliminary form of the research in this book published in late 2000 generated national and local media interest.[11]

9. Brekhus (1998).
10. Brekhus (1998).
11. Stories covering the research (Lang 2000c) appeared immediately in *USA Today,* the *Washington Post,* and the *Atlanta Journal and Constitution.* Follow-up stories included a report from the Associated Press (Hansen 2001) and the journal *Planning.* See Haya El Nasser, "Edgeless Cities Confound Efforts to Control Growth," *USA Today,* October 31, 2000, p. 4A; Jackie Spinner, "Scattered Offices Said to Fuel Traffic Woes; Report Seeks Growth in, near District," *Washington Post,* November 1, 2000, p. E1; Tony Wilbert, "Atlanta Trails only Detroit in Suburban Sprawl," *Atlanta Journal and Constitution,* November 1, 2000, p. 3E; Jeff Hansen, "State's Population Shifts Rework Cityscapes," *Birmingham News,* May 13, 2001; Knack (2000).

The media seem to love "man bites dog" stories.[12] The idea that a place such as Tysons Corner, Virginia (a large edge city outside Washington, D.C., that is heavily featured in Garreau's book) has more office space than the state capital, Richmond, is by now passé. But the fact that Washington's edgeless cities (which comprise more than a thousand scattered, low-slung buildings) cumulatively are bigger than DC's downtown is news. The public can grasp that a big, new, suburban city like Tysons Corner has surpassed an older traditional one like Richmond. It is more striking—and therefore newsworthy—to consider that, taken together, all the faceless, no-name office parks stretching to the edge of the region include more office space than is found downtown. Edgeless cities' moment in the spotlight may indeed have arrived. This book now marks the unmarked, revealing some surprising results.

Why Follow Office Space?

Following office space trends is a good way to understand metropolitan change because office space is where a large percentage of job growth occurs. In some metropolitan areas, nearly half of all newly hired employees go to work in office buildings,[13] which were the last major element of central cities to suburbanize, following residences and retail stores.[14] The rapid growth of suburban office development was so significant a trend that it sparked a series of books and articles in the late 1980s and early 1990s that sought to explain how it reshaped the American metropolis; some observers understood the meaning of this trend as early as the 1970s.[15]

The location of office space is critical in a number of public policy areas. For example, the distribution of new office space affects the extent to which a jobs/housing mismatch exists in a region.[16] It also can

---

12. The author worked on many such stories as a consultant to *USA Today* in 2001 during the release of the 2000 short-form census data.

13. Bureau of Labor Statistics (1998).

14. Leinberger (1996); Muller (1980).

15. Baldassare (1986); Bruegmann and Davis (1992); Cervero (1986, 1989); Erickson (1985); Fishman (1987, 1990); Fulton (1986); Garreau (1991); Hartshorn and Muller (1986, 1989); Leinberger and Lockwood (1986); Pivo (1990); Romanos, Chifos, and Fenner (1989); Breckenfeld (1972); Linda Greenhouse, "The Outer City: Growth Turning into a Menace," *New York Times,* June 3, 1971; John Herbers, "The Outer City; Uneasiness over the Future," *New York Times,* June 2, 1971; Douglas E. Kneeland, "The Outer City; There Is No Firm Stereotype," *New York Times,* May 31, 1971; Vance (1977).

16. Cervero (1986).

influence economic opportunity, if, for example, there is a mismatch between the locations of jobs and concentrations of minority households.[17] Office location also has an impact on urban sprawl. If much new office space is constructed at the regional edge, it extends commuter sheds for many miles into undeveloped rural areas, thereby feeding sprawl.[18] Finally, the geography of office location figures prominently in transportation analysis. If most new space is built in areas with no access to public transit, reliance on automobiles will continue to grow.

The growing importance of suburban office space in American life has even led to a new coinage: the "office park dad,"[19] who "is a suburban, non-union, stock-owning political moderate, age 25–50."[20] Office park dads, estimated to be about 15 percent of the voting age population, form a political swing group, like the minivan-driving, suburban "soccer moms" of the 1990s. The term "office park dads" works as political shorthand because these "dads" are so common—the fact that they are not "downtown dads" reflects how significant and ubiquitous a work setting suburban office space has become. And, like edgeless cities (where so many of them work), office park dads are now "marked," at least by political analysts.

While office space data are an important indicator of metropolitan change, they cannot convey the whole picture. The office space documented in the study is leased, multi-tenanted buildings; other major employment sites such as government offices, warehouses, flex space (offices combined with light-manufacturing facilities), hospitals, and universities (for more details on the data, see appendix A) are excluded. This study therefore reports only a portion of the white-collar employment, albeit a significant share, in thirteen of the nation's largest metropolitan areas. While retail space was not specifically tracked, the presence or absence of large regional malls amid office development was noted.

Also missing from the study were small office buildings such as those occupied by local professionals (for example, dentists and tax preparers). Providers of such services have long been dispersed because they fill

17. Kain (1991).

18. Ding and Bingham (2000).

19. Jill Lawrence, "Democrats Trying to Woo Suburban Dads," *USA Today,* May 21, 2002, p. A3; David Von Drehle, "For Democrats, Key Voters May Be Married to Soccer Moms: Pollster Says Party Should Target 'Office Park Dads.'" *Washington Post,* May 22, 2002, p. A8.

20. Lawrence, "Democrats Trying to Woo Suburban Dads."

local needs and therefore quickly followed people to the suburbs. Instead, this study zeros in on the type of office buildings that used to be almost exclusively found in large commercial centers, housing businesses such as advertising and finance. Had all local businesses been included in this analysis, the regions would have seemed radically decentralized, and the recent shift of higher-order economic activity from the center to the edge might have been lost in background noise.

This study measures only one type of sprawl—office sprawl. While office development is an important dimension of sprawl, it is not the only measure. Multiple sprawl measures are used in this book to offer a context for office sprawl.

Is the New Metropolitan Form Really New?

At the start of the twentieth century, almost all of America's office space could be found in its downtowns. But even in the early decades of the century, "uptowns" began to form a few miles from the original downtown, offering newer, less congested, and often more upscale business environments. Examples include the Wilshire district of Los Angeles and midtown Manhattan. Uptowns were driven by two main forces—a decentralizing population (especially wealthy people) and transportation improvements. Streetcars—and soon automobiles—loosened downtown's hold on commerce during the 1910s. The waves of decentralized office development that followed in edge cities and edgeless cities made the once distinct uptowns seem more like downtown—some of the original uptowns are now so old and so relatively close to downtown that now they are treated essentially as extensions of downtown.

Satellite cities, another form of decentralized growth, also flourished in the early twentieth century. In a 1915 publication entitled *Satellite Cities: A Case Study of Industrial Suburbs,* economist Graham Taylor described an emerging pattern of metropolitan development in which heavy industry was rapidly shifting to the suburbs in search of more space and lower costs. And more than seventy-five years ago sociologist Ernest Burgess noted that business growth, which he characterized as being "centralized-decentralized" in structure, already was evident at Chicago's edge.[21]

Early twentieth-century satellite and centralized suburbs mimicked big cities, although at a slightly lower density and on a smaller scale.

21. Burgess (1925).

Satellites included all of the features that defined a city: a main street shopping area, high-density residential neighborhoods, and, by the late nineteenth century, factory districts.[22] In the 1920s, it was even typical for larger satellite cities in the New York region, such as Newark, N.J., to have a signature Art Deco office tower, representing an already decentralizing service economy.[23]

So is the new metropolitan form really new?[24] Given the history of decentralization in America, that is a legitimate question. This study finds that most contemporary suburban business districts do not resemble traditional downtowns, uptowns, or satellite cities. Except for a few large, dense edge cities, suburban commercial districts lack, for example, a dense business core. They therefore can be seen as distinct from traditional cities—not so much in their function as in their low-density, loose spatial configuration.

Suburbia's economy reached an unprecedented diversity by the 1980s, as specialized service enterprises of every kind were established outside central business districts.[25] The multifunctional early twenty-first century "suburbs" can no longer be described by the familiar moniker "bedroom communities." They now contain all the elements of a city, including a rapidly growing number of poor households.[26] Yet even as they become more urban, suburbs maintain a distinct pattern. A new metropolitan form therefore has emerged in the past several decades: low density, automobile dependent, and dispersed. Not quite the traditional city, suburb, or exurb, but with elements of all three, it is the still-emergent America of the mall, the beltway, the subdivision, the multiplex movie theater, the drive-through fast-food outlet, the low-rise office cube, and the shopping strip.

This book shows that, as seen through the filter of rental office space development, there are many different metropolitan forms. One of the more interesting findings is that while the office building is among the most generic building types in modern America, their distribution across metropolitan areas varies tremendously and reflects regional quirks.[27]

22. Bourchert (1996).

23. Hughes, Miller, and Lang (1992).

24. "New" in this context means having emerged over the past several decades, not in, say, the 1990s.

25. Bateman (1985); Daniels (1985); Leinberger and Lockwood (1986).

26. Orfield (1997, 2002).

27. The low-rise suburban office building is now so common that it is financed through the secondary market and sold to investors as a standard real estate commodity (Leinberger 2001).

These buildings often must be fitted into existing metropolitan development patterns, which can result in some unique spatial forms.

There are, of course, some patterns to office development that reflect the region of the country. There is a distinct Texas city building style. Styles in New York and Chicago are similar, as they are Los Angeles and San Francisco. Yet the country supports many more variants of built form than would appear to be the case from a casual windshield survey of metropolitan America.[28] This study reveals how the ordinary often is quite extraordinary; the diversity that is the modern metropolis comes through in the analysis.

Not only do edgeless cities appear in all thirteen metropolitan areas, they are scattered throughout these regions. Some edgeless cities lie within the outskirts of cities, while others sweep around and between suburban edge cities, while still others ring the region at its exurban edge. The image that may best describe edgeless cities is that of low-grade commercial filler—they occupy vast areas as they fill in the various nooks and crannies of the metropolis. Their spatial form therefore varies by region, based in part on where in the metropolitan landscape they lie and how much of it they occupy.

Edge Cities, Edgeless Cities, and the New Metropolitan Form

One problem with the edge city model is that it conflates all non-downtown office space with office space that is located specifically in an edge city.[29] In fact, as this study shows, edge cities (or office clusters with more than 5 million square feet of office space, with or without major retail space) currently account for only one-third of all non-downtown office space, while edgeless cities make up the remaining two-thirds. If one were to apply the strict criteria for edge cities (that they contain 5 million square feet of office space combined, plus 600,000 square feet of retail space) the proportion would be much smaller, perhaps a little as one-fifth. The suburban office economy as it appears in the edge city model implies a polycentric regional format featuring a central business district (CBD) hub and edge city spokes, much like the older satellite city model. But often that is not the case. A closer look at the urban

28. Pressman (1985).
29. Garreau (1991, p. 5) assumes that "two-thirds of all American office facilities are in Edge Cities"—therefore, all U.S. office space outside a downtown can be found in an edge city.

form of specific edge cities (for example, Princeton, N.J.) reveals that many of them spread over tens and sometimes hundreds of square miles. Some are better categorized as edgeless.

The edge city model also assumes that the location of office space is determined by the proximity of shopping malls. Others have empirically demonstrated that that is not the case.[30] The lack of locational affinity between major retail stores and office space demonstrates how far the metropolitan form has evolved beyond current concepts. The relationship between the department store and the office building in the old downtown seems natural—a taken-for-granted reality. It is reasonable to suppose that they would pair up again in the suburbs, this time in the form of the mall and the office park. While the use of automobiles works to reduce built densities and massive parking lots encircle new suburban downtowns, the old, basic order of the city remains.[31]

However, when commerce decamped from regional cores, the connection between major retail and office space may have been lost. Because people now can drive from one location to another, commutes to offices and trips to stores need not wind up in the same place, as was often the case in a rail-based metropolis. Shopping malls and office parks are free to find independent locations that best match their respective market areas and commuter sheds. Most often, those locations are separate, which is why large edge cities (where offices cluster around shopping malls) are the exception rather than the rule. The new metropolitan form shows up less often in the Tysons Corners of the nation than in the greater Princetons. As this study finds, that is where most of the office space built outside downtowns is found.

As noted above, large metropolitan areas have long been polycentric. But today's polycentrism is different. Whereas factory towns, secondary cities, and even edge cities share a spatial logic with big cities, albeit on a smaller scale, edgeless cities represent a departure. Edge cities are perhaps the last stop on the road away from traditional urban forms. One day edge cities may be seen as a transitional urban form—an attempt to build auto-based, low-density downtowns before developers realized that for the most part, cars made such places unnecessary.

Perhaps most important, edgeless cities are not edge cities waiting to happen. Instead they represent a concurrent, competing, and more decentralized form of office development. In fact, the office data

30. Pivo (1990).
31. Leinberger and Lockwood (1986).

presented in this book indicate that edge cities and edgeless cities grew up more or less together. But edge cities did experience a burst of growth in the mid- to late 1980s, at the time that Garreau was observing them. Edge city growth has since slowed, while edgeless cities seem to have grown at a steadier pace.

Ironically, some big edge cities face the same land cost and congestion pressures as old downtowns, for now they too are central places. It therefore appears that even many edge cities are starting to lose their edge.[32] Edgeless cities may be the ultimate result of a metropolitan process that has been tearing apart concentrated commercial development for the better part of a century.[33] One alternative title considered for this book was *The Rise and Fall (or Stall) of Edge Cities*. In many ways, the study is as much about the fate of edge cities as it is a depiction of edgeless cities.

Book Organization and Topics

This book first addresses ways to categorize office location environments; this includes a discussion of the literature on the topic. A presentation and analysis of office data follow. Next, the fates of edge cities and edgeless cities are considered. How office development fits within the regional context is then explored, and new methods to measure metropolitan sprawl and urban density are presented. Finally, some of the public policy and business investment implications of edgeless cities are considered.

Chapter 2 reviews some of the literature describing the new metropolitan form. The review covers efforts to analyze the emerging suburban metropolis, focusing on office location patterns and the role they play in shaping metropolitan development. Next, which urban functions are likely to remain downtown despite the predominance of non-CBD office development are considered. The chapter ends with a synthesis and reformulation of theory that frame the data analyses that follow.

The first part of chapter 3 reviews efforts to label the new metropolis, presenting several summary tables to show the difficulty of capturing in a single term this still emerging phenomenon. Definitions form the core of this study. The edgeless city is a newly identified category of office space, so maps, photos, and illustrations are provided to demonstrate its

32. Fulton (1996).
33. Mills (1988).

uniqueness relative to traditional office categories. The office categories described here are used throughout the rest of the book in data analysis.

Chapter 4 examines the distribution of office space in downtowns, edge cities, and edgeless cities in the thirteen metropolitan areas covered in the study. The profiles contain the names and office space inventories for all of the downtowns and edge cities in these areas, including some analysis of historic growth trends within regions and across metropolitan areas. The chapter ends with regional comparisons, in which metropolitan spatial types are developed based on the data.

Chapter 5 covers ways to map and measure the new metropolitan form. It begins with a descriptive typology of edgeless cities and includes maps showing the distribution of office space in four metropolitan areas—Chicago, Detroit, Philadelphia, and San Francisco—selected to show a range of urban spatial forms.

Chapter 6 examines the types, locations, and evolution of edge cities. Two classes of edge cities derived from a descriptive interpretation of the office space data are established, and an analysis of very large edge cities is given. Next, a life cycle model showing how edge cities form and mature is presented. The discussion finally turns to why edgeless cities appear to be have been flourishing for at least the last several decades.

In chapter 7, edgeless cities are placed in a regional context. Office sprawl is just one dimension of metropolitan form. Three other schemes that look at housing, urbanized area, and built density also are considered and compared. The chapter organizes recent research on sprawl into a comprehensive analysis that places rental office development in a regional context in the thirteen metropolitan areas covered in the study.

The emergence of edgeless cities challenges policymakers and practitioners who favor more compact regions to rethink some of their planning strategies. New urbanist architects and developers, smart growth advocates, transportation and land use planners, environmentalists, politicians interested in regional social equity, and many others are directing much of their attention to curbing the type of urban sprawl that edgeless cities exemplify. Chapter 8 considers the relationship of edgeless cities and several regional growth issues. It also explores the market and investment conditions that edgeless cities present.

CHAPTER 2

Centrists versus Decentrists:

The Debate over the New City

A key divide emerges in the literature conceptualizing the new metropolitan form. One side argues that the pattern of decentralized commerce is still influenced, to varying degrees, by the traditional urban forces that shaped the old metropolis. Members of this camp are referred to here as the "centrists" because they emphasize the emergence of central places in the suburbs. Others see a bigger break with the past and highlight instead the forces that pull the elements of the old metropolis apart. They are called the "decentrists." The two divergent lines of argument—clustering versus scatteration—are typified in the writings of Christopher Leinberger (centrist) and Robert Fishman (decentrist).

The Centrist View

Leinberger proposes what he refers to as the "urban village," which is analogous to an edge city.[1] In his view, suburban commerce is becoming increasingly concentrated. The urban village concept owes some intellectual debt to Ebenezer Howard's "garden cities."[2] The key connection is the idea of retaining what is desirable about the city in terms of services, convenience, and opportunity while improving on its physical environment.

1. Leinberger (2001, 1996, 1995, 1990, 1989, 1988, 1984); Leinberger and Lockwood (1986).
2. Howard (1965 [1902]).

According to Leinberger, the development of urban villages can be traced in part to the transition from a manufacturing to a service economy (Leinberger assumes that manufacturing was concentrated in cities), which has enabled businesses to cluster with residences because service businesses generally do not produce noxious byproducts, such as environmental pollutants. Another cause is the shift from rail to truck transportation, which favors peripheral locations in the suburbs instead of central cities. A third factor is advanced communications technology, which enables businesses to set up shop with little concern for their physical location. The lower-priced land in the suburbs also induces businesses to locate there.

After citing several material causes for the emergence of urban villages, Leinberger shifts his emphasis to social forces. He argues that technological and economic influences on their own "might have only encouraged more suburban sprawl had not another factor come into play: most Americans like cities and the concentration of services they provide."[3]

In Leinberger's view, Americans actually prefer cities but they do not want the congested and often unsafe environment that traditional urbanization brings. So, equipped with their automobiles and fax machines (and now the Internet) and driven by land costs and a new economy, they remade their urban world to reflect their desire for urban amenities, this time in a more appealing and controlled lower-density suburban setting.

In Leinberger's view, the decentralized metropolis is now a reality. However, it also has become substantially re-centered: all the elements of a city are still sewn together, even if the urban fabric has become very loose. People may have to glance across a spacious lawn or cut across an enormous parking lot to see the connection between the mall and the office tower, but they remain inexorably linked. While urban villages typically have such low densities that they may look like an altogether new style of city building, an important connection to satellite cities of the past nonetheless remains.

Leinberger notes that many older satellite cities have been redeveloped as contemporary urban villages. Examples include Pasadena, California, in the Los Angeles region and Stamford, Connecticut, in the New York metropolitan area—both pre-auto satellites of their respective central cities.

3. Leinberger and Lockwood (1986), p. 46.

The problem with this argument is that, in spatial terms, redeveloped satellite cities still resemble their regional cores more than they resemble most new office development. Take, for example, a comparison between Stamford and Princeton, New Jersey, that Leinberger mentions in discussing office decentralization in the New York region.[4] Leinberger treats Stamford and Princeton as one and the same phenomenon; yet a closer look reveals that the two are as different in urban form as night and day. While they are about the same size in total office market, Princeton's office development, according to the analysis in the study reported in this book, is *more than 100 times less dense* than Stamford's.

Stamford's compact urban core seems far closer to being a medium-sized central business district than does the sprawling edgeless city around Princeton. Both places benefit from office decentralization in the New York region, and both are home to many equally prestigious office tenants, but they are spatial opposites. Part of the problem may be that the old suburban/urban dichotomy has been lost, replaced by a continuum.

Rodney Erickson and Peter Daniels offer another variation on Leinberger's urban village model.[5] They argue that suburban agglomeration economies have drawn together a diverse array of services into increasingly significant concentrations of businesses. Their historical analysis of the suburbanization of the service sector finds an original pattern of random spillover and dispersal, followed in turn by a more recent phase of recentralization into suburban business nodes.

Leinberger also implies an agglomerative effect by arguing that urban villages in Los Angeles have begun to specialize: the insurance, aerospace, and entertainment industries, he notes, have come to dominate individual urban villages.[6] Efficiencies are created in such instances by sharing the producer services that assemble around related industries. An example in Los Angeles would be that of talent agencies locating near major studios.

While this is a credible argument for suburban commercial clustering, it also directly contradicts an earlier point made about the impact of improved telecommunications on business location decisions. If fax machines freed businesses from downtowns, why do businesses now need to reassemble by industry in specialized urban villages? After all, they could, in theory, move anywhere in a metropolitan area and still be

4. Leinberger and Lockwood (1986).
5. Erickson (1983, 1985); Daniels (1985).
6. Leinberger and Lockwood (1986).

in intensive contact with consultants and clients. Gordon and Richardson in fact argue that agglomeration economies now exist on the regional scale.[7] Further, if agglomerative efficiencies help produce urban villages, then they also certainly serve to maintain downtowns, perhaps even more given downtowns' size and density.

The Decentrist View

To Robert Fishman, concepts developed to describe regional process based on traditional patterns of urbanization are becoming increasingly irrelevant. In his view, today's sprawling suburban regions can no longer be judged by the standards of the old metropolis, in part because the new suburban form "lacks any definable borders, a center or a periphery, or clear distinctions between residential, industrial and commercial zones."[8] Fishman offers a new theoretical understanding of the contemporary metropolis on its own terms. Ironically, Fishman, an urban historian, appears to develop an approach liberated from the past; in reality, his new conceptualizations are deeply rooted in the history of both events and ideas.

To begin, Fishman's description of the new suburban form differs considerably from that of those who identify a latent spatial order. "Technoburbs," a term he originally coined to characterize today's suburbs, are "a hopeless jumble of housing, industry, commerce and even agricultural uses."[9] Where some find coherence, Fishman sees chaos. And yet, in spite of all of the disarray that typifies suburbia, he still argues "that the new city has a characteristic structure."[10]

It is over the issue of what constitutes "structure" that Fishman's analysis diverges most from that of the centrists. The term "structure," as used by urban geographers and planners, usually implies an empirically knowable and generalizable spatial pattern. To Fishman, structure need not relate so particularly to an aggregate pattern of regional land use; it can instead derive from an individual's daily use of space. Consequently, a region's focal point is no longer found at its geographic center, nor has it been redistributed among several peripheral centers. It is now the person, or more precisely, the household. This new urban reality is

---

7. Gordon and Richardson (1996).
8. Fishman (1990), p.189.
9. Fishman (1987), p. 190.
10. Fishman (1990), p. 30.

not the result of some evolutionary shift in city structure but "departs radically . . . from the old metropolis [and] all cities of the past."[11]

The key element in Fishman's new structural framework is what he refers to as "household networks." Three major household networks exist, based around personal contacts, consumptive desires, and productive requirements. Each network entails a separate set of trips or destination points. Fishman notes that "the pattern formed by these destinations represents 'the city' for that particular family or individual."[12] More important, these networks overlap and in most ways are unrelated to one another; correspondingly, each also possesses its own "spatial logic." Fishman uses a comparison of shopping malls (consumption) and primary schools (production) to demonstrate his point. The location of a primary school is based on the local distribution of a school age population, while the siting of malls involves a calculus of road access, population density, and income.

Urban planners have long understood that the diverse requirements of households help shape urban patterns. In 1963, Christopher Alexander challenged a planning concept known as the "neighborhood unit principle," which held that there are natural and roughly analogous catchment areas of community facilities such as primary schools and local shops.[13] His criticism was that a more complex settlement pattern already had produced overlapping fields for shops and schools. Jane Jacobs made a similar case around the same time.[14]

In aggregate terms, the diverse requirements of household networks add up to a region characterized by the unconnected "juxtaposition and interpenetration" of different types of space. The mall may very well wind up next to the office building, but because their spatial relationship to the household differs significantly, it does not have to. This would explain the empirical finding that major retailing is disconnected from office space.[15] To Fishman, when commerce decentralizes from the core of a region or even a satellite city, it is not likely to be reconstituted in new multicentered, low-density settings. The resulting urban form is likely to be more chaotic than the ordered polycentric structure described by centrists. This point is best illustrated in Fishman's depiction of a technoburb:

11. Fishman (1990), p. 26.
12. Fishman (1990), p.30.
13. Hall (1982).
14. Jacobs (1961).
15. Pivo (1990); Lang (1994a).

[T]he Technoburb has no proper boundaries; however defined, it is divided into a crazy quilt of separate and overlapping political jurisdictions, which make any kind of coordinated planning virtually impossible.[16]

Compared even to a traditional suburb, [a Technoburb] at first appears impossible to comprehend. It has no clear boundaries; it includes discordant rural, urban, and suburban elements; and it can best be measured in counties rather than in city blocks. Consequently, the new city lacks any recognizable center to give meaning to the whole. Major civic institutions seem scattered at random over an undifferentiated landscape.[17]

Fishman's analysis also is far less materialistic than that of most centrists. He does not argue that technological and economic forces inevitably lead to any particular type of metropolitan form. He looks instead to cultural characteristics such as the emphasis on individualism in the United States and asks what kind of city such a society is likely to build—what types of economic and technological instruments it will deploy to achieve its goals. This helps account for important differences between Anglo-American and European cities.[18] When the car was invented (in late nineteenth-century Germany), Europeans regarded it as a luxury item for the rich, while Americans mass produced it and used it to radically decentralize their metropolitan areas. Same technology, but different outcomes based on different cultural predilections, as well as differences in existing transportation networks, distances to be covered, and amount of land available to build roads.

The decentrist view also has its problems—for one, edge cities do exist and are fairly common. That fact is not well accounted for in a metropolitan model that argues that the new city is "everywhere or nowhere." Clearly, much of the new metropolis is somewhere, and that somewhere often is an edge city. In addition, it can be reasonably argued that some centralizing forces do remain and that they influence the form and function of a region. In a study comparing the spatial form of the Silicon Valley to that of Boston's route 128 high-tech corridor, Saxenian finds that the former is much denser and concentrated.[19] She also concludes that this density supports a creative milieu in which social net-

16. Fishman (1987), p. 190.
17. Fishman (1987), p. 203.
18. Fishman (1987).
19. Saxenian (1996).

Table 2-1. **Centrist versus Decentrist Perspectives on the New Metropolis**

Element	Centrist	Decentrist
New metropolitan center	Edge cities, urban villages	Households
New metropolitan form	Polycentric	Post-polycentric
Key structuring force	Agglomeration economies	Personal mobility
Connection to traditional urban structure	Strong	Weak
Clustering of key urban elements (malls, offices)	More common, predictable, with clear borders	Less common, random, with fuzzy borders

works develop and ideas are frequently exchanged. Saxenian concludes that part of Silicon Valley's comparative advantage over route 128 is a dense spatial form that helps foster innovation.

Table 2-1 summarizes the contrast in centrist and decentrist thinking on the new metropolis. For centrists, the new focal point for regions is decentralized clusters. For decentrists, metropolitan areas now center on individual households, creating an unfocused spatial structure and a new basis for urbanization.

What of the Old Monocentric Metropolis?

Given that the metropolitan literature now is divided between polycentric and post-polycentric camps, what is left of the old monocentric model? Ernest Burgess, using Chicago as his case study, developed the classic monocentric model of the metropolis.[20] Burgess saw the region as a series of "concentric zones." Beginning at the regional core (or the Loop in Chicago) and moving to the edge, each zone became successively less dense. At the center of the metropolitan zones was downtown, ringed by warehouses and factories, which were surrounded by "working men's homes." The next zone contained middle-income residences, which were surrounded in turn by a ring of luxury housing at the edge of the region.

As old-fashioned as Burgess's concentric zone theory may seem given the new metropolitan form, it still informs a good deal of modern thinking on the region. Consider, for example, Myron Orfield's work on inner-ring suburbs.[21] Orfield finds that the older ring of suburbs that

20. Burgess (1925).
21. Orfield (1997).

surround central cities are themselves now experiencing a type of urban distress that once was found exclusively in cities. The zone of working men's homes that Burgess identified in 1925 has expanded to include areas that used to be middle- and upper-income rings as the whole scale of metropolitan regions expanded with use of the automobile. Orfield's work shows that at least some of Burgess's thinking remains relevant.

It is interesting to consider Burgess's enduring relevance given the critiques his thinking has sustained over the years. For example, twenty years after the concentric zone model was introduced, some, such as Harris and Ullman, argued that it was false to assume that most or even a majority of metropolitan areas were actually monocentric.[22] Clearly, specific elements of Burgess's model, such as which land use fills which zone, no longer apply. Yet his fundamental assumption—that distance from the core structures land use—may still hold. It may even help determine how suburban office development is arrayed.

In a similar vein, William Alonso's bid-rent curve model is essentially an analytical adjunct to Burgess's concentric-zone theory.[23] The independent variable in this instance, distance from the center, causes a change in the dependent variable, cost of land, which ultimately affects land use. However, this hypothesis, which also assumes monocentricity, can be adjusted to different geographic scales. More specifically, bid-rent curves need not be calculated at the regional level from just one center; they also can apply to a local context. For example, major highway interchanges have economic value because they offer a valuable commodity, transportation access to the rest of the region. That, in turn, can affect land values on a small scale as land radiates from this central point.[24] In such instances, the land nearest the interchange goes for what is termed the "highest and best use," which most often means office buildings. That use is followed by a variety of other land uses, all of which are determined by their cost.

Every major highway interchange thus represents a microcosm of the same spatial structuring principle (distance from the center) that also occurs on successively larger geographic scales throughout the region. Metropolitan areas can, therefore, be multinucleated and yet simultaneously governed by a unifying geographic process that is oriented around a single regional center. The validity of this postulate would be

22. Harris and Ullman (1945).
23. Alonso (1960).
24. Erickson and Gentry (1985).

strengthened if it were found empirically that the land use patterns surrounding localized central points (for example, those at interchanges)
are influenced by their geographic position in the larger region. If that
were demonstrated and a consistent pattern of variance emerged, it
would indicate that metropolitan-scale spatial processes could influence
even multinucleated regions—that there may still remain a latent mecha-
nism of regional unification, even in the face of apparent fragmentation.
There are two separate but interrelated scales of land use structuring
occurring at every location in a metropolitan area.[25] One is based on the
region's center and applies to a metropolitan area. The other is based on
key transportation access points, which influence the local land market.
This can be thought of conceptually as a spatial form of a nested hierarchy in which all local development must ultimately be understood in the
context of the entire region. Thus the center may indeed hold, but it
would extend its influence by indirectly structuring land uses in multiple
subcenters surrounding it.

The New Metropolitan Form and the Future of Downtowns

Suburban office construction over the last three decades has so outpaced
growth in high-density urban settings that many observers have predicted a continued and even accelerated relative decline of downtowns.
A forceful advocate of this perspective is economist Edwin Mills, who
asserts that "nearly all center city employment is footloose."[26] Mills further contends that "there appears to be no powerful factor that holds
manufacturing, construction, FIRE [finance, insurance, and real estate]
and business and professional services in central cities."[27] Mills is not
surprised that cities have recently lost so much ground to the suburbs,
noting that the decentralization of people and commerce has been
occurring since the mid-nineteenth century. He finds that generally people dispersed first, followed by different categories of business, until
even the highest-order economic functions had decentralized.

While Mills predicts an especially grim outlook for cities, the boom
in suburban office space raises a legitimate question: what role remains
for dense urban cores? In particular, what is the role of downtowns in
the new suburban-oriented metropolis? The answer is complicated

25. Lang (1994b).
26. Mills (1988).
27. Mills (1988), p. 252.

because the fate of cities varies depending on their size, location, history, politics, and industry. But as a whole, downtowns still play a critical role in the social and economic life of the nation. Large downtowns, because of their scale and density, offer a unique environment in which inventive and enterprising populations flourish.[28] Big cities nurture a dynamic confluence of ideas and trends that, although they may be considered unconventional by the general population at first, ultimately are absorbed by society.[29]

On the surface it appears that downtowns will decline to the point of irrelevance. But looking at just the shift in office space ignores which types of businesses remain downtown and which have relocated to the suburbs. Major downtowns retain a significant share of the information-intensive industry—for example, market exchanges and business services.[30] The suburbs also claim a good share of this employment; however, the more significant suburban businesses in terms of total employment involve back-office and routinized operations such as billing.[31] Even companies that have moved their headquarters to a suburb often find it necessary to maintain an office in a national or international downtown in order to benefit from business services that the company cannot provide internally.[32] Because it is expensive to maintain employees downtown, if work can be shipped to the suburbs, it will be.[33] The market has been quite efficient at sorting out the types of work that need to be downtown and those that do not. In the regional division of labor, downtowns will probably continue to grab a significant portion of higher-order, specialized employment.

A city's unique advantage may emerge unexpectedly. Take the case of the high-tech sector. High technology practically defined the initial suburban locational advantage. From Bell Labs in suburban New Jersey to the sprawling computer industry in California's Silicon Valley, suburbs appeared to own the industry. But recently, as these industries evolved to the point that the creative focus shifted toward the application of technology to fields such as multimedia, the role that cities can play in driving high-tech business has become clear. Several years ago, as "new

28. Glaeser (1994); Florida (2002).
29. Fischer (1975).
30. Hall (1998); Raines (2000).
31. Sassen (1994).
32. Moss and Dunau (1987).
33. Daniels (1985); Soja (1989); Sassen (1994).

media" emerged in such fields as CD-ROMs and computer graphics, high-tech businesses became increasingly content driven.

An even more recent explosion in the Internet and e-commerce further reinforced this shift.[34] Many technology companies recently have returned to the urban core in search of the creative talent they need to supply the Internet's demand for content. This trend has given rise to New York's Silicon Alley, built around the city's graphic and advertising industry, and to the densely packed West Side of Los Angeles, where writers and artists now contribute to what is perhaps the nation's largest conglomeration of new media companies. LA's downtown has emerged as a national center for telecommunications companies. The continued viability of downtown also helps explain why so many dotcoms, despite their inherently footloose existence in cyberspace, remain disproportionately concentrated in the cities that stand at the center of the new information economy.[35]

The emergence of suburban business centers notwithstanding, downtowns often maintain their rank as first among equals in the metropolitan economy. If, as some have predicted, the sprawling postwar metropolis has reached its limits, viable downtowns may be in a position to solidify that role.[36] This means that downtowns must find their niche, both within their region and in the new international economy.[37] They need to cultivate dense concentrations of businesses by sector: publishing in Boston's Back Bay; fashion in Miami Beach's South Beach; entertainment in Los Angeles's West Side; lobbying in Washington, D.C.; headquarters services and advertising in New York City's midtown Manhattan and financial services in lower Manhattan. The office data presented in this book show that downtowns did well in the 1990s, especially the older and denser ones in the Northeast and Midwest.

Downtowns and their adjacent neighborhoods foster the development of rich communicative milieus that even in an information age may not be fully replicable in the lower-density suburbs. Businesses can communicate by fax and e-mail, but it is hard to establish the personal networks that often are necessary to support the high-end downtown economy. People still need to be in the middle of the action, and that means that at least some players in virtually any information-intensive

34. Raines (2000).
35. Hall (1998); Florida (2002).
36. Leinberger (1996).
37. Raines (2000).

industry will remain downtown.[38] Counterintuitively, the continued evolution of edgeless cities may make the high-density business cores of large cities all the more important because they may be the only places left where all the elements of the fractured metropolis still come together.[39]

The diverse lifestyles nurtured in big, vital downtowns, the neighborhoods surrounding them, and the people attracted to them play a critical role in keeping America competitive. The skills such people bring to the city are important, but perhaps more significant for many industries are the creative milieus that thrive in big cities. Sociologist Claude Fischer argues that large, dense cities such as New York, Chicago, and Boston sustain innovative subcultures (Richard Florida recently drew on and extended this work).[40] Big cities support unconventional subcultures and lifestyles that find full expression in what are called bohemian enclaves. Industries such as fashion, entertainment, advertising, and publishing, all major businesses in New York, draw heavily from the city's diverse subcultures as a source for new ideas. Thus, large, dense cities with significant bohemian communities have a competitive advantage in industries that are fueled by unconventional thinking, which today constitute the leading edge of the economy.

Theory Synthesis

A key determinant of the distribution and density of suburban office development is the tension between the efficiencies gained through agglomeration and the diseconomies of scale that result from increasing density. In large central business districts (CBDs) such as Manhattan, the diseconomies of scale are very costly; however, a business may consider the costs justified by the benefits of being in a central location where it can make use of the most specialized types of producer services. The dynamic in an edge city is much the same, although the costs and benefits are considerably less.

Manhattan and the nation's other large, vital CBDs exist in a dynamic equilibrium between diseconomies and efficiencies. The risk that they run is that some day the diseconomies will substantially outweigh the efficiencies. For some economic sectors, they already do. Over

38. Sassen (1994).
39. Raines (2000).
40. Fischer (1975).

the years, many CBD-based businesses have left, judging the location too costly.[41] The loss has been at least partly offset by the influx of new industries that prefer downtown.

Edge cities appear to be on the verge of the same predicament. Some may prove so efficient, so essential, that most businesses will pay the price of remaining there.[42] But as Fulton noted, some edge cities face relative decline as they seek to remain competitive by expanding while nearby residents limit their growth.[43] The not-in-my-backyard (NIMBY) sentiment of some suburbs may simply trap edge cities in a noncompetitive position—big and dense enough to be high cost but unable to fully exploit their future growth prospects.

Metropolitan form represents in part a compromise between forces that centralize and those that decentralize. The respective power of the two forces shifts with changes in technology, culture, economic production, regional scale, intergroup relations, social and political organization, physical and regulatory constraints, demographic composition, and popular tastes. The existing built environment also is influenced by centralizing and decentralizing forces. As described above, in regions with strong cores, distance from the center may still shape metropolitan structure at the edge. Many of these variables differ dramatically from region to region, producing a nation of different contexts, different compromises, and correspondingly different metropolitan forms. Those multiple forms are one reason why both centrist and decentrist perspectives can coexist. Each can point to a region or a part of a region and find evidence of its view. The centrists do case analysis of big edge cities, while the decentrists focus on the post-polycentric metropolis.

Better understanding is needed to be able to to delineate the urban from the nonurban on the metropolitan continuum. This is not just a trivial matter for people obsessed with geographic categorization. When someone declares Princeton, New Jersey, and Stamford, Connecticut, to be analogous phenomena, as Leinberger did, something clearly is off. This study separates Princeton from Stamford and presents data on both types of metropolitan development. The division is crude, but at least it is a starting point. Hopefully, further analysis by the author and others will greatly refine it.

41. Mills (1988).
42. The high-tech cluster at Tysons Corner, Virginia, may be one example.
43. Fulton (1996).

The data that follow show how large these two types of metropolitan development—centrist edge city and decentrist edgeless city—are relative to one another. We also can get a sense for the direction in which they are heading. Right now edgeless cities have almost twice the office space found in edge cities. By the best estimate, the relative percentages have been equal for about twenty years. Essentially, edge cities and edgeless cities have grown up together—one marked and well documented, the other unmarked and ignored. Another non-CBD real estate boom like the one in the 1980s is needed to get a clear sense of which (if either) will prevail. At least now we may have a better sense of what to track.

CHAPTER 3

A Field Guide to

the New Metropolis

Americans have long been inventive in labeling their urban world. In the early twentieth century, they coined the term "skyscraper" to describe tall downtown office buildings. But no one has devised a compelling term to depict the typical low-slung buildings found in edgeless cities. Skyscraper sounds heroic, modern, soaring. But its logical antonym, "ground hugger," sounds—well, not very heroic, or modern, or soaring. There is little chance that the label will catch on. Yet ground huggers define the new metropolis just as skyscrapers do the traditional downtown. The problem is that the language to describe the new metropolis never quite hits the target the way terms such as "skyscraper" and "downtown" did.

Definitions form the core of the study on which this book is based, and this chapter reviews efforts to label the emerging suburban metropolis. The term "edgeless city" identifies a new category of office space. Through photos and maps, this chapter shows how edgeless cities differ from traditional office areas. The office categories described are used throughout the rest of the book as the basis for data analysis.

"What Do You Call This Place?"

Much of the literature naming the new metropolitan form focuses on relabeling suburbs. An early critic of urban sprawl defined a suburb as a "city trying to escape the consequences of being a city while still remaining a city."[1] American suburbs began as an ambiguous urban subcategory wedged between city and countryside. Outgrowths of the Industrial Revolution, they are works in progress—forever provisional, much like cities themselves. For many decades the term "suburb" captured the essence of the new form, but the 1950s changed all that. Exurbs arose as a low-density, upscale residential ring between older suburbs and rural areas. Major retailing then found a new home on the highway, signaling a far more fundamental shift. Within a generation, suburbs attained economic, social, and demographic parity with cities, often supplanting them. Yet suburbs have maintained a distinct pattern even as they have become more urban in function.

Urban scholars have been attempting to characterize this change for the past three decades. As Sharpe and Wallach note:

> In the early 1970s, as concern about the inner-city crisis waned and the decentralization of the metropolis reached new proportions, "the urbanization of the suburbs" suddenly became a topic of national interest. The ensuing flurry of articles and books introduced neologisms such as "outer city," "satellite sprawl," "new city," "suburban 'city,'" "urban fringe," and "neo city" to describe this phenomenon.[2]

Thus a new metropolitan form proliferates: low density and automobile dependent, often dispersed and edgeless. There is no single name for it. Observers instead use an inventive array of names, suggesting that planners, developers, journalists, and academics do not yet fully understand it. Part of the problem is that they are bound by language that continues to rank living space hierarchically—urban, suburban, exurban, rural—when the old hierarchy no longer applies. Whereas the old delineation in space was sharp edged, a new "soft-edged" division between city and country has emerged.[3] In the new metropolis, density, scale, and function may no longer correlate.[4]

The U.S. Census Bureau is left to grapple with distinguishing an "urbanized area" from a "metropolitan area," which today can be a vast, low-density environment that includes many of the traditionally urban functions. The bureau now has come to accept two definitions of spatially noncoterminous areas: an urbanized area is a higher-density

1. Taylor (1915).
2. Sharpe and Wallach (1994), p. 4.
3. Kostof (1992), p. 59.
4. Meltzer (1984).

(more than 1,000 people per square mile) subset of a metropolitan area, which also includes largely rural counties at the fringe linked to the metropolis through commuter sheds.[5] Properly naming the new metropolitan form is an important step in better understanding it. As Lewis notes: "Language is important. We cannot talk about a phenomenon unless we posses the vocabulary to describe it, and many observers still cannot agree on what to call this new amorphous form of urban geography."[6] Even news accounts of the 2000 census noted that the geographic categories used to report the numbers seem old and outdated. Haya El Nasser of *USA Today* noted that "with people spreading out from cities, the old labels of urban, suburban and rural don't cut it." She adds that "now, the 'suburbs' are not 'sub' to anything because they often have as many, if not more, jobs than cities" and that "'rural' seems too quaint to describe places where modern homes are going up on 5-acre lots next to farms."[7]

Table 3-1 lists some of the terms applied to the new metropolitan form.[8] The list certainly supports the observation that we cannot agree on what to call these places or even on which places need labeling.[9] The new metropolis is such a conceptual mess that almost four dozen names appear on the list—and it is only a partial list.[10] In a 1992 Columbia University conference on the new suburbs, more than 200 names were listed that identified the entirety or elements of the new metropolis.[11] The names in the table were selected because of their relevance to this study and the diversity of their sources and perspectives. Common terms such as "office park," "sprawl," and "exurb" were omitted because they have entered wide use.

The names in table 3-1 collectively convey the image of a spread-out "regional city" based more on the postindustrial service economy than on the industrial economy. Most include common words like "city" and "village," but mix them in novel, often contradictory ways, thus coining

5. Palen (1995).

6. Lewis (1995), p. 61.

7. Haya El Nasser, "Language Doesn't Fit USA's Profile," *USA Today,* August 9, 2001, p. 3A.

8. For other summaries of naming the new metropolitan form see Romanos, Chifos, and Fenner (1989) and Sharpe and Wallach (1994).

9. Brown and Hickok (1990).

10. And new names keep getting added, for instance, the "limitless city" (Gillham 2002) and the "exit ramp economy" (Bruce Katz, "Welcome to the 'Exit Ramp' Economy," *Boston Globe,* May 13, 2001).

11. Columbia University (1992).

Table 3-1. Partial List of Names Given to the New Metropolitan Form

Term	Year	Author
Anticity	1985	Louv
Cities à la carte	1990	Fishman
Concentrated decentralization	1985	Daniels
Countrified city	1984	Doherty
Disurb	1987	Baldassare and Katz
Edge city	1991	Garreau
Edgeless city	2000	Lang
Exopolis	1997	Soja
Galactic city	1983	Lewis
Major diversified center	1983	Baerwald
	1983	Huth
Megacenter	1985	Orski
	1986	Cervero
Megacounty	1987	Church
Metropolitan-level core	1986	Hartshorn and Muller
Metropolitan suburb	1986	Baldassare
Metrotown	1988	Romanos, Schifos, and Fenner
Mini-city	1972	Breckenfeld
	1976	Muller
Mini-downtown	1986	Cervero
Multicentered net	1961	Lynch
Net of mixed beads	1990	Pivo
New downtown	1978	Baerwald
Outer city	1976	Muller
	1987	Stevens
Outtown	1987	Goldberger
Penturbia	1987	Lessinger
Regional city	2000	Calthorpe and Fulton
Regional town center	1985	Hutton and Davis
Ruburbia	1988	Sternlieb and Hughes
Servurb	1988	Malin
Slurbs	1973	Huxtable
Spillover city	1972	Packard
Spread city	1960	Regional Plan Association
Stealth city	1992	Knox
Subcenter	1996	Gordon and Richardson
Suburban business center	1986	Hartshorn and Muller
Suburban downtown	1982	Baerwald
	1989	Hartshorn and Muller
Suburban employment center	1989	Cervero
	1998	Freestone and Murphy
Suburban freeway corridor	1978	Baerwald
Suburban growth corridor	1986	Hughes and Sternlieb
Suburban nucleation	1985	Erickson and Gentry
Technoburb	1987	Fishman
The new heartland	1986	Herbers
Urban core	1990	Leinberger
Urban galaxy	1961	Lynch
Urban realm	1964	Vance
Urban village	1984	Leinberger
	1986	Leinberger and Lockwood

such titles as "edge city," "countrified city," "urban village" and "concentrated decentralization." This book adds the label "edgeless city" to this already long list.

Many observers seeking to name the new metropolitan form stress office development, for it has been the most recent city element to suburbanize and its decentralization has become the symbol of the new metropolis.[12] A few visionaries like Kevin Lynch and James Vance foresaw suburbia's future in the 1960s, but most of the names are more recent, with the biggest flurry coming in the late 1980s. Many of the names labeling office development refer to large, dense clusters, therefore the terms "mega," "major," "concentrated," "downtown," and "core." Some of the labels, such as "slurbs" and "disurb" are overtly disapproving; some, such as "anticity," "exopolis," "spread city," "spillover city," and "edgeless city," are more slyly disparaging. Among the forty-four terms, ten contain the word "city"; eight, "suburb" or "suburban"; four, "urban"; three, "downtown"; three, "town"; three, "metro" or "metropolitan"; two, "core"; and one each, "village," "rural," and "country." Garreau's "edge city" is the only label on the list that has entered common use and will likely earn a dictionary definition.

The naming does not stop here; within many of these labels are sublabels. Figure 3-1 shows three examples. The sub-labels point to a highly pluralized region—not simply a multinucleated one, but one comprising various densities, scales, functions, contexts, and structures. They also indicate how closely labeling is tied to the actual research methods and categories used for gathering office data. The first set of sub-labels in figure 3-1 was developed by the author in the early 1990s to categorize office space in northern New Jersey.[13] The labeling process starts with the context and age of development (traditional versus modern), then spatial form; next, scale and spatial form further subdivide modern development. Traditional development is divided only by scale. The divisions result in six office location categories: central business district (for example, Newark); county seat complex (New Brunswick); edge city—or 5 million–plus square feet of office space (Parsippany); sub-edge city—or 2 to 5 million square feet of office space (Secaucus); corridor (route 287 from Edison to Bridgewater); and scatter (Monmouth County). The biggest category was "modern unfocused," which contained more than half of northern New Jersey's 140 million square feet

12. Mills (1988).
13. Lang (1994a, 1994b).

Figure 3-1. Sub-Labels for Metropolitan Office Locations

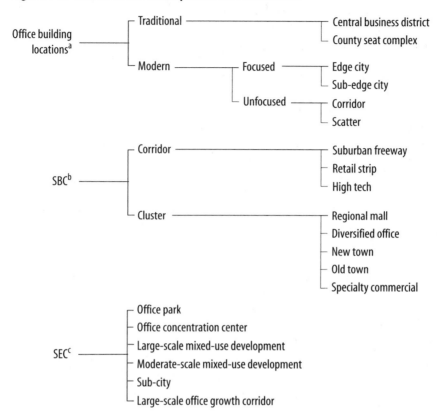

a. Typology developed for the *Rutgers Regional Report,* Department of Urban Planning (Robert Lang).
b. Suburban business center (Truman Hartshorn and Peter Muller).
c. Suburban employment center (Robert Cervero).

of office space.[14] The traditional office locations held about one-quarter of the space; edge cities and sub-edge cities accounted for another fifth.

The other two sets of sub-labels in figure 3-1 also were developed to help determine the locational characteristics of office space. Hartshorn and Muller split corridors from clusters and then divide locations further on the basis of age and economic function.[15] Cervero used multivariate

14. Lang (1994a, 1994b).
15. Hartshorn and Muller (1986).

techniques (cluster analysis) to provide order to a database of office locations, sorting office locations by scale, form, density, and function.[16]

The Big Picture versus the Basic Elements

In almost all fields of inquiry there are two camps: those who try to understand the big picture and those who seek out the basic elements—the old "forest versus the trees" dichotomy. Figure 3-2 shows that research on the new metropolitan form is no different; it encompasses both those who try to capture the macro and those who identify the micro features. As shown below, those who take a broad view of the new metropolis tend to see chaos and those who focus on the basic elements often find order.

Figure 3-2 lists each label that appears in table 3-1 under the headings "big picture" or "basic elements." It then further subdivides the terms on the basis of what they describe. In the big-picture category, ten of the terms describe regional structure; interestingly, five of them label the metropolitan fringe. The observation that the suburban metropolis now supports urban activities across a wide area without necessarily assuming a traditional city form is captured in the terms "technoburb" and "servurb," which focus on function.

The names describing the basic elements are especially complicated and diverse. Almost all refer to office development, but the particular aspect they seek to identify varies widely. Many identify where office development occurs in the region, including the terms "edge city," "outer city," and "outtown." Most names describe the form of office development, with all three major variants—cluster, corridor, and diffuse—represented. The cleverly named "stealth city" applies to all three types.[17] Seven names label clustering, while two each identify corridors and diffuse forms. All of the eight regional location names also secondarily identify clustered development. Were it not for the inclusion of "edgeless city," only Gordon and Richardson's "subcenters" would describe diffuse office locations, and even that label includes the word "center."

"Edgeless cities" labels those parts of metropolitan areas that often have large volumes of office space that is not clustered enough to form edge cities. It does not describe regional structure per se but rather subregional structure. It identifies specific but amorphous places across

---

16. Cervero (1989).
17. Knox (1992).

Figure 3-2. The Big Picture versus the Basic Elements

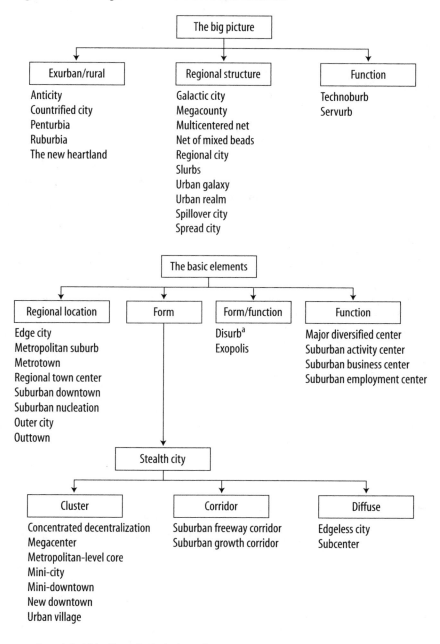

a. Dense, industrial, self-contained suburban region.

different, often large, scales. "Edgeless city" is an urban geographic concept, but an elusive one. Throughout this book the term appears primarily in the plural form because there are always several edgeless cities per region.

From Downtowns to Edgeless Cities: The Office-Density Continuum

Density, and often specifically office density, is a key delineating element in the various labels reviewed above. In this study, the office-density continuum is divided into four main segments. The ends are the primary downtowns and edgeless cities; in between are secondary downtowns and edge cities. Table 3-2 summarizes these types and identifies their place in the office-density gradient.

Primary and Secondary Downtowns

Downtowns can be found throughout older parts of metropolitan areas. The "primary downtown," or central business district (CBD), lies at the center of the region; it is the original site of significant commercial development. In some cases, such as Manhattan, the CBD may be split between an original downtown and a midtown that emerged in the twentieth century. In such instances, the two downtowns are combined into one general primary downtown. Figure 3-3 shows Atlanta's primary downtown. (Note that Atlanta's midtown, which looms in the background, was folded in with its downtown for the statistical analysis.) What are referred to here as "secondary downtowns" are the centers of major suburbs and uptowns in central cities that developed a relatively modest, though focused, commercial center early in the twen-

Table 3-2. Office Types

Category	Scale	Office density	Basic units	Boundary
Primary downtown	A square mile or a few square miles	Very high to high	City block	Sharp; well delineated
Secondary downtown	A square mile or a few square miles	High to medium	City block	Mostly well delineated, with some soft edges
Edge city	Several square miles	Medium to low	Freeway interchange	Fuzzy, but with a recognizable edge
Edgeless city	Tens or hundreds of square miles	Very low	Municipality or county	Indeterminate, very hard to delineate

Figure 3-3. Downtown Atlanta

Aerial photo by Georgia Aerial Services, Inc.

tieth century. Secondary downtowns are scaled down, slightly less dense versions of primary downtowns. They have their origin in the streetcar and early auto era and therefore support some pedestrian presence. Figure 3-4 shows Atlanta's Buckhead, the area's leading uptown.

Secondary dowtowns often emerged in what some urban historians refer to as residential city suburbs.[18] These suburbs represented the first generation of major population centers outside central cities and often replicated many of the CBD's features, including retail and commercial development. Residential suburbs even contained a modest amount of high-density, low-income residences surrounding their downtowns.

Edge Cities

In the literature on suburban office development, edge cities have a specific definition. While Joel Garreau first used the term "edge city" in

18. Bourchert (1996).

Figure 3-4. Buckhead, Atlanta

1991, he defined it by using the same criteria real estate consultant Christopher Leinberger used earlier to identify what Leinberger referred to as urban villages.[19] As defined by Garreau, edge cities are places that

—have 5 million square feet or more of office space

—have 600,000 square feet or more of retail space

—have more jobs than bedrooms

—are perceived by the population as one place

—were nothing like a "city" as recently as thirty years ago.[20]

Garreau finds that edge cities are dense relative to their suburban surroundings. Leinberger also emphasizes density when describing urban

---

19. In a personal conversation with the author, Chris Leinberger indicated that Joel Garreau was the first person to contact him after the publication of his piece with Charles Lockwood (1986) in the *Atlantic Monthly*, which listed the criteria for an urban village.

20. Garreau (1991), pp. 6–7.

Figure 3-5. Perimeter Center, Atlanta

Aerial photo by Georgia Aerial Services, Inc.

villages, which he depicts as "business, retail and entertainment focal points amid a low-density cityscape" having "a core—a kind of new downtown—where the buildings are the tallest, the daytime population the largest, and the traffic congestion the most severe."[21] In the study reported in this book, edge cities are defined only by total square feet of office space, the first of the five criteria listed above. The number of edge cities varies depending on metropolitan area, with larger office markets typically containing several. (For a complete list of edge cities, see appendix C.) Most edge cities are found along interstate beltways and major arterial roads that run through the mature suburban parts of metropolitan areas. Perimeter Center outside of Atlanta, shown in figure 3-5, constitutes a large edge city.

21. Leinberger and Lockwood (1986), p. 43.

Edgeless Cities

Edgeless cities, along with edge cities, identify a subset of non-CBD office space. As the term implies, edgeless cities lack a well-defined boundary or edge. They may extend over tens and, in a few cases, hundreds of square miles of urban space, and although their individual components often have a name ("So-and-so" office park), edgeless cities seldom strike a casual observer as unified in any meaningful way. Therefore, unlike edge cities, edgeless cities are *not* perceived as a place. Gertrude Stein's famous comment about Oakland, California—"When you get there, there isn't any there, there"—would apply even more aptly to edgeless cities.

Edgeless cities capture all non-downtown office space that is not in an edge city. They scatter far and wide across the region, some ringing the metropolitan edge, others lying between edge cities or covering the outskirts of cities. Places such as northern New Jersey contain vast swaths of office buildings—some grouped in small clusters and corridors, others solitary, tucked into hill and dale. Edgeless cities are so large and dispersed that it is difficult to refer to them individually. It is not always possible to say, for example, "Consider this particular edgeless city." Rather, because of their scale, they have to be described in general terms: "Edgeless cities constitute X percent of a region's office space." Edgeless cities are more diffuse, less glamorous cousins of edge cities. Edgeless cities are as elusive and hard to define as urban sprawl, of which, essentially, they constitute a major part.[22] Saying "edgeless city" is in fact a polite way of saying "office sprawl." Figure 3-6, which shows a nondescript area north of Atlanta, illustrates the point.

Delineating Office Location Types

Despite the relatively straightforward distinctions in the types of office locations in the accompanying photographs, much of the nation's office space exists across a spectrum of built environments that sometimes are hard to delineate. This study assigned all of the office space in the thirteen major markets examined to one of the four categories already described (figure 3-7).

22. Lang (2000c).

Figure 3-6. Edgeless City North of Atlanta

Aerial photo by Georgia Aerial Services, Inc.

Distinguishing Primary Downtowns from Secondary Downtowns

The distinction between primary and secondary downtowns was clear cut. Primary downtowns are the original core of commercial development. The only difficulty lay in determining what space to include in the primary downtowns of New York City and Los Angeles. If, despite being many miles apart, midtown Manhattan and lower Manhattan (the financial district) together constitute a single downtown, could the same be true of separate areas in other cities? The only other city for which such a conclusion seemed reasonable was Los Angeles. Besides tradition, a key fact supporting the view that midtown Manhattan and the financial district are linked as a single CBD is that a spine of development that runs along Broadway joins the two. The "Broadway" of Los Angeles is

Figure 3-7. Office Location Types

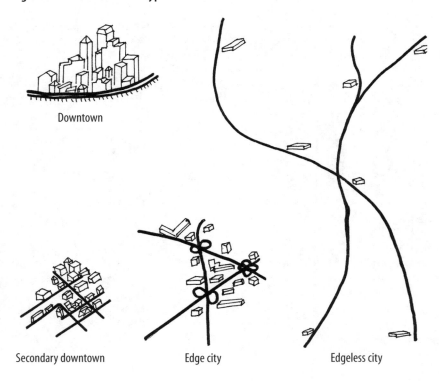

Downtown

Secondary downtown   Edge city   Edgeless city

Wilshire Boulevard.[23] Commercial development runs the length of Wilshire, beginning in Los Angeles's downtown and running west to the Pacific in Santa Monica, with only occasional breaks.[24] According to analysis of the office data in this study, nearly 85 million square feet of office space can be found within a half-mile of the street. Therefore, if Broadway defines downtown New York, Wilshire Boulevard defines downtown Los Angeles.

Distinguishing Secondary Downtowns from Edge Cities

The distinction between secondary downtowns and edge cities is based primarily on context. Secondary downtowns appear in locations

23. Abbott (1990).

24. In fact, Abbott refers to Wilshire Boulevard as the "first linear downtown" (1990, p. 64).

that traditionally have been regional satellite centers. For example, places such as Jersey City, New Jersey, are not edge cities. Jersey City has two large office clusters: one is Journal Square, its traditional commercial core; the other is Exchange Place, a new office area built directly across the Hudson River from lower Manhattan. Exchange Place also has a stop on the Port Authority Trans-Hudson (PATH) train. Although Exchange Place is new, its context is old. In fact, Exchange Place is really a spillover of development from lower Manhattan. Secondary downtowns also differ from edge cities in terms of streetscape. Secondary downtowns maintain a city-like street grid, and the buildings connect to the streets rather than sit in a sea of parking and landscaped lawns. Urban morphology therefore helps separate secondary downtowns from edge cities.

Delineating secondary downtowns from edge cities is important in public policy terms. When places such as Jersey City gain more office space, their growth does not create the same set of issues that accompanies similar development in the suburbs. For the most part, concerns about open space, transportation, and mismatching of jobs and housing are not present. Smart growth proposals, which seek to direct growth to areas that already are built up, often recommend developing secondary downtowns.

Separating secondary downtowns from edge cities was most difficult for New York City, Washington, D.C., and Los Angeles. The three regions have plenty of both, and they also are the nation's biggest office markets. In instances in which the decision was difficult, edge city was used as the default category. Places such as Morristown, New Jersey, and Crystal City in Arlington, Virginia, are older, and according to the census definition they are central cities. However, the office development they feature does not connect to an older context. In Morristown, most of the development sprawls outside the older urban core; Crystal City, created in the 1960s, is an isolated office environment disconnected from the older city of Arlington. By contrast, the office development that occurred in Arlington along Wilson Boulevard was designed to fit the context of the city and therefore formed secondary downtowns.[25]

Distinguishing Edge Cities from Edgeless Cities

The distinction between edge cities and edgeless cities is more a matter of degree than of absolute difference. A gradient exists for both the

25. Porter (1997).

size and density of office clusters. Five million square feet of office space is used as the primary cut-off point for size because that is the figure used by Garreau and by Leinberger and Lockwood.[26] At some point, all edge cities were edgeless cities in that they did not possess enough office space to qualify as edge cities. Had a longitudinal analysis been performed in this study, the specific edge cities identified would have been somewhat different at different data points. The issue does not arise in a historical analysis of current office stock (or panel data), as was done in this study (see appendix B for details). In addition, it appears that most current edgeless cities are not edge cities waiting to grow up. New office space is added to them at such low densities that most edgeless cities are not coalescing into the type of dense clusters that would meet the criteria for being an edge city. Contrary to some theories,[27] the data show that most non-CBD office space did not migrate to the big clusters that were forming during the 1970s and 1980s.

Building heights generally tend to be higher in edge cities than in edgeless cities. Edge cities also tend to have some signature structures that rise high above their surroundings and thereby create a citylike impression. This is especially true of larger edge cities, such as those with more than 10 million square feet of office space. Edge cities in the 7 to 9 million-square-foot range exhibit some of these characteristics but they are less pronounced.

A decision was made not to use the additional edge city criterion requiring 600,000 square feet of retail space. As was predicted in theory,[28] studies have shown no correlation between the location of retail and office space.[29] Had this criterion been added, the amount of space assigned to edge cities would have dropped dramatically, resulting in less useful findings for this study.

The data analysis that follows shows seventeen edge cities with more than 10 million square feet of office space. (A full listing of edge cities by region and size appears in chapter 5.) Such places were clearly distinguishable from edgeless cities. That was not unexpected. Most of the places that Garreau focuses on have more than 10 million square feet of office space. However, according to the analysis here, big edge cities represent only 30 percent of the edge city total. The edge cities that were

---

26. Garreau (1991); Leinberger and Lockwood (1986).
27. Daniels (1985); Erickson (1983, 1985); Erickson and Gentry (1985).
28. Fishman (1990)
29. Lang (1994a); Pivo (1990).

just over the 5 million-square-foot cut-off point were a bit harder to distinguish from edgeless cities, but even these small edge cities clustered in a way that made them denser than edgeless cities. Because they are discrete and bounded, edge cities also can be counted the way satellite cities can. Edgeless cities cannot be counted because they do not have an edge.

Black's Guide Data and Maps

Office market statistics are not collected by government agencies but by a variety of real estate brokers, consulting firms, realty and building associations, and online data providers. Given the diversity of the sources, with their correspondingly varied focuses and interests, no uniform guidelines exist for determining even basic attributes of office markets, such as total size. In fact, there is not even general agreement on what should be categorized as an office building. Therefore any compilation of office statistics must to some extent be customized and data selected on the basis of their relevance to the task at hand (for more details, see appendix A).

The major source of office data in the study examined in this book is *Black's Guide to Office Leasing*, a directory of office space published by a company based in Gaithersburg, Maryland. *Black's Guide* was until very recently the only national office data source that allowed central city space to be separated from suburban space; no other national office survey listed buildings by address.[30] *Black's Guide* lists multitenanted rental office buildings of 15,000 square feet or more, identified as "existing," "under construction," or "proposed." Inventory data, by which total market size is determined, include buildings under construction at the time of the survey but not those proposed, even if a starting date is given. *Black's Guide* surveys even the smallest suburban office markets, making it possible to compare data across regions. Buildings are listed in the publication at no cost to owners or developers, and the guide, whose primary source of revenue was display advertising, is distributed free to companies and institutions involved in office leasing.

Black's Guide's best feature is its maps, which show the exact location of all of the offices that appear in the directory. The maps clearly indicate how widely buildings are dispersed across a region. Examples of

30. In 2000, a number of online data sources were established, such as Reality IQ; however, the dotcom bust affected these start-ups, and now it is increasingly hard to get online office data.

these maps are shown at the end of this chapter. The challenge for those mapping office buildings is to find the right blocks of space to show clusters of office development. For downtowns, the process is simple. Find the downtown, draw a perimeter, and then map the buildings. The same is true for edge cities, which exist as either a cluster or a relatively dense corridor. But how does one map edgeless cities? Not easily. If there is a question about the existence of edgeless cities, a quick glance at the maps in *Black's Guide* will dispel any doubt. Edgeless cities appear across multiple pages—a few buildings here, some more buildings there—some in small clusters, others scattered like buckshot. *Black's Guide* often uses dozens of maps to show all of the buildings in large markets. A single map usually depicts the downtown; the region's edge cities take up several more; and the rest of the maps—often thirty to forty—show edgeless cities. The maps by themselves tell a compelling story of how America's office economy has grown in ways that are hard to measure.

Field Guide for the Study

Examples of a primary downtown, a secondary downtown, an edge city, and an edgeless city based on the maps in *Black's Guide* follow.

Primary Downtown: Houston, Texas

Houston's downtown is a relatively compact cluster of several dozen large office buildings that fit into a space of fewer than 100 city blocks. It contains just over 38 million square feet of office space, much more than even the largest edge city. The center of the downtown is the intersection of Travis and Walker streets. The blocks bounded by Louisiana Street to the west, San Jacinto to the east, Capitol to the north, and McKinney to the south contain the densest development. Over the last twenty years, the center of the downtown shifted west toward Sam Houston Park and the city hall complex, stranding some of the pre–World War II office towers.[31] The continuity of downtown is broken in parts by empty lots that provide surface parking.

As figure 3-8 shows, many of the major buildings downtown are connected by tunnels and overhead walkways to provide protection from Houston's stifling heat and humidity in the summer and security all year round. (The walkways have been criticized for reducing the pedestrian presence on the street.) Houston's is a fairly typical Sunbelt downtown that caters to the nine-to-five office worker and offers little to tourists or

31. ULI (1999).

Figure 3-8. Downtown Houston

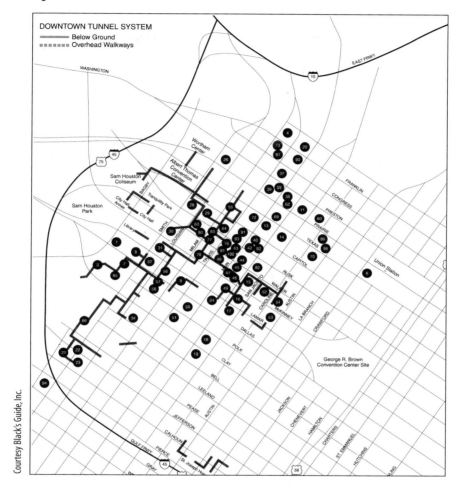

Courtesy Black's Guide, Inc.

residents. In recent years some of the old office buildings have been converted into housing in an attempt to introduce some life after 5:00 p.m.[32] While that has helped, the downtown seems more like an edge city on steroids than a Boston or San Francisco CBD.

Secondary Downtown: Pasadena, California

Downtown Pasadena, made famous by the Rose Bowl Parade and a song, "The Little Old Lady from Pasadena," made popular by Jan and

32. Sohmer and Lang (2000).

Figure 3-9. Downtown Pasadena, California

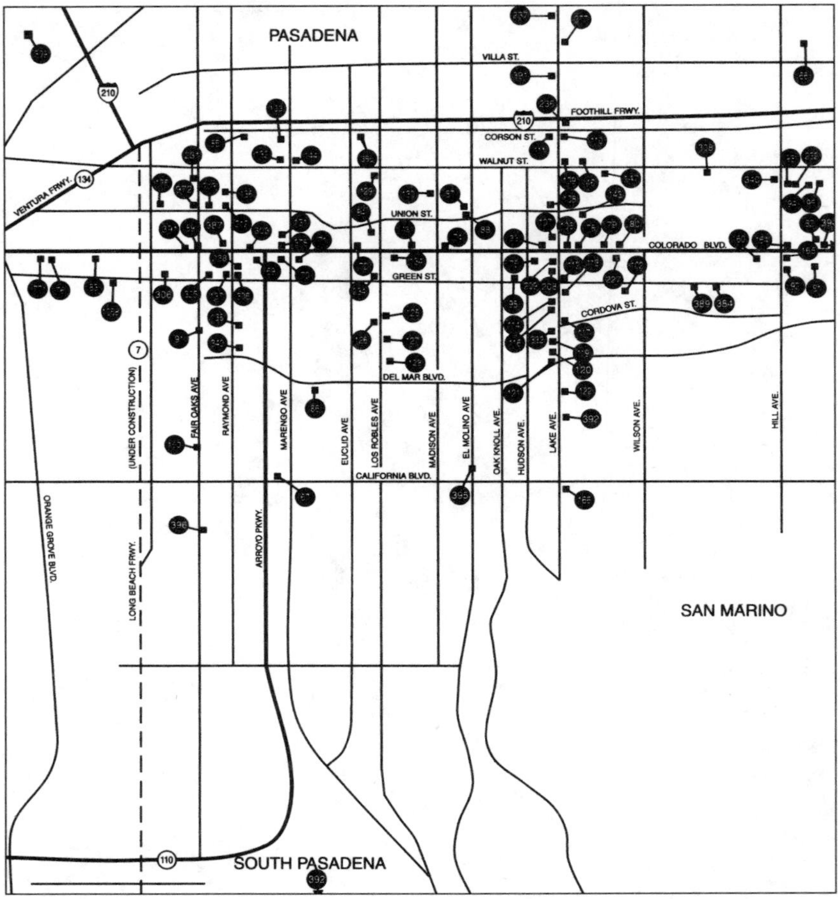

Courtesy Black's Guide, Inc.

Dean in the 1960s, is a late nineteenth-century satellite city northeast of downtown Los Angeles (figure 3-9). The city was so important that it received the first freeway (along the Arroyo Seco) to downtown in the early 1940s. The heart of Pasadena's downtown runs about a dozen blocks along Colorado Boulevard. Within this stretch lies most of the city's nearly 8 million square feet of office space, an amount typical of many secondary downtowns. The stretch includes a pedestrian-friendly shopping district. Pasadena was in decline as recently as the 1970s, but its Victorian and Craftsman homes dating from the turn of the twentieth century proved an inviting target for gentrification. The city is typical of upscale secondary downtowns around the county, such as Cambridge, Massachusetts, and Bethesda, Maryland. To some, these places are more attractive, human-scaled alternatives to the primary downtown.

Edge City: Tysons Corner, Virginia

Tysons Corner seems to be everybody's favorite Edge City—almost any account of suburban office development in the late 1980s contained some mention of it. Tysons Corner even appears in before-and-after photographs on the inside leaves of Joel Garreau's *Edge City*. Looking at figure 3-10, it is easy to see why. Tysons Corner is a dense (for the suburbs) cluster of office buildings surrounding two large regional malls. It is the nation's third-largest edge city, with nearly 18 million square feet of office space, most of which lies within a triangular area well-bounded by the Dulles Toll Road, Leesburg Pike, and Magarity Road.

While Tysons Corner has been well profiled as the ultimate marked edge city, it is hardly typical. It is bigger and denser and features more mixed uses than many of its more humble fellow edge cities. But Tysons Corner does have several notable peers. It belongs to a family of edge cities referred to in this book as glamorous galleria edge cities. Post Oak (Houston), the LBJ Freeway (Dallas), and Cumberland Galleria (Atlanta) are close cousins to Tysons Corner. They are all big (the second-, fourth-, eighth-, and third-largest, respectively, of the edge cities ranked by analysis here), and they all have large, upscale regional malls with the label "Galleria." In addition, they all have been featured, as early as the 1970s, as representing suburbia's future.[33] They are in fact the flagships of the new metropolis, and they are surrounded in the suburban sea by an armada of frigates (smaller edge cities) and countless patrol boats (edgeless cities).

The developer of several Galleria malls, Gerald Hines, played a key role in building many of the nation's largest edge cities. In order to prevent downscale retail centers from cutting in on his market, Hines had the land surrounding his malls zoned for office space, hotels, and multifamily housing, and the zoning promoted the formation of large-scale, mixed-use edge cities. In this, Hines was the Baron von Haussmann of edge cities.[34]

33. Breckenfeld (1972).
34. Von Haussmann was the master planner who redesigned Paris in the late nineteenth century, giving the city its signature wide boulevards (Fishman 1987).

Figure 3-10. Tysons Corner, Virginia

Figure 3-11. Coconut Creek, Margate, and North Lauderdale, Florida

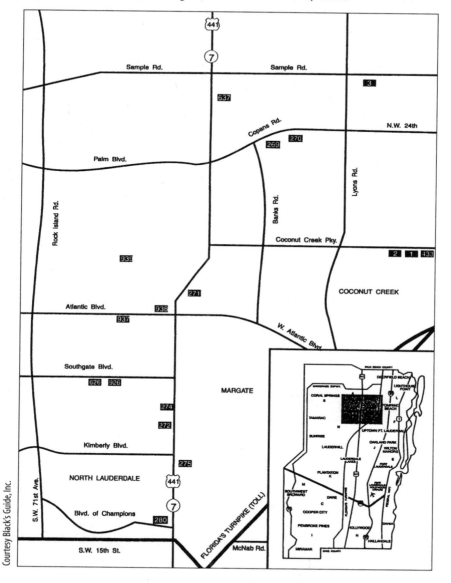

Edgeless City: Space in Coconut Creek, Margate, and North Lauderdale, Florida

The patch of south Florida that appears in figure 3-11 is a bit hard to describe. It represents just under fourteen square miles and contains 684,758 square feet of office space. There is no center. If the map were shifted a mile or two in any direction to show a slightly different area, some buildings would slip off while new ones would appear. What the map shows is just a routine stretch of suburbia—an occasional office building among strip malls and single-family homes. Here the office building is like another strip mall. No glamorous galleria mall anchors it to a soaring suburban city. The area probably has never been highlighted in a national study on office development in suburbia. It probably has never been heralded as the new urban form. But this little corner of suburban south Florida and countless other places around the country more or less like it add up to what metropolitan America is really all about. They are the latest result of a decentralizing pattern that began in the mid-nineteenth century and has continued into the twenty-first.

CHAPTER 4

The Battle for Number One:

Downtown versus Edgeless Cities

By the mid 1980s, there was far more office space in Edge Cities around America's largest metropolis, New York, than there was at its heart—Midtown Manhattan.

—JOEL GARREAU (1991)

Garreau's announcement of the triumph of edge cities over the nation's largest cluster of office space makes for good reading. It has a David-and-Goliath sort of appeal: the once humble suburbs, home to Levittown and pink flamingo lawn ornaments, had enough office space to take on Manhattan, the titan of commerce. A good story, and almost true. Although Garreau based his definition of "edge city" on Leinberger's criteria for an urban village, he applied the term loosely, including many office clusters that did not meet those criteria. And there is another problem—the midtown's real competitor is not edge cities, but its much humbler suburban cousin, the edgeless city.

As table 4-2 shows, as of 1999 the amount of office space in Manhattan was almost twice the total amount found in the New York metropolitan area's edgeless cities. In contrast, Manhattan's office space dwarfed that in the area's edge cities by more than nine to one. Despite Garreau, Manhattan's dominance of the New York region is safe for the time being. But the same cannot be said for downtowns in eleven of the thirteen metropolitan areas studied. In the regional battle for the number-one spot in total office space, edgeless cities beat primary downtowns except in New York City and Chicago. In places such as Boston and Washington, D.C., the gap was narrow, but in Philadelphia and especially Miami, it ranged from large to enormous. In comparison, there were just five regions—Atlanta, Dallas, Detroit, Houston, and Miami—where the edge city total surpassed that of downtown. And in

Table 4-1. Historical Analysis of Office Space in Thirteen Metropolitan Areas, 1999[a]

| Location | Office space 1999 | | By year built[b] | | | | | |
| | | | 1990–99 | | 1980–89 | | Pre-1980 | |
	Square feet	Percent[c]	Square feet	Percent[c]	Square feet	Percent[c]	Square feet	Percent[c]
Downtown	1,175,546,637	43.7	205,991,927	40.0	395,715,246	31.3	573,839,464	63.0
Primary	1,013,603,948	37.7	165,015,561	32.1	312,911,334	24.8	535,677,053	58.8
Secondary	161,942,689	6.0	40,976,366	8.0	82,803,912	6.6	38,162,411	4.2
Edge city	532,944,733	19.8	108,864,284	21.1	322,615,829	25.5	101,464,620	11.1
Edgeless city	980,993,488	36.5	199,935,211	38.8	545,425,995	43.2	235,632,282	25.9
Total	2,689,484,858	100.0	514,791,422	100	1,263,757,070	100	910,936,366	100

Source: *Black's Guide to Office Leasing.*

a. The thirteen metropolitan office markets are Atlanta, Boston, Chicago, Dallas, Denver, Detroit, Houston, Los Angeles, Miami, New York, Philadelphia, San Francisco, and Washington, D.C.

b. For an explanation of the historical anaysis used in this study see appendix B.

c. Percent of total square feet in the thirteen metropolitan areas.

each of those places, except Dallas, the edgeless cities were as large as or even larger than the edge cities.

Chapter 4 examines the distribution of office space in downtowns, edge cities, and edgeless cities in the thirteen metropolitan areas covered in the study. The profiles that follow contain the names and office space inventories for all of the primary downtowns, secondary downtowns, and edge cities. The tables show the percentage of current office space in each of these categories as well as edgeless cities; they also feature historical data, allowing for tracking of the expansion and contraction of downtowns, edge cities, and edgeless cities during the 1980s and 1990s. The chapter ends with an analysis of office space trends in the 1990s and an effort to group the various metropolitan areas on the basis of office space distribution.

National Historical Analysis

Table 4-1 shows the historical analysis of current office inventory in the study's office location categories. Note that although this analysis is not the same as a longitudinal study, it can serve as a proxy for one (for details, see appendix B). The boom of the 1980s and the bust of the 1990s clearly register in table 4-1. Even though the 1990s are more recent, the bulk of space in the current inventory dates from the 1980s. Almost half (47 percent) of the existing office space in the thirteen mar-

Table 4-2. Summary of Office Space in Thirteen Metropolitan Areas, 1999[a]

Metropolitan area	Primary downtown Square feet	Percent	Secondary downtown Square feet	Percent	N	Edge city Square feet	Percent	N	Edgeless city Square feet	Percent	Total square feet
Atlanta	31,132,327	23.6	13,049,980	9.9	1	33,501,999	25.3	2	54,486,457	41.2	132,170,763
Boston	56,666,727	37.4	6,995,406	4.6	1	28,426,987	18.8	4	59,345,046	39.2	151,434,166
Chicago	134,285,726	53.9				48,546,947	19.5	6	66,250,174	26.6	249,082,847
Dallas	30,607,818	20.5	6,779,628	4.5	1	60,084,103	40.3	6	51,554,463	34.6	149,026,012
Denver	23,522,232	30.4	3,263,748	4.2	1	22,753,338	29.4	4	27,722,095	35.9	77,261,413
Detroit	16,754,461	21.3				31,085,327	39.5	2	30,813,711	39.2	78,653,499
Houston	38,046,467	23.0				62,557,748	37.9	6	64,470,742	39.1	165,074,957
Los Angeles	85,037,104	29.8	22,109,801	7.8	4	72,324,970	25.4	6	105,412,452	37.0	284,884,327
Miami	12,678,884	13.1	4,374,329	4.5	1	16,077,609	16.6	2	63,774,416	65.8	96,905,238
New York	390,143,000	56.7	49,711,600	7.2	6	43,006,777	6.2	6	205,503,635	29.9	688,365,012
Philadelphia	54,818,180	34.2	5,196,698	3.2	1	14,199,849	8.9	2	85,899,853	53.6	160,114,580
San Francisco	60,114,661	33.9	15,606,968	8.8	2	24,612,366	13.9	4	76,968,744	43.4	177,302,739
Washington, D.C.	79,796,361	28.6	34,854,531	12.5	5	75,766,713	27.1	8	88,791,700	31.8	279,209,305
Average	81,872,635		16,543,634		2.4	41,620,228		4.7	77,208,919		213,109,508
Median	55,742,454		6,995,406		1.0	37,046,052		5.0	65,360,458		162,594,769
Total	1,013,603,948	37.7	161,942,689	6.0	23	532,944,733	19.8	58	980,993,488	36.5	2,689,484,858

Source: *Black's Guide to Office Leasing*. New York's primary downtown figure comes from Cushman & Wakefield and the Real Estate Board of New York.

a. N: Number of secondary downtowns and edge cities; percent: percent of total square feet in the thirteen metropolitan areas.

kets studied was added in the 1980s, when both edge cities and edgeless cities boomed—well over half of their existing space dates to that decade. It also was a boom time for secondary downtowns, which added about half (51 percent) of their current space during those years. While primary cities also gained a significant amount of space, more than half of their stock dates to the 1970s and earlier. Primary downtowns had so much inventory by 1980 that it would have been difficult for them to double it in the 1980s. Even so, both edge cities and especially edgeless cities also outpaced primary downtowns in absolute terms during the decade.

Historical analysis of existing office inventory suggests that the current edgeless cities and edge cities grew up more or less together. In percent terms, they expanded about equally in the last two decades of the twentieth century. In absolute terms, however, edgeless cities significantly outpaced edge cities. More space was added to edgeless cities during the 1980s alone (545 million square feet) than is now found in edge cities (533 million square feet). Comparing the two over time is complicated a bit by the fact that edge cities once were edgeless. Yet it is reasonable to assume that these two variants of non-downtown office space development have coexisted and will continue to do so.

National Metropolitan Summary

Table 4-2 shows the distribution of office space for downtowns, edge cities, and edgeless cities in the study's thirteen metropolitan areas. Primary downtowns maintain the largest share of office space, with 38 percent of the total. Edgeless cities follow close behind, with 37 percent. Edge cities contain one-fifth of the office space in these major markets, and secondary downtowns have the smallest share, just 6 percent. The study identified thirteen primary downtowns, twenty-three secondary downtowns, and fifty-eight edge cities; all other space was counted as edgeless cities (see appendix C for the complete list).

Primary downtowns have just over 1 billion square feet of office space; edgeless cities contain nearly a billion. Together they account for three-quarters of the office space in the thirteen regions studied. These numbers constitute a major research finding. The fact that edgeless cities, which are so deconcentrated, have achieved parity with the primary downtowns of the nation's biggest markets is astonishing. A revolution in metropolitan form occurred in the past several decades—the regional office hierarchy has been turned upside down.

Most metropolitan office space exists in either high-density downtowns or low-density edgeless cities. The middle-density office environments of edge cities and secondary downtowns, which total eighty-one places in the study, account for one-quarter of metropolitan space. Clearly, edge cities do not capture all or even most non-CBD office space; in fact, they contain less than one-third of all such space. Edge cities are a major office location category, but on their own they do not represent the entire or even the predominant pattern of non-CBD office development.

The distribution of office space across the categories developed in the study varies significantly by metropolitan area. In some regions, edge cities proliferate, while in others edgeless cities balloon. The share of edgeless space ranges from 66 percent in Miami to 27 percent in Chicago. Edge city percentages range from 40 percent in Dallas to 7 percent in New York. Three metropolitan areas lack secondary downtowns altogether, while New York, Washington, D.C., and Los Angeles maintain several.

Edge cities are best represented in Dallas, Detroit, and Houston, yet all three of these regions also maintain a large share of office space in edgeless cities. Edge cities contain a larger percentage of regional space in just two metropolitan areas, Dallas and Detroit. New York and Chicago were the only metropolitan areas where the majority of office space was found in the area's primary downtown.

Five metropolitan areas (Boston, Washington, D.C., Denver, Los Angeles, and San Francisco) had near parity in their amounts of primary downtown and edgeless city office space. However, all five had more space in their edgeless cities than in their primary downtowns. Four metropolitan areas (Dallas, Houston, Atlanta, and Detroit) show a wider disparity between downtown and edgeless city office space. While the Philadelphia metropolitan area still has an average amount of office space in its primary downtown, more than half (54 percent) of its office space is located in edgeless cities. Miami, the only other area with more than half (almost two-thirds) of its office space in edgeless locations, has the least amount of space in its primary downtown (13.1 percent), giving it by far the highest disparity between downtown and edgeless city office space.

Interestingly, while the percentage of office space in downtowns dips almost to single digits and the percentage in edge cities and secondary downtowns drops to single digits or to zero, edgeless cities always represent at least one-quarter of total regional office space. In that way, edgeless cities are the most ubiquitous feature of the modern metropolis.

Metropolitan Area Profiles

The thirteen metropolitan areas for which data were collected (see tables 4-3 through 4-15) are scattered throughout the United States, ranging in size from New York (the largest office market) to Denver (the smallest). Their profiles follow below.

Atlanta: The Sprawling Metropolis

Recent research has shown Atlanta to have more sprawl than any large region in America.[1] Atlanta, like much of the Southeast, is a product of a regional culture that has never built large dense cities.[2] The South's great coastal centers, Savannah and Charleston, began their relative decline at the end of the eighteenth century, and they now are

1. Galster and others (2001).
2. Lang (2000a).

Table 4-3. Metropolitan Atlanta Office Space, 1999[a]

| Location | Current | | By year built | | | | | |
| | | | 1990–99 | | 1980–89 | | Pre-1980 | |
	Square feet	Percent	Square feet	Percent	Square feet	Percent	Square feet	Percent
Downtown	44,182,307	33.4	13,928,484	35.2	16,702,543	27.4	13,551,280	42.9
Atlanta	31,132,327	23.6	9,971,160	25.2	9,126,403	15.0	12,034,764	38.1
Buckhead	13,049,980	9.9	3,957,324	10.0	7,576,140	12.4	1,516,516	4.8
Edge city	33,501,999	25.3	7,491,376	18.9	20,943,615	34.3	5,067,008	16.0
Cumberland/ Galleria	17,620,553	13.3	5,061,684	12.8	9,520,126	15.6	3,038,743	9.6
Perimeter Center	15,881,446	12.0	2,429,692	6.1	11,423,489	18.7	2,028,265	6.4
Edgeless city	54,486,457	41.2	18,142,428	45.9	23,351,444	38.3	12,992,585	41.1
Total	132,170,763	100	39,562,288	100	60,997,602	100	31,610,873	100

Source: Author's calculations.

a. Percent: percent of total square feet in Atlanta metropolitan area.

tourist towns. The region's current big cities, Atlanta and Charlotte, are for the most part creations of the post–World War II era. The South's topography and climate provide no natural limit to how far a metropolitan area can spread, unlike physical conditions in the Western half of the Sunbelt.[3] Atlanta is primarily a horizontal city, although anyone who has flown over the region can pick out the skylines of the four areas that contain much of Atlanta's office space.

Atlanta has few major centers, but they are substantial. The region has two edge cities, Cumberland Galleria and Perimeter Center, that are among the top ten in the nation, and it has the largest secondary downtown, Buckhead. In fact, all three are larger than Miami's primary downtown. These centers, plus Atlanta's downtown, account for almost 60 percent of the region's office space. Despite Atlanta's sprawl, much of the region's office employment is concentrated in a few locations.

Most of Atlanta's office space lies north of the downtown in a "favored quarter" that has been well documented by Christopher Leinberger;[4] the region's wealthy and largely white residential areas also lie mostly north of downtown. The area around Buckhead is especially affluent. Atlanta's south, in contrast, has a substantial African American

3. Lang, Popper, and Popper (1997); Lang (2000c).
4. Leinberger (1996).

Table 4-4. Metropolitan Boston Office Space, 1999[a]

| Location | Current | | By year built | | | | | |
| | | | 1990–99 | | 1980–89 | | Pre-1980 | |
	Square feet	Percent	Square feet	Percent	Square feet	Percent	Square feet	Percent
Downtown	63,662,133	42.0	16,909,088	48.2	31,891,773	38.2	14,861,272	45.1
Boston	56,666,727	37.4	15,376,588	43.9	27,745,044	33.2	13,545,095	41.1
Cambridge	6,995,406	4.6	1,532,500	4.4	4,146,729	5.0	1,316,177	4.0
Edge city	28,426,987	18.8	6,518,560	18.6	17,282,405	20.7	4,626,022	14.0
Burlington-Woburn	5,988,741	4.0	973,033	2.8	4,052,389	4.9	963,319	2.9
Framingham-Natick	6,267,958	4.1	2,931,327	8.4	2,576,165	3.1	760,466	2.3
Quincy-Braintree	5,619,711	3.7	195,000	0.6	4,478,864	5.4	945,847	2.9
Waltham-Newton	10,550,577	7.0	2,419,200	6.9	6,174,987	7.4	1,956,390	5.9
Edgeless city	59,345,046	39.2	11,620,652	33.2	34,270,090	41.1	13,454,304	40.8
Total	151,434,166	100	35,048,300	100	83,444,268	100	32,941,598	100

Source: Author's calculations.

a. Percent: percent of total square feet in Boston metropolitan area.

population and is far less wealthy. Despite being focused in a few key nodes, much office employment is far removed from the residences of less well-off commuters, creating a regional jobs/housing imbalance and some of the nation's worst traffic.

Although Atlanta's non-CBD clusters are among the largest in the nation, edgeless cities still capture a larger share of the region's office space. According to historical analysis of current inventory, Atlanta's edgeless city office space accounts for the most space added to the region in the 1990s, more than twice the space added to edge cities. Atlanta not only sprawls, it also appears to be growing more edgeless.

Boston: The Prototypical Region

Who would guess that among the nation's largest metropolitan areas, the Boston area, with its unique New England character, would come closest to representing the average metropolitan office development form? The region has an average amount of office space, and that space is distributed among office locations in a way that closely matches the percentages for the nation as a whole. It has an average-sized downtown, a secondary downtown, four (mostly small) edge cities, and lots of edgeless city space. The historical data indicate that the current inventory has been added in the different office location categories at about the same relative pace.

Boston's edge cities ring the downtown in all directions. Boston's secondary downtown is located in Cambridge, home to Harvard University and the Massachusetts Institute of Technology; this cluster, as well as the edge cities that line route 128 (Boston's main beltway), contains many high-tech firms. The downtown office economy features the standard complement of financial services firms, but it also specializes in such knowledge industries as publishing.

Chicago: The Monocentric Metropolis

In the 1920s the Chicago School of Sociology developed a model of the early twentieth-century American metropolis based on concentric zones of progressively lower-density development extending outward from the region's predominant commercial core.[5] Chicago was used as the model, and the model still applies better to Chicago than perhaps any other city in the nation.

As discussed earlier, no twentieth-century American region has ever been completely monocentric. There have long been industrial satellites and big mixed-use suburbs that had distinct identities. But Chicago captured the key idea of the monocentric metropolis, which held that the center structured the space in the rest of the region. Despite the recent emergence of substantial edge cities, the region still revolves around Chicago's downtown.

Chicago's downtown maintains the majority (54 percent) of office space in the region. This space lies in one large cluster—the second-largest in the United States following midtown Manhattan—beginning in the Loop and running along the Magnificent Mile north of the Chicago River. Chicago's six edge cities together account for another fifth (20 percent) of space. The region's edgeless cities add more than one-quarter (27 percent) of all office space. Much of the growth in the region's edge cities occurred in the 1980s, especially in Schaumberg, which appears to be almost purely a product of the 1980s.

5. Burgess (1925).

Table 4-5. Metropolitan Chicago Office Space, 1999[a]

| Location | Current | | By year built | | | | | |
| | | | 1990–99 | | 1980–89 | | Pre-1980 | |
	Square feet	Percent	Square feet	Percent	Square feet	Percent	Square feet	Percent
Downtown	134,285,726	53.9	14,269,506	41.6	36,325,627	40.1	83,690,593	67.5
Edge city	48,546,947	19.5	8,724,122	25.4	28,637,644	31.6	11,185,181	9.0
Chicago O'Hare	8,157,332	3.3	900,247	2.6	5,049,525	5.6	2,207,560	1.8
Deerfield/North-								
brook	7,122,374	2.9	1,348,908	3.9	4,019,229	4.4	1,754,237	1.4
Lombard	6,451,516	2.6	1,478,187	4.3	4,004,509	4.4	968,820	0.8
Naperville	7,306,689	2.9	2,370,597	6.9	4,391,971	4.8	544,121	0.4
Oakbrook	10,823,162	4.3	1,891,648	5.5	4,812,161	5.3	4,119,353	3.3
Schaumburg	8,685,874	3.5	734,535	2.1	6,360,249	7.0	1,591,090	1.3
Edgeless city	66,250,174	26.6	11,345,465	33.0	25,712,096	28.4	29,192,613	23.5
Total	249,082,847	100	34,339,093	100	90,675,367	100	124,068,387	100

Source: Author's calculations.

a. Percent: percent of total square feet in Chicago metropolitan area.

Dallas: The Big D Has Big Edge Cities

Like all things Texan, Dallas's edge cities are big. Three of the six in Dallas have more than 10 million square feet of office space, and even the smallest has more than 7.5 million square feet. Dallas's edge cities fit into a favored quarter to the north and west of the downtown, and upscale residential areas surround most, especially Las Colinas. Historical data on the current inventory show that edgeless cities constitute the newest space and that they may be gaining on edge cities. The data also show that the downtown has experienced remarkably diminished building activity since the crash in the 1980s. The downtown, already small relative to the region, will fall even further behind if the trend continues.

Office development occurs along freeway corridors more in Texas than perhaps anywhere else in the country.[6] The Texas freeway system, which features long stretches of frontage road running parallel to the highway, has facilitated this type of growth. These roads function as local lanes to the freeway's express lanes, allowing motorists to leave the

6. See Baerwald (1978, 1982) for a description of the same type of development in metropolitan Minneapolis.

Table 4-6. Metropolitan Dallas Office Space, 1999[a]

| | Current | | By year built | | | | | |
| | | | 1990–99 | | 1980–89 | | Pre-1980 | |
Location	Square feet	Percent	Square feet	Percent	Square feet	Percent	Square feet	Percent
Downtown	37,387,446	25.1	5,304,141	13.4	20,513,231	24.2	11,570,074	46.9
Dallas	30,607,818	20.5	3,258,329	8.2	16,639,341	19.6	10,710,148	43.4
Fort Worth	6,779,628	4.5	2,045,812	5.2	3,873,890	4.6	859,926	3.5
Edge city	60,084,103	40.3	15,824,146	40.0	36,761,324	43.4	7,498,633	30.4
Far North Dallas	12,257,981	8.2	5,666,376	14.3	6,235,932	7.4	355,673	1.4
Las Colinas	7,775,891	5.2	657,185	1.7	6,252,982	7.4	865,724	3.5
LBJ Corridor	13,223,639	8.9	3,100,561	7.8	8,272,239	9.8	1,850,839	7.5
Oaklawn (Midtown)	10,366,787	7.0	2,197,375	5.6	7,431,261	8.8	738,151	3.0
Plano/Richardson	7,521,566	5.0	1,967,222	5.0	5,128,480	6.0	425,864	1.7
Stemmons Freeway	8,938,239	6.0	2,235,427	5.6	3,440,430	4.1	3,262,382	13.2
Edgeless city	51,554,463	34.6	18,447,477	46.6	27,500,524	32.4	5,606,462	22.7
Total	149,026,012	100	39,575,764	100	84,775,079	100	24,675,169	100

Source: Author's calculations.

a. Percent: percent of total square feet in Dallas metropolitan area.

freeway and drive alongside it for miles (as people do at times to avoid traffic). In most of metropolitan America, a location at the intersection of a freeway and a major arterial road is a prime location for large-scale commercial development. The space along the highway between these intersections, however, is at a distinct disadvantage for edge city development because one would have to enter the local street system to access the space. But that is not the case in Texas. The frontage road is an adjunct to the highway; location along its length only slightly diminishes the access available at a major intersection. Along many stretches of the freeway network, the frontage road functions as a quasi-extra lane and has multiple points of entry to the highway, helping to elongate development into corridors. Dallas's LBJ Freeway is one prominent example of this office development form.

Denver: The Prototypical "Smaller" Region

Denver is essentially a smaller version of Boston, with the same complement of non-CBD office clusters. The percentages of space in the

Table 4-7. Metropolitan Denver Office Space, 1999[a]

| Location | Current | | By year built | | | | | |
| | | | 1990–99 | | 1980–89 | | Pre-1980 | |
	Square feet	Percent	Square feet	Percent	Square feet	Percent	Square feet	Percent
Downtown	26,785,980	34.7	2,973,119	25.0	18,594,273	37.7	5,218,588	32.5
Denver	23,522,232	30.4	2,281,546	19.2	16,966,509	34.4	4,274,177	26.6
Boulder	3,263,748	4.2	691,573	5.8	1,627,764	3.3	944,411	5.9
Edge city	22,753,338	29.4	2,982,912	25.1	15,039,200	30.5	4,731,226	29.5
Cherry Creek	6,206,844	8.0	812,795	6.8	3,268,974	6.6	2,125,075	13.2
Denver Tech- nology Center	5,779,654	7.5	889,719	7.5	4,222,600	8.6	667,335	4.2
Greenwood Plaza	5,939,986	7.7	450,718	3.8	4,268,725	8.7	1,220,543	7.6
Inverness/Cen- tennial Airport	4,826,854	6.2	829,680	7.0	3,278,901	6.6	718,273	4.5
Edgeless city	27,722,095	35.9	5,924,492	49.9	15,701,934	31.8	6,095,669	38.0
Total	77,261,413	100	11,880,523	100	49,335,407	100	16,045,483	100

Source: Author's calculations.

a. Percent: percent of total square feet in Denver metropolitan area.

office categories match figures for both Boston and the nation. The region's edge cities, such as the Denver Technology Center, specialize in high-tech enterprises. Denver's one secondary downtown is in the town of Boulder, home to the University of Colorado.

Much of Denver's non-CBD office space is south of the downtown. Almost 30 percent of the region's office space falls in edge cities, and another 36 percent can be found in edgeless cities. Edgeless cities gained half of the office inventory built during the 1990s, while the downtowns and edge cities each added one-quarter. During the boom years of the 1980s, the distribution among the three office development categories was far more equal.

During the early 1980s, savings and loan companies invested heavily in office construction. When Denver was hit hard by recession in the late 1980s, the earlier overbuilding left the region with a large excess inventory as it entered the 1990s. According to historical analysis of current stock, the region experienced a sharp 75 percent drop in office construction during the 1990s. The slowdown affected all parts of the region, although Denver's edgeless cities fared a bit better.

Table 4-8. Metropolitan Detroit Office Space, 1999[a]

| Location | Current | | By year built | | | | | |
| | | | 1990–99 | | 1980–89 | | Pre-1980 | |
	Square feet	Percent	Square feet	Percent	Square feet	Percent	Square feet	Percent
Downtown	16,754,461	21.3	3,370,056	14.2	3,058,850	8.5	10,325,555	55.0
Edge city	31,085,327	39.5	10,432,675	44.0	15,752,083	43.6	4,900,569	26.1
Troy	13,580,655	17.3	5,128,076	21.6	7,502,680	20.8	949,899	5.1
Southfield	17,504,672	22.3	5,304,599	22.4	8,249,403	22.8	3,950,670	21.0
Edgeless city	30,813,711	39.2	9,919,754	41.8	17,331,044	48.0	3,562,913	19.0
Total	78,653,499	100	23,722,485	100.0	36,141,977	100.0	18,789,037	100

Source: Author's calculations.

a. Percent: percent of total square feet in Detroit metropolitan area.

Detroit: The Big Three

The Big Three in Detroit typically refers to the big three automobile manufacturers—General Motors, Ford, and Chrysler (now Daimler Chrysler). In this case it refers to the three office clusters that dominate the region—Southfield, downtown Detroit, and Troy. Note that Southfield is listed *before* downtown, because of the thirteen metropolitan areas studied Detroit is the only one in which a single edge city surpasses the CBD. Detroit historically has been known for racial problems and white flight. Following urban riots in the 1960s, many businesses and people left the city for its suburbs, reducing its population by half. The region's suburban/urban split is perhaps the starkest in the nation, and many suburban residents do not treat Detroit as the center of the region.

The region's suburbanites instead have supported the emergence of large suburban centers. Detroit has the second-smallest office market in this study (just ahead of Denver's), and yet its only two edge cities rank in the top ten. These edge cities, along with an equal amount of edgeless city space, account for almost four-fifths (79 percent) of all of the office space in the region. According to historical analysis of the current inventory, edgeless cities contain the newest office space; they have been gaining ground on the downtown at least since the 1980s and probably before.

The Detroit region suffered the smallest bust in the 1990s of any metropolitan area in the study, in part because Detroit experienced the smallest boom during the 1980s. Construction activity varied widely

Table 4-9. Metropolitan Houston Office Space, 1999[a]

| Location | Current | | By year built | | | | | |
| | | | 1990–99 | | 1980–89 | | Pre-1980 | |
	Square feet	Percent	Square feet	Percent	Square feet	Percent	Square feet	Percent
Downtown	38,046,467	23.0	7,131,025	26.5	19,142,156	21.6	11,773,286	23.7
Edge city	62,557,748	37.9	11,397,839	42.4	31,985,835	36.1	19,174,074	38.6
Clearlake	4,965,400	3.0	589,299	2.2	3,438,816	3.9	937,285	1.9
Greenspoint	8,734,170	5.3	1,777,303	6.6	5,113,808	5.8	1,843,059	3.7
Greenway Plaza	10,345,432	6.3	2,039,842	7.6	3,360,619	3.8	4,944,971	10.0
Katy Freeway	7,647,034	4.6	1,342,231	5.0	4,009,219	4.5	2,295,584	4.6
Post Oak	21,118,568	12.8	4,406,234	16.4	9,280,098	10.5	7,432,236	15.0
Westchase	9,747,144	5.9	1,242,930	4.6	6,783,275	7.7	1,720,939	3.5
Edgeless city	64,470,742	39.1	8,382,648	31.1	37,399,421	42.2	18,688,673	37.7
Total	165,074,957	100	26,911,512	100	88,527,412	100	49,636,033	100

Source: Author's calculations.

a. Percent: percent of total square feet in Houston metropolitan area.

across metropolitan Detroit during the last two decades of the past century—the downtown languished while the suburbs gained. During the 1980s, Detroit's edge cities and edgeless cities added more than 33 million square feet of office space to the area's current inventory while the city added only 3 million square feet. The space in Detroit's suburbs also is remarkably new: almost 90 percent of all existing edge city and edgeless city office space in the region has been built since 1980.

Houston: Master-Planned Edge Cities

Houston is a city of logos. Its built environment, like that of most big Sunbelt metropolises, is divided up into large-scale, named private developments. In most places, naming is limited to master-planned communities, but in Houston and to a degree Dallas, the appellations extend to edge cities, which in many cases also are master planned. Most edge cities are named by local real estate people trying to identify a submarket. A large regional mall often identifies an area,[7] and a major highway also can serve as a label. But in Houston, many edge cities are named as if they were master-planned communities. With no irony intended, these centers of business are named as if they were woodsy, suburban gated

7. Garreau (1991).

enclaves; Houston, for example, features edge cities called Greenspoint, Clearlake, and Post Oak.

Most edge cities in Houston also have separate chambers of commerce and business improvement districts (BIDs), which operate the way a homeowner's association does—they provide maintenance and security services and generally ensure that the quality of the public environment does not deteriorate. The BIDs attempt to create an integrated streetscape that gives the edge city a distinctive look, and they also formalize its name.

Houston's half-dozen edge cities are arrayed to the west of the downtown, either at or past the inner beltway. Although most major cities feature photos of their downtown skyline on postcards, Houston is perhaps the only city that has a postcard featuring multiple skylines, including Post Oak, Greenway Plaza, the Texas Medical Center, the Astrodome/Astroworld, and downtown. Despite their size and number, Houston's edge cities collectively are just a bit smaller than the region's edgeless city space. Together, the two categories account for more than three-quarters (77 percent) of the metropolitan area's office space.

Because the energy industry is heavily concentrated in the city, the region suffered a tremendous bust in the mid-1980s when energy prices collapsed. Houston's economy took many years to recover to the point that it could absorb excess office inventory; therefore, very little space was built in the 1990s compared with the prior decade. The region's edge cities did a bit better than its downtown and edgeless cities during the 1990s.

Los Angeles: A Metropolis of Urban Realms

Los Angeles is a big, complex, and dispersed region. It is really several regions, or what James Vance calls "urban realms," folded into one.[8] These realms bump up against one another and may even overlap somewhat, but their cores are largely autonomous. Orange County, south of Los Angeles, constitutes one of the region's realms. Others include the Inland Empire, anchored by the cities of San Bernardino and

8. To Vance (1964), urban realms are a natural function of the growth of cities; the city has changed structurally, becoming a collection of realms that has grown "one stage beyond that of a metropolis" (p. 78). The core-periphery relationship weakens as realms become more equal. The basic organization of the region becomes more cooperative as the shared urban and cultural identity of the urban realms creates what Vance calls a "sympolis" rather than a metropolis.

Table 4-10. Metropolitan Los Angeles Office Space, 1999[a]

Location	Current Square feet	Current Percent	By year built 1990–99 Square feet	1990–99 Percent	1980–89 Square feet	1980–89 Percent	Pre-1980 Square feet	Pre-1980 Percent
Downtown	107,146,905	37.6	36,921,897	49.1	40,297,752	27.3	29,927,256	48.1
Primary downtown	85,037,104	29.8	31,068,066	41.3	27,314,506	18.5	26,654,532	42.8
Beverly Hills	17,398,390	6.1	5,267,210	7.0	5,069,031	3.4	7,062,149	11.3
Los Angeles	44,818,372	15.7	17,857,750	23.8	15,696,148	10.6	11,264,474	18.1
Santa Monica	8,320,447	2.9	3,684,324	4.9	3,799,253	2.6	836,870	1.3
Mid Wilshire	14,499,895	5.1	4,258,782	5.7	2,750,074	1.9	7,491,039	12.0
Secondary downtown	22,109,801	7.8	5,853,831	7.8	12,983,246	8.8	3,272,724	5.3
Glendale	6,179,136	2.2	2,899,877	3.9	2,689,056	1.8	590,203	0.9
Long Beach	8,059,753	2.8	1,636,529	2.2	5,553,121	3.8	870,103	1.4
Pasadena	7,870,912	2.8	1,317,425	1.8	4,741,069	3.2	1,812,418	2.9
Edge city	72,324,970	25.4	18,070,629	24.0	42,048,480	28.5	12,205,861	19.6
Costa Mesa/Irvine/ Newport	28,496,983	10.0	4,927,660	6.6	17,137,472	11.6	6,431,851	10.3
Santa Ana	5,649,978	2.0	1,173,663	1.6	3,199,756	2.2	1,276,559	2.0
Sherman Oaks	8,651,478	3.0	3,081,483	4.1	3,719,417	2.5	1,850,578	3.0
South Bay/LAX	11,626,533	4.1	3,962,707	5.3	6,920,863	4.7	742,963	1.2
West Los Angeles	11,111,940	3.9	3,221,033	4.3	6,878,172	4.7	1,012,735	1.6
Woodland Hills	6,788,058	2.4	1,704,083	2.3	4,192,800	2.8	891,175	1.4
Edgeless city	105,412,452	37.0	20,175,353	26.8	65,093,076	44.1	20,144,023	32.3
Total	284,884,327	100	75,167,879	100	147,439,308	100	62,277,140	100

Source: Author's calculations.

a. Percent: percent of total square feet in Los Angeles metropolitan area.

Riverside, to the east, and the valleys stretching north and west to Ventura. The Los Angeles basin is the oldest and densest of these realms. Locally the region is referred to in its entirety as the Southland.

New York, the nation's other gigantic region, has realms as well. But Manhattan is so strong a core that it does a good job of holding the region together;[9] the same is true for Chicago's loop. But Los Angeles, as Robert Fishman argues, was born decentralized.[10] Its core simply cannot hold it together.[11]

9. Lang (1994a, 1994b).
10. Fishman (1987).
11. Fulton (1997).

Los Angeles may be the most fractured region in the nation, and the best way to understand it is to treat it in parts. The LA basin contains the majority of the region's office space. In addition to the large primary downtown office strip along Wilshire Boulevard, there is a mid-sized secondary downtown in Long Beach and large edge cities at the Los Angeles International Airport and on the city's West Side south of Wilshire. In sum, the LA basin's space is essentially polycentric. In Orange County, Costa Mesa dominates. Beyond these centers things begin to break apart. There is an edge city here and there, but for the most part there is just a lot of edgeless space.

According to historical analysis of existing inventory, it looks as if the 1980s was the decade of the edgeless city: almost half of the space added in LA in the 1980s was added there. That is remarkable considering that there are ten non-CBD and four CBD nodes competing for space. The finding indicates that office development in the region as a whole is post-polycentric and scattered in a way that fits no existing urban spatial model.[12]

Interestingly, the same historical analysis suggests that Los Angeles's primary downtown is making a comeback. Much of this space was begun late in the 1980s, when Japanese investors went on an office-buying spree. When their economy went bust in the early 1990s, so did California's, and the resulting recession created huge vacancies downtown.[13] But slowly, as the economy recovered, this space was occupied. The downtown, now home to many new media and telecommunications companies, has become Los Angeles's Silicon Alley or, more appropriately, its Silicon Boulevard.

No mention of Los Angeles would be complete without considering the role that its street system plays in structuring office development. Like parts of Texas, Los Angeles has a road network that tends to promote linear development. Interestingly, the region's fabled freeway system is not the major determinant of office location; that is determined by the grid of broad boulevards that lace the Southland.[14] As in Texas, LA's boulevards, or surface streets, are the local lanes to the expressway network, and the region's major commercial enterprises, from malls to office buildings, locate along their length. The boulevards predate the

12. Gordon and Richardson (1996).
13. Cushman and Wakefield, *Southern California: Real Estate Forecast and Review* (1997).
14. Pivo (1990).

Table 4-11. Metropolitan Miami Office Space, 1999[a]

| | Current | | By year built | | | | | |
| | | | 1990–99 | | 1980–89 | | Pre-1980 | |
Location	Square feet	Percent	Square feet	Percent	Square feet	Percent	Square feet	Percent
Downtown	17,053,213	17.6	3,542,330	15.5	8,837,543	16.0	4,673,340	24.8
Miami	12,678,884	13.1	1,451,558	6.4	6,887,664	12.5	4,339,662	23.0
Fort Lauderdale	4,374,329	4.5	2,090,772	9.2	1,949,879	3.5	333,678	1.8
Edge city	16,077,609	16.6	5,658,359	24.8	9,253,906	16.8	1,165,344	6.2
Boca Raton	6,870,513	7.1	2,757,411	12.1	3,653,398	6.6	459,704	2.4
Miami Airport	9,207,096	9.5	2,900,948	12.7	5,600,508	10.1	705,640	3.7
Edgeless city	63,774,416	65.8	13,625,873	59.7	37,148,553	67.2	12,999,990	69.0
Total	96,905,238	100	22,826,562	100	55,240,002	100	18,838,674	100

Source: Author's calculations.

a. Percent: percent of total square feet in Miami metropolitan area.

freeways, which were added to alleviate the traffic that by the mid-twentieth century had filled these streets, by many years. The boulevards help create a pattern of dispersed, mostly undifferentiated growth with focal points scattered about at random.[15]

Miami: The Edgeless Metropolis

Miami is like a chunk of Los Angeles that broke off and found its way to the East Coast. However, the part of Los Angeles that Miami resembles is *not* the LA basin—Miami is more like an urban realm of edgeless cities. South Florida is the edgeless metropolis incarnate. It is simply the most centerless large region in the nation—Los Angeles minus the focal points. The ocean and the Everglades hold its sprawl in check, but within the urbanized space there are few major centers.

Two-thirds (66 percent) of South Florida's office space can be found in edgeless cities; the rest is about evenly split between downtown (18 percent) and edge cities (17 percent). Miami has the smallest primary downtown of the thirteen cities in this study, and Fort Lauderdale, the secondary downtown, is the second smallest. The development around Miami International Airport is the region's only major edge city. The edge cities and Fort Lauderdale did add a significant amount of space in the 1990s, indicating that Miami may have reached its limits of edgelessness.

15. Pressman (1985).

Table 4-12. Metropolitan New York Office Space, 1999[a]

| Location | Current | | By year built | | | | | |
| | | | 1990–99 | | 1980–89 | | Pre-1980 | |
	Square feet	Percent	Square feet	Percent	Square feet	Percent	Square feet	Percent
Downtown	439,854,600	63.9	50,582,288	59.9	76,491,235	34.1	312,781,077	82.4
Manhattan	390,143,000	56.7	37,143,000	44.0	53,800,000	24.0	299,200,000	78.8
Brooklyn	5,493,600	0.8	3,260,000	3.9	115,000	0.1	2,118,600	0.6
Jersey City	10,183,136	1.5	3,342,282	4.0	5,925,754	2.6	915,100	0.2
Newark	11,524,262	1.7	3,678,500	4.4	3,123,000	1.4	4,722,762	1.2
New Haven	5,158,075	0.7	2,093,923	2.5	2,030,140	0.9	1,034,012	0.3
Stamford	11,774,490	1.7	762,417	0.9	7,966,914	3.6	3,045,159	0.8
White Plains	5,578,037	0.8	302,166	0.4	3,530,427	1.6	1,745,444	0.5
Edge city	43,006,777	6.2	5,403,473	6.4	26,540,814	11.8	11,062,490	2.9
Garden City	9,322,876	1.4	623,498	0.7	6,129,221	2.7	2,570,157	0.7
Franklin/ Piscataway	6,915,291	1.0	61,200	0.1	6,132,025	2.7	722,066	0.2
Lake Success	5,220,105	0.8	307,800	0.4	2,300,773	1.0	2,611,532	0.7
Melville	5,552,987	0.8	1,170,270	1.4	2,303,750	1.0	2,078,967	0.5
Morristown	5,949,485	0.9	1,165,976	1.4	3,091,484	1.4	1,692,025	0.4
Parsippany	10,046,033	1.5	2,074,729	2.5	6,583,561	2.9	1,387,743	0.4
Edgeless city	205,503,635	29.9	28,517,350	33.7	121,096,153	54.0	55,890,132	14.7
Total	688,365,012	100	84,503,111	100	224,128,202	100	379,733,699	100

Source: Author's calculations.

a. Percent: percent of total square feet in New York metropolitan area.

New York: Manhattan Island in an Edgeless Ocean

Were it not for Manhattan Island's massive stock of office space, the New York region would be, without qualification, the great edgeless metropolis. As it stands, New York outside of Midtown and Wall Street has the nation's largest inventory of edgeless office space—a whopping 206 million square feet, almost double the amount in Los Angeles, which has the next-largest inventory. More than 121 million square feet of that space was added in the 1980s alone, an amount almost equivalent to the Atlanta region's total. It is apparent from the case of New York that edgeless cities are not edge cities in waiting. The New York region has enough non-CBD office space for a dozen large edge cities; instead, it has just a dozen mostly small edge cities.

Northern New Jersey in particular houses a vast supply of edgeless city space. Consider, for example, Princeton, New Jersey, which often is mentioned in books on the new suburbs, including Garreau's *Edge City*.

In this book, Princeton is listed as an edge city, represented by a small dot about where the town stands. But if readers open up *Black's Guide* and try to locate the Princeton edge city, as they would Tysons Corner, they will find that it simply does not exist—as a center, at least. Instead they will be confronted with about a dozen maps that together represent more than 100 square miles of central New Jersey between Princeton and New Brunswick. In those maps they can find just over 11 million square feet of space, but they will not find anything even closely resembling a Tysons Corner or a Post Oak.

The Big Apple certainly is big. It has by far the nation's largest office inventory. The New York metropolitan area also maintains the nation's oldest office stock, much of it located in Manhattan. The region features many satellite central cities. Places such as Newark, New Jersey, and Stamford, Connecticut, have large office markets that are nonetheless dwarfed by New York City's market. The city's office space is divided between two very large clusters, midtown Manhattan and lower Manhattan, which constitute the first- and third-largest concentrations of space in the nation. There also are good-sized office nodes in the outer boroughs of Queens and Brooklyn.

Philadelphia: The Edgeless Metropolis of the North

Like New York, Philadelphia is proof that the edgeless metropolis is not just a Sunbelt phenomenon. In fact, the region appears to be the south Florida of the north, the major difference being that Philadelphia

Table 4-13. Metropolitan Philadelphia Office Space, 1999[a]

| Location | Current | | By year built | | | | | |
| | | | 1990–99 | | 1980–89 | | Pre-1980 | |
	Square feet	Percent	Square feet	Percent	Square feet	Percent	Square feet	Percent
Downtown	60,014,878	37.5	7,317,702	21.4	35,913,222	41.4	16,783,954	42.7
Philadelphia	54,818,180	34.2	6,683,702	19.6	32,389,160	37.4	15,745,318	40.1
Wilmington	5,196,698	3.2	634,000	1.9	3,524,062	4.1	1,038,636	2.6
Edge city	14,199,849	8.9	2,987,279	8.8	9,019,918	10.4	2,192,652	5.6
King of Prussia	6,173,563	3.9	1,209,429	3.5	3,776,267	4.4	1,187,867	3.0
Malvern-Paoli-Wayne	8,026,286	5.0	1,777,850	5.2	5,243,651	6.0	1,004,785	2.6
Edgeless city	85,899,853	53.6	23,827,588	69.8	41,773,524	48.2	20,298,741	51.7
Total	160,114,580	100	34,132,569	100	86,706,664	100	39,275,347	100

Source: Author's calculations.

a. Percent: percent of total square feet in Philadelphia metropolitan area.

does have a decent-sized downtown. Philadelphia's two modest-sized edge cities are north and west of the downtown. Malvern-Paoli-Wayne is along Philadelphia's Main Line, a commuter line that runs through the region's older affluent suburbs. The King of Prussia edge city is built around a regional mall, near the intersection of the region's major interstates. Interestingly, the New Jersey side of the Philadelphia metropolitan area contains no office cluster that qualifies as either a downtown or an edge city. Places such as Cherry Hill, New Jersey, which features one of the oldest enclosed malls in the nation, lacks the size required to be called an edge city. The old industrial satellite city of Camden, New Jersey, has fallen on hard times and, unlike Newark and Jersey City, has not been redeveloped as a secondary downtown.

Not only does Philadelphia have large edgeless cities; they are the fastest-growing office development category of late. About 70 percent of the office space in the current inventory added during the 1990s was built in edgeless cities. Meanwhile edge cities captured 9 percent and downtowns 21 percent.

San Francisco: The Fragmented Metropolis

Like Los Angeles, San Francisco comprises several regions. The big factor here is not absolute size or the lack of a strong center, but physical form.[16] Many underestimate the impact that the Bay Area's scenic geography has on its urban form and subsequently its office development pattern. If one were to outline the urbanized area of most American regions the result would look something like an amoeba. But tracing San Francisco's urbanized area produces something very different. Its urban space rings a large bay, and it slips around mountains—in short, it has many breaks. The Bay Area's physical reality produced an early polycentrism, as secondary downtowns such as Oakland and San Jose grew along with San Francisco.

After Miami and Philadelphia, San Francisco has the highest percentage of edgeless city space. The downtown and edgeless city space combine to total 86 percent of the region.

Outside its original satellite cities, the San Francisco metropolitan area has only four small edge cities. According to historical analysis of current inventory, the region's edge cities, which accounted for just 5 percent of the space added in the 1990s, have not been thriving of late. Downtowns, meanwhile, accounted for half of the region's current

16. Vance (1964, 1977).

Table 4-14. Metropolitan San Francisco Office Space, 1999[a]

| Location | Current | | By year built | | | | | |
| | | | 1990–99 | | 1980–89 | | Pre-1980 | |
	Square feet	Percent	Square feet	Percent	Square feet	Percent	Square feet	Percent
Downtown	75,721,629	42.7	10,714,441	49.8	39,770,351	37.3	25,236,837	51.5
San Francisco	60,114,661	33.9	8,189,697	38.1	32,199,414	30.2	19,725,550	40.2
Oakland	10,130,041	5.7	1,474,744	6.9	4,149,901	3.9	4,505,396	9.2
San Jose	5,476,927	3.1	1,050,000	4.9	3,421,036	3.2	1,005,891	2.1
Edge city	24,612,366	13.9	1,141,687	5.3	19,129,662	17.9	4,341,017	8.9
North San Jose	7,742,562	4.4	0	—	7,234,501	6.8	508,061	1.0
Pleasanton	5,017,613	2.8	85,027	0.4	4,626,062	4.3	306,524	0.6
San Ramon	5,017,579	2.8	606,932	2.8	4,058,227	3.8	352,420	0.7
Walnut Creek	6,834,612	3.9	449,728	2.1	3,210,872	3.0	3,174,012	6.5
Edgeless city	76,968,744	43.4	9,658,348	44.9	47,841,622	44.8	19,468,774	39.7
Total	177,302,739	100	21,514,476	100	106,741,635	100	49,046,628	100

Source: Author's calculations.

a. Percent: percent of total square feet in San Francisco metropolitan area.

space added in the 1990s, and edgeless cities approached this number by capturing 45 percent. San Francisco's urban form is now heading in a post-polycentric direction—a South Florida with mountains and chilly summers.

Interestingly, the San Francisco metropolitan area experienced one of the steepest declines in office growth rates during the 1990s, dropping almost 80 percent from the 1980s rate. Four key factors explain the decline. First, the national recession of the early 1990s lasted a bit longer in California. Second, office space in the city of San Francisco was quite overbuilt in the 1980s and new space was in little demand during the 1990s, when consolidations in the banking industry resulted in the loss of the headquarters facilities of two major downtown banks. Third, growth restrictions in the city of San Francisco prevented developers from launching a speculative building boom there during the late 1990s. Fourth, office growth in the Bay Area is not as important an indicator of the economy as it is in other regions. Metropolitan San Francisco's major industry is high tech, much of it housed in what are known as flex buildings, which contain a hybrid of office and manufacturing space. Flex buildings also are important in Los Angeles, although less so than in San Francisco. Because *Black's Guide* does not fully track

Table 4-15. Metropolitan Washington, D.C., Office Space, 1999[a]

| Location | Current | | By year built | | | | | |
| | | | 1990–99 | | 1980–89 | | Pre-1980 | |
	Square feet	Percent	Square feet	Percent	Square feet	Percent	Square feet	Percent
Downtown	114,650,892	41.1	33,027,850	50.3	48,176,690	32.2	33,446,352	52.3
Washington	79,796,361	28.6	24,821,328	37.8	31,316,660	20.9	23,658,373	37.0
Arlington-Rosslyn/ Court House	9,734,636	2.1	2,211,286	4.1	4,951,532	1.5	2,571,818	1.5
Arlington-Ballston/ Clarendon	5,922,570	2.1	2,672,925	4.1	2,300,549	1.5	949,096	1.5
Downtown Alexandria	5,694,042	2.0	926,710	1.4	3,668,876	2.5	1,098,456	1.7
Downtown Bethesda	7,583,288	2.7	912,909	1.4	3,507,662	2.3	3,162,717	4.9
Downtown Silver Spring	5,919,995	2.1	1,482,692	2.3	2,431,411	1.6	2,005,892	3.1
Edge city	75,766,713	27.1	12,231,227	18.6	50,220,943	33.6	13,314,543	20.8
Greenbelt	7,082,018	2.5	1,160,513	1.8	4,981,332	3.3	940,173	1.5
Chantilly/Dulles	8,203,804	2.9	1,831,115	2.8	6,327,308	4.2	45,381	0.1
Crystal City	10,305,673	3.7	435,040	0.7	5,947,333	4.0	3,923,300	6.1
Fairfax Center	5,277,217	1.9	1,047,645	1.6	4,229,572	2.8	0	—
Reston	9,545,763	3.4	1,185,203	1.8	7,484,530	5.0	876,030	1.4
Rockville/North Bethesda	10,666,670	3.8	2,155,555	3.3	5,920,678	4.0	2,590,437	4.0
Shady Grove	6,744,909	2.4	856,603	1.3	4,110,866	2.7	1,777,440	2.8
Tysons Corner	17,940,659	6.4	3,559,553	5.4	11,219,324	7.5	3,161,782	4.9
Edgeless city	88,791,700	31.8	20,347,783	31.0	51,206,514	34.2	17,237,403	26.9
Total	279,209,305	100	65,606,860	100	149,604,147	100	63,998,298	100

Source: Author's calculations.

a. Percent: percent of total square feet in Washington, D.C., metropolitan area.

flex space, much of the region's high-tech boom is not captured in office statistics.

Washington, D.C.: Land of Edge Cities

As a *Washington Post* writer, Joel Garreau was at ground zero when he wrote *Edge City*. Washington is a land of edge cities, including three that have more than 10 million square feet of office space. Washington also is a mature polycentric metropolis. It has more non-CBD office centers with 5 million or more square feet of space (eight edge cities and five secondary downtowns) than any other metropolitan area in the country. In that measure it surpasses even larger regions such as New York and Los Angeles.

Most of Washington's office space lies in the western half of the region. Like Atlanta, Washington is a region divided by income and race.[17] The line that divides the region runs along 16th Street in the center of Washington and into the suburbs of Virginia and especially Maryland. The area west of the line is for the most part affluent and white. The area east of the line is substantially African American and less affluent, although Prince George's County, Maryland, outside the Washington beltway, is home to a large number of middle-income black households.

Northern Virginia, where edge cities along the Dulles airport toll road have exploded with high-tech growth, has been the region's boom area for much of the last two decades. Suburban Maryland also has flourished from downtown Bethesda near the District of Columbia outward to Rockville and Shady Grove. Despite the fact that there has been tremendous auto-dependent office development in Washington's suburbs, it appears that that the region's subway system (Metro) still plays a major role in supporting polycentric growth. The primary and all secondary downtowns have subway stations that are close to most of the office space to make it easier for commuters to walk to work. In addition, four edge cities have stations, one of which, Crystal City, allows for easy pedestrian access to nearby office buildings. Thus, almost half of the office space in the Washington region is within reasonable walking distance of the Metro. The hub-and-spoke arrangement of the Metro system supports a similar pattern of development for much of the region's office space.

Metropolitan Washington has the nation's third-largest office economy, just barely behind Los Angeles and well ahead of Chicago. The size of the market is especially interesting given that *Black's Guide* excludes government offices from its office space figures.

Office Growth Trends in the 1990s

Table 4-16 shows office space growth trends in the 1990s for the thirteen metropolitan areas in the study. The analysis is based on a comparison of the regional share captured by each office location type compared

17. Orfield (1999).

Table 4-16. Office Space Growth Trends in the 1990s[a]

Metropolitan area	Gain in office space	Loss in office space
Atlanta	Edgeless cities	Edge cities
Boston	Downtown	Edgeless cities
Chicago	Edgeless cities	Edge cities
Dallas	Edgeless cities	Downtown
Denver	Edgeless cities	Downtown/edge cities
Detroit	Downtown	Edgeless cities
Houston	Downtown/edge cities	Edgeless cities
Los Angeles	Downtown	Edgeless cities
Miami	Edge city	Edgeless cities
New York	Downtown	Edge/edgeless cities
Philadelphia	Edgeless cities	Downtown/edge cities
San Francisco	Downtown	Edge cities
Washington, D.C.	Downtown	Edge cities

Source: Author's calculations.

a. Based on regional share in the 1990s compared with share in the 1980s.

with its share in the 1980s. Note that in cases in which the percent share was essentially flat it was treated as neither a gain nor a loss.

Table 4-16 shows that, relative to the 1980s, the 1990s were a good decade for downtown. Seven metropolitan areas—Boston, Detroit, Houston, Los Angeles, New York, San Francisco, and Washington—saw their regional share of downtown office space increase when compared with the 1980s. In contrast, the downtown share of office space dropped in only three regions—Dallas, Denver, and Philadelphia.

The 1990s were not as good for edge cities. Only two regions, Houston and Miami, saw an uptick in the share of edge city office space during the 1990s. Conversely, seven metropolitan areas—Atlanta, Chicago, Denver, New York, Philadelphia, San Francisco, and Washington, D.C.—saw a drop. Edge cities were essentially the mirror opposite of downtown during the 1990s; the struggle that some of them experienced during the decade is discussed more fully in chapter 6.

Edgeless cities' share of regional office space varied in the 1990s. Five regions saw an expansion in the share of edgeless city office space, while six metropolitan areas experienced a contraction. The gaining metropolitan areas were Atlanta, Chicago, Dallas, Denver, and Philadelphia; the losing regions were Boston, Detroit, Houston, Los Angeles, Miami, and New York.

Table 4-17. Typology of Metropolitan Areas, 1999

Metropolitan area	Percent office space in primary downtown	Percent office space in secondary downtown	Percent office space in edge cities	Percent office space in edgeless cities	Percent difference between primary downtowns and edgeless cities
Core Dominated					
Chicago	53.9		19.5	26.6	27.3
New York	56.7	7.2	6.2	29.9	26.8
Balanced					
Boston	37.4	4.6	18.8	39.2	−1.8
Washington, D.C.	28.6	12.5	27.1	31.8	−3.2
Denver	30.4	4.2	29.4	35.9	−5.5
Los Angeles	29.8	7.8	25.4	37.0	−7.2
San Francisco	33.9	8.8	13.9	43.4	−9.5
Dispersed					
Dallas	20.5	4.5	40.3	34.6	−14.1
Houson	23.0		37.9	39.1	−16.1
Atlanta	23.6	9.9	25.3	41.2	−17.6
Detroit	21.3		39.5	39.2	−17.9
Edgeless					
Philadelphia	34.2	3.2	8.9	53.6	−19.4
Miami	13.1	4.5	16.6	65.8	−52.7

Source: Black's Guide to Office Leasing.

Regional Comparisons and Metropolitan Types

The thirteen regions surveyed feature multiple metropolitan office development forms. As would be expected, no two are exactly alike, but it seems that most are not even close to being alike. Office development around the nation, despite being a product of a highly standardized design, finance, and construction process, is nonetheless subject to regional quirks, many of which are highlighted in the survey.

The office data show that there is no single new metropolitan form—there are many. The hallmark of modern American metropolises is difference—difference from cities of the past and difference from one another. The commonalties are chaotic form and massive decentralization. While is hard to discern a consistent pattern in the way office space is distributed in the thirteen metropolitan areas studied, regions can be grouped by the proportion of their space (see table 4-17). The key basis for this grouping is the comparative amount of primary downtown and edgeless city office space.

According to a comparison of the amount of space in the various office location types, the metropolitan areas fit into four categories. There are two "core-dominated" regions, New York and Chicago, where primary downtown space greatly exceeds edgeless city space. There are "balanced" metropolitan areas, where the percentage of edgeless city space exceeds that of primary downtown space, but only by single digits. Five regions meet that criterion—Boston, Denver, Los Angeles, San Francisco, and Washington, D.C. In "dispersed" metropolitan areas—Atlanta, Dallas, Detroit, and Houston—the percentage of edgeless city space exceeds that of primary downtown office space by double digits. Edge cities in dispersed regions also exceed the amount of office space in downtowns by a wide margin. Finally, there are "edgeless" regions, where the edgeless cities account for more than half of the office space in the metropolitan area. Only Miami and Philadelphia fall into this category.

CHAPTER 5

Charting the

Elusive Metropolis

It is a city where all the traditional urban elements float in space like stars and planets in a galaxy, held together by mutual gravitational attraction but with large empty spaces in between.

—PEIRCE LEWIS (1995)

Peirce Lewis's cosmological metaphor, "the galactic city," indirectly raises a key issue that physicists have been working on for years—the fate of the universe. In particular, they debate the content of the empty spaces between the stars because that content will determine whether the universe will go on expanding forever or eventually collapse back on itself. If the seemingly empty spaces are actually full of "dark matter," then there might be enough gravitational attraction to slow down and ultimately reverse the expansion of the universe that started with the Big Bang. But if the empty spaces are in fact mostly empty, then the universe will expand forever—and die in icy darkness.

The galactic city also has dark matter in the spaces between its brightly lit centers. The fate of the universe does not hang on their composition, of course, but the nature and direction of the modern metropolis will be determined in part by what is in these spaces. To carry Lewis's metaphor a bit further, edgeless cities are the dark matter of the galactic city. Identifying, categorizing, and charting these places will add much to knowledge about the metropolitan universe.

Chapter 5 covers ways to map the new metropolitan form and roughly categorize edgeless city office space. It presents and analyzes maps showing the distribution of office space in four metropolitan areas that illustrate the range of urban spatial forms identified in the previous chapter.

Classifying Edgeless Cities

Classifying edgeless cities is like trying to nail Jell-O to the wall. But despite their largely indeterminate nature, edgeless cities can be distinguished in part on the basis of where they lie in the region. The three basic types are "in-towners," "in-betweeners," and "outposts." The maps that follow show each of these variants.

The edgeless city categories developed here are hardly definitive. They derive from a qualitative assessment of how office space is distributed based on viewing numerous *Black's Guide* maps and looking at the municipal distribution of office data. Follow-up research by the author and others will more precisely measure and group the types of edgeless cities. At this preliminary stage, it is useful to briefly consider the general ways edgeless office space appears across the region.

In-towners

In-towner edgeless cities are found in the denser parts of metropolitan areas such as central cities or older suburbs. This is by far the smallest edgeless city category, according to a reading of the *Black's Guide* maps and outputs of municipal-level office data. Most office space in cities appears in distinct centers. There are, however, regions such as Los Angeles where good portions of edgeless city office space are in dense, urban-like settings. As the sprawl analysis in chapter 7 shows, given the overall spatial form of the Los Angeles region, that should be expected.

In-betweeners

In-betweener edgeless cities are located in the general vicinity of other clusters, such as secondary downtowns and edge cities. Sometimes they trail away from denser office development, like tails on a comet. In other instances, they fill in the gaps between edge cities. In all cases, they are far enough away from other more concentrated developments not to be part of them.

Outposts

Outposts, which lie at the edge of the region, often in the lowest-density settings, and in-betweeners constitute the big categories of edgeless cities. Outposts serve as development spearheads in the exurban frontier. They are probably the biggest public policy concern because they extend commuter sheds deep into a region's semi-rural hinterlands. Much of northern New Jersey's office space is in this category.

Figure 5-1. Chicago Region: Total Square Footage of Office Space by One-Square-Mile Area Cells

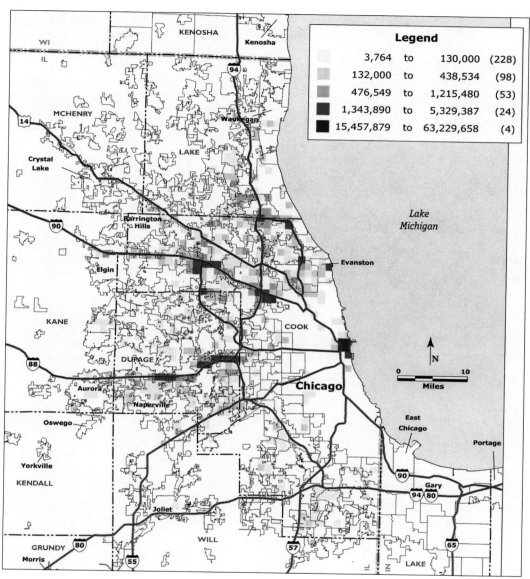

Legend

3,764 to 130,000	(228)
132,000 to 438,534	(98)
476,549 to 1,215,480	(53)
1,343,890 to 5,329,387	(24)
15,457,879 to 63,229,658	(4)

Source: data, CB Richard Ellis; map, courtesy Metropolitan Area Research Corporation.

Figure 5-2. San Francisco Region: Total Square Footage of Office Space by One-Square-Mile Area Cells

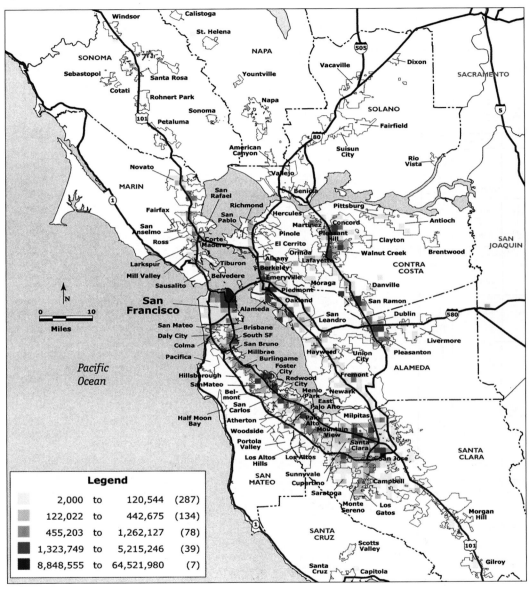

Legend

2,000	to	120,544	(287)
122,022	to	442,675	(134)
455,203	to	1,262,127	(78)
1,323,749	to	5,215,246	(39)
8,848,555	to	64,521,980	(7)

Source: data, CB Richard Ellis; map, courtesy Metropolitan Area Research Corporation.

FIGURE 5-3. Detroit Region: Total Square Footage of Office Space by One-Square-Mile Area Cells

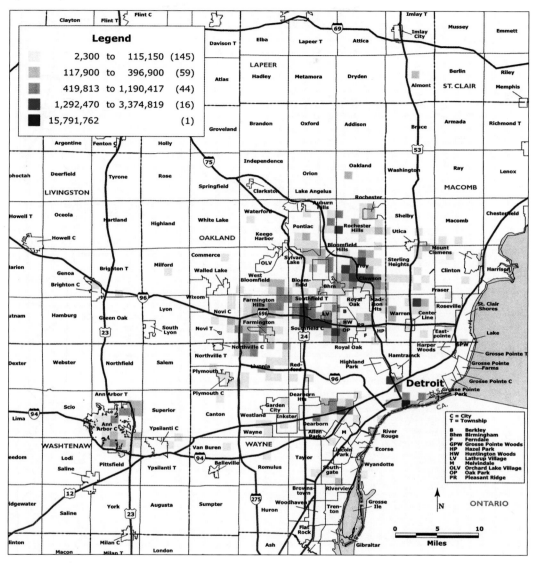

Source: data, CB Richard Ellis; map, courtesy Metropolitan Area Research Corporation.

Figure5-4. Philadelphia Region: Total Square Footage of Office Space by One-Square-Mile Area Cells

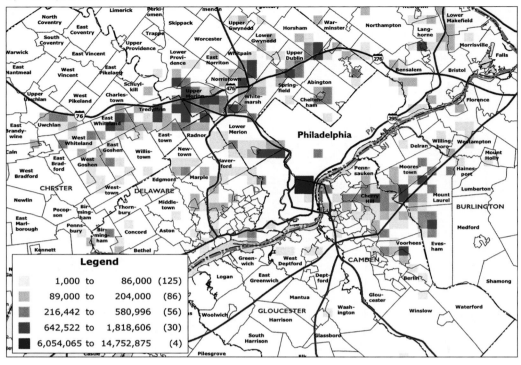

Legend			
1,000	to	86,000	(125)
89,000	to	204,000	(86)
216,442	to	580,996	(56)
642,522	to	1,818,606	(30)
6,054,065	to	14,752,875	(4)

FIGURE 5-5. Philadelphia Region: Clustering of Quarter-Mile Area Cells with Total Square Footage Greater than 100,000

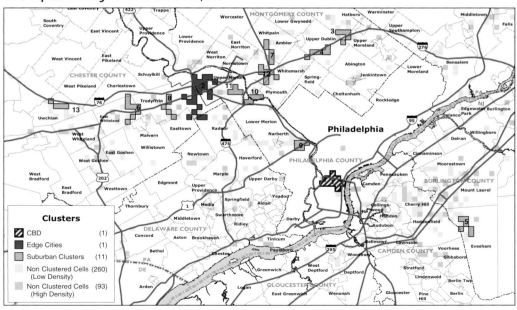

Clusters	
CBD	(1)
Edge Cities	(1)
Suburban Clusters	(11)
Non Clustered Cells (Low Density)	(260)
Non Clustered Cells (High Density)	(93)

Source: data, CB Richard Ellis; map (top), courtesy Metropolitan Area Research Corporation; map (bottom), courtesy Ameregis.

Office Data Maps

The preceding maps show the distribution of office space in four of the thirteen metropolitan areas in the study. The Metropolitan Area Research Corporation (MARC) of Minneapolis prepared the maps; the office data were provided by CB Richard Ellis. (See appendix A for a comparison of these data to *Black's Guide* data.)

The office building location maps were divided into cells representing one square mile. The total square footage of office space for each cell was then mapped and ranges assigned to natural break points in the data (ranges also appear in the data tables that follow). In addition to office space, the maps include two other important features: municipal boundaries and major highways.

Four metropolitan areas—Chicago, San Francisco, Detroit, and Philadelphia—were picked to represent a range of office location patterns, using the typology discussed in chapter 4 and shown in table 4-17.[1] There is one metropolitan area for each of the four types shown in the table, which groups regions by comparing the ratios of their primary downtown to their edgeless city office space. The four categories are "core dominated," "balanced," "dispersed," and "edgeless."

Chicago: Core Dominated

Figure 5-1 indicates that metropolitan Chicago, despite being core dominated, has fairly widely dispersed non-CBD office space across dozens of municipalities. Two clear patterns emerge. The first is that Chicago has a favored quarter—or half. The region north and west of the Loop, Chicago's downtown, contains the great bulk of the region's office space. The second pattern is the distinct clustering of edge cities around the intersections of the region's main beltway and arterial highways. Around some of these clusters are some in-betweener edgeless cities, and some outpost edgeless cities lie in the far north, south, and west of the metropolitan area.

However, not all highway intersections have office space; there is a distinct absence of office development around the big intersections south of Chicago. The region traditionally has been rich to the north

---

1. Maps were provided by MARC for several other regions as well, such as Miami and Denver. Office space scatters widely in most of the maps. The maps shown here document the range of the distribution, from relatively clustered to more scattered. The other maps typically depict office space to be sprawled across much of the region.

Table 5-1. Metropolitan Chicago Office Space, 2001

Size range	Square foot range	Total cells	Total square feet in range	Number of buildings	Average size of building
Range 1	3,764–130,000	228	12,142,849	326	37,248
Range 2	132,000–438,534	98	23,487,382	360	65,243
Range 3	476,549–1,215,480	53	38,929,936	402	96,841
Range 4	1,343,890–5,329,387	24	52,669,564	382	137,878
Range 5	15,457,879–63,229,658	4	125,945,273	423	297,743
Total		407	253,175,004	1,893	133,743

Sources: MARC and CB Richard Ellis.

and poor to the south—a pattern first documented by early twentieth-century sociologists in the Chicago School.[2] It appears that a community's affluence may be more important in attracting office development than having a major highway intersection. This finding is consistent with the pattern that Orfield found in an analysis of office space prepared by MARC.[3]

Table 5-1, which shows the data that underlie figure 5-1, indicates that Chicago's office space sweeps across 400 square miles. Range 5 includes almost half of this space, which can be found in just four square miles in Chicago's downtown, covering both the Loop and the office development running north along Lake Michigan. Range 4 captures the region's edge city space, which includes a fifth of the metropolitan area's office space, in a total of twenty-four square miles. Ranges 1 through 3 track the region's edgeless city space, which accounts for 29 percent of Chicago's office space and covers a total of 379 square miles.

The average building sizes closely follow the size ranges. Range 1 cells, representing the most diffuse development, contain the smallest buildings, just 37,248 square feet on average. In contrast, range 5 (downtown Chicago) includes buildings that average 279,743 square feet.

San Francisco: Balanced

The physical features of the Bay Area—mountains and sea—substantially shape the region's urban development. Figure 5-2 would appear to

2. Burgess (1925).
3. Orfield (2002).

Table 5-2. Metropolitan San Francisco Office Space, 2001

Size range	Square foot range	Total cells	Total square feet in range	Number of buildings	Average size of building
Range 1	2,000–120,544	287	11,648,852	615	18,941
Range 2	122,022–422,675	134	31,693,412	1,034	30,651
Range 3	455,203–1,262,127	78	57,879,835	1,217	47,559
Range 4	1,323,749–5,215,246	39	82,652,025	1,450	57,001
Range 5	8,848,555–64,521,980	7	179,471,919	1,918	93,572
Total		545	363,346,043	6,234	58,285

Sources: MARC and CB Richard Ellis.

show that the San Francisco region is dominated by long office corridors. Office buildings line route 101 (running west of the San Francisco Bay), interstate 880 (lying east of the bay), and interstate 680 (connecting Concord and Pleasanton). But almost all development of every type lines these highways because there is limited developable land in the region, due to such factors as slope, open-space preservation, and geological fault lines.[4] West of the development along the peninsula is a large open-space preserve. East of the East Bay cities are the Berkeley Hills and Rocky Ridge, which cannot be built on due to the steep slope of the terrain. The highways in the San Francisco region therefore are rough indicators of where urban growth is possible. Finally, the Bay Area's office development lies almost entirely south of the city. The region's northern counties contain vineyards, precluding sprawling office development.

According to the data provided by CB Richard Ellis, the San Francisco region has a tremendous amount of office space (table 5-2; appendix A). San Francisco's downtown, covering seven square miles in the northeast part of the city, accounts for almost half of this space. The Bay Area's secondary downtowns and edge cities also have a large share, with 23 percent of total inventory. They occupy 39 square miles, while the region's vast edgeless cities fill 499 square miles, much of it in the form of outpost edgeless cities at the southern end of the region.

4. Had the Denver map been used as the example of the "balanced" region, office space would have been shown to be much more scattered. Despite mountains to the west, the Denver metropolitan area's development spreads widely along the high plains, lining the Front Range of the Rockies. Office development follows this regional pattern.

Table 5-3. Metropolitan Detroit Office Space, 2001

Size range	Square foot range	Total cells	Total square feet in range	Number of buildings	Average size of building
Range 1	2,300–115,150	145	6,700,636	208	32,215
Range 2	117,900–396,900	59	12,553,820	205	61,238
Range 3	419,813–1,190,417	44	30,777,630	375	82,074
Range 4	1,292,470–3,374,819	16	33,195,157	214	155,118
Range 5	15,791,762–15,791,762	1	15,791,762	54	292,440
Total		265	99,019,005	1,056	93,768

Sources: MARC and CB Richard Ellis.

Detroit: Dispersed

Figure 5-3 shows that, like Chicago's, Detroit's office development lies mostly north and west of downtown. Once again, office location throughout the region is tied to the major highways. But Detroit's big ring roads (highway 23 and interstate 69) have no office development except around the college town of Ann Arbor, indicating that the region's office space has yet to diffuse to its farthest reaches.

Detroit's three big office clusters—Southfield, Troy, and downtown—clearly turn up on figure 5-3. There also is a good-sized patch of office space around Dearborn and one far to the west in Ann Arbor. Outside and between these clusters lie large arrays of in-towner and outpost edgeless cities. The city of Detroit has an uptown in addition to its downtown.

Downtown Detroit is compact; table 5-3 indicates that all of it fits within one square mile. According to the CB Richard Ellis data, Detroit's downtown, which includes nearly 16 million square feet of office space, accounts for about 16 percent of the total stock in the region. With more than 33 million square feet of office space, Detroit's edge cities, which cover sixteen square miles, account for one-third. The other half of Detroit's regional space lies in edgeless cities, which contain 50 million square feet of office space spread over 248 square miles.

Philadelphia: Edgeless

Figure 5-4 shows that office development spills all over and around greater Philadelphia. There are big patches to the west of the city and

Table 5-4. Metropolitan Philadelphia Office Space, 2001

Size range	Square foot range	Total cells	Total square feet in range	Number of buildings	Average size of building
Range 1	1,000–86,000	125	5,495,659	183	30,031
Range 2	89,000–204,000	86	11,765,605	232	50,714
Range 3	216,442–580,996	56	18,145,841	326	55,662
Range 4	642,522–1,818,606	30	30,118,564	419	71,882
Range 5	6,054,065–14,752,875	4	38,483,700	128	300,654
Total		301	104,009,369	1,288	80,753

Sources: MARC and CB Richard Ellis.

across the Delaware River in southern New Jersey. (Note that the map does not include office data from Wilmington, Delaware; if it did, office development would also spill substantially south of the city.) On the Philadelphia map, the color red does not indicate dense concentrations of office space. In Philadelphia's case, the office square footage range indicated by the color red (range 4) is only a one-third as dense as Chicago's and San Francisco's range 4 red cells (see figures 5-1, 5-2, and 5-4 and tables 5-1, 5-2, and 5-4).

Unlike with Chicago, San Francisco, and Detroit, it is hard to separate the edge cities and edgeless cities in the office data that underlie Philadelphia's office space map (see figure 5-4 and table 5-4). The data in ranges 1 through 4 capture the edgeless cities, while range 5 clearly indicates Philadelphia's downtown. In total, edgeless cities spread over 297 square miles and account for 63 percent of the region's office space. The downtown fits into just four square miles and contains the remaining 37 percent of office inventory. The downtown's office buildings, averaging more than 300,000 square feet, also dwarf those in edgeless cities, which range from 30,031 to 71,882 square feet. Philadelphia's metropolitan area features all variants of edgeless city office space. Outpost edge cities ring the region, in-betweeners fill the gaps between the few small office nodes that exist, and in-towners pepper the region's older suburbs.

The findings in the four metropolitan office maps are consistent with recent work that shows the regional distribution of office space. In an analysis of land use in Atlanta, French, Frank, and Bachman found that more than one-fifth of all the cells (or what they call centroids) in the region contain some office space.[5] While office buildings are more concentrated than residences or other commercial properties, the fact that they diffuse to this extent demonstrates how far twenty-first century office development has evolved beyond a monocentric or, in some cases, even a polycentric form. Collectively, the office data maps tell an interesting story. They show that office development occupies a large share of the developable land in many metropolitan areas. The maps also highlight the fact that office development is often arrayed very differently from one region to the next.

Figure 5-5 represents a sample (also showing metropolitan Philadelphia) of the next-generation office maps now under development by the ameregis, the successor of MARC. This map is part of a series that Tom Luce of ameregis prepared using the same office data used in the four preceding maps. Luce sought to structure the office data by size and density categories in order to tease out some of the sub–edge city divisions in the data—and to find some order in the chaos. The sections are drawn in quarter-mile cells, a unit of analysis that often is used in transit studies because it captures a pedestrian scale (a quarter-mile from a transit stop often is the threshold tolerance that a commuter has for walking to work). A quarter-mile also is smaller than the scale of even a modest CBD, and it is much smaller than the scale of an edge city.[6]

Luce's Philadelphia map identifies just one edge city (a cluster having more than 5 million square feet of office space), and eleven sub–edge city clusters of varying size. He also finds ninety-three "non-clustered cells" with "high-density" office development (more than 100,000 square feet of office space)[7] and 260 "non-clustered cells" with low-density development. The vast majority of Philadelphia's non-CBD office space lies outside its edge city. Most is split between the smaller "suburban clusters" and the high-density non-clustered cells. Thus it takes more than 100 discrete, noncontiguous office locations to account for the majority of Philadelphia's non-CBD office space.

5. French, Frank, and Bachman (2000).

6. Quarter-mile cells also produce the impression of a more clustered metropolis because they limit the area in which office space is shown. In contrast, French, Frank, and Bachman (2000) used several-mile-square cells (centroids). The previous four maps fall in the middle, with one-mile-square cells.

7. This would represent a typical cluster of two to three average non-CBD office buildings. A "high-density" cluster would be one in which two to three buildings are found within a quarter-mile space.

Figure 5-5 shows that office development spreads throughout the region. In New Jersey, towns such as Cherry Hill and Mount Laurel fill up with low-density office development. Another low-grade patch of development occurs just west of the city in Delaware County. Some in-town edgeless city space can be found north and west of downtown Philadelphia. Finally, a long, spread-out corridor of development, stretching the western length of metropolitan Philadelphia's urbanized area, accounts for much of the region's non-CBD office space.

CHAPTER 6

Are Edge Cities
Losing Their Edge?

The title of this chapter comes from an article in *Planning* magazine by Bill Fulton in which he suggested that edge cities may be at risk of being outcompeted by more decentralized, sprawling commercial development. Fulton found that "edge cities are becoming increasingly land locked. They are no longer the land-rich emerging districts where office buildings or shopping centers can be built more quickly and cheaply than elsewhere."[1] Fulton's observation is borne out by the data presented in this book. As noted in chapter 4, edge cities in many regions lost ground to both downtowns and edgeless cities. This chapter seeks to answer why that occurred.

Chapter 6 examines the types, locations, and evolution of edge cities. The chapter begins by establishing two classes of edge cities derived from an interpretation of the office space data and then moves to an analysis of very large edge cities. Next, a life cycle model of how edge cities form and mature is presented, followed by a discussion of why edgeless cities appear to be flourishing, often at the expense of edge cities.

Edge City Hierarchy

Not all edge cities are the same. As the data show, several are very large, with more than 17 million square feet of office space, while many more

1. Fulton (1996), p. 5.

have 5 to 10 million square feet.[2] Because edge cities come in different sizes, it is worth briefly considering the top edge cities as a distinct group. While some studies have used multivariate statistical methods to distinguish different types of non-CBD office development,[3] an analysis of *Black's Guide* maps and office space data suggests that a rough, but relatively clear, division can be made between two common types of edge cities:

   —*Glamour Galleria Edge Cities.* Glamour galleries are large mixed-use edge cities with at least 10 million square feet of office space. The "galleria" in the name refers to the presence of a large, typically upscale regional mall, recognizing the important role that Gerald Hines, the developer of several Galleria shopping centers, played in sparking the growth of several large edge cities. "Glamour" comes from the kinds of businesses these places attract. Big edge cities are direct competitors of the nation's largest downtowns for prestige tenants, including corporations looking for headquarters locations.

   Glamour also refers to the fact that these places grab the headlines. They powerfully demonstrate that even many of the nation's largest companies—headquarters and all—have left the big city. Glamour galle-rias also have entered the public consciousness, and to many (including many planners and academics) they now represent all edge cities. Post Oak, in Houston, and Tysons Corner, in northern Virginia, are two leading glamour galleria edge cities.

   —*Smaller Utility Version (SUV) Edge Cities.* SUVs, as the name implies, function as more basic cousins of the glamour galleries. They are smaller (most have less than 10 million square feet of office space) and unlikely to be anchored by a regional mall. SUVs also have fewer major corporate headquarters (according to a reading of the literature) and fewer signature buildings such as the sixty-two-story skyscraper found in Post Oak than glamour galleries do.

   The abbreviation SUV is, of course, popularly attached to "sport util-ity vehicle," a class of big, utilitarian vehicles that as of 2002 made up almost half of new car sales in the United States. The edge city SUV is similar: although smaller than glamour galleries, it certainly is big rela-tive to edgeless cities and arguably serves a more utilitarian purpose than many places in the metropolis. And auto SUVs wind up being

   2. Edge cities appear as a definitive cluster, making locating, naming, measuring, and ranking them a more straightforward process than it is with the more elusive edgeless city.
   3. See Cervero (1989).

driven around SUV edge cities more than any wilderness setting. The Franklin/Piscataway area in central New Jersey and the Denver Technology Center south of Denver are examples of SUV edge cities.

The Top Ten Edge Cities

Table 6-1 shows the top ten edge cities according to square footage of office space as derived from the *Black's Guide* data shown in chapter 5. The top ten represent the glamour galleria edge cities; together they contain almost one-third (32 percent) of all the office space in edge cities. Besides the top ten, seven more edge cities have more than 10 million square feet of office space, ranging in size from 11 million to an even 10 million square feet. (The full list of edge cities and their sizes appears in chapter 4.) After these, the size of edge cities drops off sharply, resulting in a large cluster in the 6 to 8 million-square-foot range. The seventeen edge cities that exceed 10 million square feet of office space account for almost half (45 percent) of the edge city total inventory reported in this study. Another 41 edge cities have from 5 to 10 million square feet of office space.

While the top ten edge cities turn up all over the country, there is a definite concentration in the Sunbelt, with Atlanta, Dallas, and Los Angeles each having two edge cities on the list and Houston having one. Detroit (with two edge cities) and Washington, D.C., are the only regions outside the Sunbelt on the list. The second-largest (Post Oak) and eighth-largest (LBJ Freeway) edge cities lie within the central cities of Houston and Dallas respectively. All others on the list are outside the central city of the region.

Most top ten edge cities are bigger than the downtowns of such major cities as Detroit and Miami. Together, they represent more than 169 million square feet of office space. Although that sounds like an impressive amount, it is not much larger than Chicago's downtown and considerably smaller than midtown Manhattan. More significant, it is much smaller than the amount of office space in the vast edgeless cities of the New York metropolitan area. Furthermore, many of these places are not growing very fast, especially compared with smaller and more scattered locations.

Table 6-1 also shows the location of the big edge cities relative to the downtown and the distance between them. Most are about ten miles from the downtown. The closest (Post Oak) is six miles and the farthest (Costa Mesa) is thirty-three miles from the CBD. They are the two largest edge cities and the only ones with more than 20 million square feet of space; five more glamour galleria edge cities follow them in size, ranging from around 18 million to 11.5 million square feet.

Table 6-1. Office Space, Top Ten Edge Cities, 1999

Edge city	Square feet (millions)	Metropolitan area	Direction from CBD[a]	Miles from CBD
Costa Mesa	28.5	Los Angeles	South and East	33
Post Oak (Uptown)	21.1	Houston	West	6
Tysons Corner	17.9	Washington	West	10
Cumberland Galleria	17.6	Atlanta	North and West	10
Southfield	17.5	Detroit	North and West	13
Perimeter Center	15.9	Atlanta	North	12
Troy	13.6	Detroit	North	17
LBJ Freeway	13.2	Dallas	North	10
Far North Dallas	12.3	Dallas	North	17
South Bay/LAX	11.6	Los Angeles	South	10
Total	169.2			

Source: *Black's Guide to Office Leasing.*
a. CBD: central business district.

Costa Mesa and Post Oak illustrate the contrast in how glamour galleria edge cities are situated in their region. Post Oak is essentially an extension of the downtown—or a modern version of an uptown. In fact, its chamber of commerce is in the process of having its name officially changed to Uptown. Post Oak's relationship to Houston's downtown is not unlike the one between midtown and lower Manhattan. Midtown Manhattan is a mid-twentieth-century uptown built around the juncture of the New York region's commuter rail system, which had a less direct connection to lower Manhattan. Midtown thus became the new downtown, built to accommodate the boom in suburban rail commuting.

Likewise, Post Oak is a late twentieth-century uptown built around Houston's interstate beltway—a version of midtown Manhattan, complete with the sixty-two-story Transco Tower, the tallest office building outside a central business district. Just as Midtown eventually overtook the Wall Street area in lower Manhattan, Post Oak someday may usurp Houston's old downtown in size and importance.

Costa Mesa, meanwhile, represents a break from downtown Los Angeles (recall that Los Angeles is a region of realms).[4] Rather than a

4. The Costa Mesa edge city actually encompasses much of Central Orange County and spreads into cities such as Irvine and Santa Ana. Its anchor mall is the South Coast Plaza. Costa Mesa, Irvine, and Santa Ana are large suburban cities that Lang and Simmons (2001) refer to as "boomburbs." In fact, Santa Ana is the second-largest such suburban super-city in the United States, surpassing such traditional cities as Pittsburgh and Cincinnati in population.

Table 6-2. Ten Largest Non-CBD Office Markets, 1997

Market	Square feet (millions)	Location/state	Metropolitan area
Post Oak/West Loop	22.9	Houston, Texas	Houston
South Coast	22.8	Costa Mesa/Irvine/Newport Beach, California	Los Angeles
Central Perimeter	19.2	Fulton County, Georgia	Atlanta
LBJ Freeway	18.6	Dallas, Texas	Dallas
Schaumburg	18.1	Schaumburg, Illinois	Chicago
Tysons Corner	17.9	Tysons Corner, Virginia	Washington
Oak Brook	17.3	Oak Brook, Illinois	Chicago
Route 128 West	14.6	Middlesex/Norfolk Counties, Massachusetts	Boston
Stamford	14.1	Stamford, Connecticut	New York
Las Colinas/Dallas/ Fort Worth Airport	13.2	Irving, Texas	Dallas
Total	178.7		

Source: Cushman and Wakefield Research.

relocated downtown, it is essentially the central business district of Orange County, California, and it claims its own major airport (John Wayne) and sports franchises in baseball (Angels) and hockey (Mighty Ducks). Costa Mesa forms the center of an Orange County urban realm that has broken from downtown and now has its own commuter and market sheds.[5] Post Oak and downtown Houston are the binary stars of the same regional solar system; Costa Mesa and downtown Los Angeles are the stars of separate solar systems. The difference is important, and it underscores the subtle distinctions that exist in the vastly expanded twenty-first century American metropolis.

As table 6-2 shows, the real estate firm of Cushman and Wakefield also follows big edge cities, what it refers to as "large non-CBD markets" (for details on Cushman and Wakefield office data see appendix A).[6] The list substantially overlaps with the list of top ten edge cities derived from *Black's Guide* office data. Five places appear on both tables 6-1 and 6-2: Costa Mesa ("South Coast" in Cushman and Wakefield), Post Oak, Tysons Corner, Perimeter Center, and the LBJ Freeway. The lists do not entirely overlap because the criteria for their selection vary—for example, "office building" is defined differently—but there

5. Vance (1964, 1977).
6. Cushman and Wakefield's office data are shown here to demonstrate how "marked" large edge cities have become.

are similarities in the total size of the top-ten non-CBD markets and the biggest edge cities.

Interestingly, Detroit, a region whose edge cities turn up twice on the *Black's Guide*–derived top-ten list, has no representatives on Cushman and Wakefield's list. Yet Chicago, which registers no edge cities on the *Black's* list, has two in Cushman and Wakefield's top ten.

Favored Quarters

In many cases non-CBD office space is concentrated in a large wedge of a metropolitan area, in what some now refer to as the "favored quarter." Leinberger developed the favored-quarter concept to account for the fact that, for the most part, wealthy households, high-end retail, and suburban corporate offices seem to cluster in one quadrant of the region.[7] The favored-quarter idea has its roots in the work of Homer Hoyt, an economist with the Federal Housing Administration during the 1930s. Hoyt found that high-income housing radiated mostly from the core in one wedge—often beginning at the corner of the central business district that contained the financial services industry. Hoyt's "sector hypothesis" was based on the movement of high-rent districts in 142 American cities in 1900, 1915, and 1936.[8]

The favored-quarter model explains the location of some office space reported in this study, including that in the glamour galleria edge cities. Previous research has established the statistical association between office space location and affluent municipalities in New Jersey.[9] The office space presented in this study (and an analysis of the data in *Black's Guide* maps) indeed shows a favored-quarter (or favored-half) pattern in several of the regions, especially those in the South. Atlanta and Dallas have distinct favored quarters, the former to the north of the downtown and the latter to the north and west. Chicago, Houston, and Washington, D.C., exhibit favored halves: the half of the region north of the Loop in Chicago and the halves to the west of Houston and Washington (more favored-quarter analysis appears in the discussion of office space maps in chapter 7).

Urban theory has long held that the more affluent parts of metropolitan areas tend to be located to the north and west because the prevailing winds in North America come from that direction and therefore would blow pollution to the south and east.[10] As table 6-1 shows, all but one of

7. Leinberger (1995, 1996).
8. Hoyt (1939).
9. Lang (1994a, 1994b); Orfield (2002).
10. Hoyt (1939); Harris and Ulman (1945); Vance (1977).

the glamour galleria edge cities are located to the north and west of the downtown.

Edge Cities: Twenty-First Century Urban Renewal Projects?

The office data reported in this book should concern those who seek to build better suburbs, especially those looking to improve the design of edge cities. Given the poor prospects for building urban centers out of edgeless cities, edge cities may be as good as it gets for those seeking to establish a more urban pattern of development in the suburbs.

Many observers have been hoping that edge cities would some day grow up and become more like old downtowns.[11] They could grow denser, provide mass transit service, offer some cultural attractions, and eventually become true centers of the new metropolis. For example, Brown and Hickok suggest that edge cities can be improved by selectively adding more density to them.[12] They argue that because concentrating more people and commerce in edge cities will reduce trip generation, it can reduce congestion. They note that there is plenty of developable land left in edge cities between the buildings because floor-to-area ratios (FARs) on most buildings remain lower there than in traditional downtowns.[13] Using Tysons Corner as an example, they assert, "Although Tysons, by far the largest office and shopping center in Virginia, may indeed have too many people using its current infrastructure, it's hard to argue that too many people occupy its land."[14]

Apparently, however, the prospects for improving most edge cities by increasing their density seem grim. In a recent study on edge city morphology, Scheer and Petkov concluded that they "do not expect that the Edge Cities now developing can be adapted to be more like traditional downtowns."[15] Part of the problem they identify is introducing a citylike street network into places that are now built to accommodate automobiles. In a way, edge cities are trapped. Increasing their density when the street network is built for low-density land use immediately translates into increasing congestion. The initial competitive advantage that most

11. Barnett (1992); Bruegmann (1995); Bruegmann and Davis (1992); Garreau (1991); Leinberger (1996); Langdon (1990).

12. Brown and Hickok (1990).

13. The floor-to-area ratio is a measure of how much space a building takes up relative to its lot. A one-floor, one-acre-sized building on a one-acre lot would have an FAR of 1.

14. Brown and Hickok (1990), p. 20.

15. Scheer and Petkov (1998), p. 308.

edge cities have enjoyed—a low-cost, open-space, and winding-street suburbia—often becomes a disadvantage when development eventually concentrates. Traditional urban grids, with their multiple points of entry and dispersed route patterns, do a far better job of managing congestion in densely built areas.

In edge cities increases in density often come from increasing building height rather than covering more ground. For example, consider the recent efforts to transform Tysons Corner into a more traditional urban environment. In 1994, Fairfax County, Virginia (home to Tysons), approved the Tysons Corner urban center plan, which proposed transforming the edge city into a city center. The plan allowed for greater building density, although it still remains low compared with that of most downtowns. However, according to an early assessment, the plan has not had the desired effect:

> Instead, what is emerging at Tysons Corner is a slightly taller version of what was there before: The buildings are still set apart from one another, remote islands in a sea of driveways, plazas, berms and parking garages—a place, in other words, that remains better suited to automobiles than pedestrians.[16]

One problem is that despite the goals of the plan, Fairfax County officials remain reluctant to allow zoning changes that would promote the kinds of urban design and density reforms needed to build a true city center.[17] To some extent, their fear is rational: they know that Tysons Corner's road network is ill designed for the type of traffic congestion that would accompany much higher density.

Edge City Life Cycle

Figure 6-1 shows a proposed model for the life cycle of an edge city, although not all edge cities necessarily go through the stages shown here. The model, which is more applicable to larger edge cities but not necessarily limited to them, derives from the author's interpretation of the edge city literature and data and extensive field notes gathered on the ground in edge cities.

---

16. Peter Whoriskey, "Fairfax's Elusive Downtown," *Washington Post*, April 1, 2001, p. A1.

17. For perspective consider that building FARs in Tysons Corner range from 1 to 2, while FARs in downtown Washington, D.C., run from 5 to 9 and in downtown Bethesda from 4 to 5.

Figure 6-1. Life Cycle of a Big Edge City

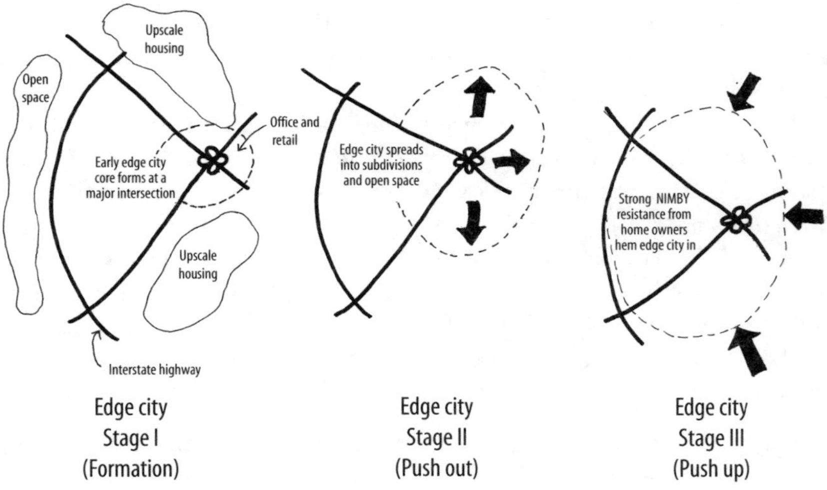

Edge city
Stage I
(Formation)

Edge city
Stage II
(Push out)

Edge city
Stage III
(Push up)

—*Stage 1*. An edge city takes hold at a major highway intersection in a metropolitan area, developing at relatively low density. At this stage it has a significant cost advantage over the downtown; it also enjoys good commuter access. The road network comprises exit ramps and feeder roads, and building sites develop as independent pods off these roads. Inexpensive surface parking surrounds most buildings. The area may or may not have a major shopping mall. The new edge city begins to establish a reputation as a major commuter destination in the region.

—*Stage 2*. The edge city expands, at a relatively low density but in a fairly contiguous manner, pushing out into both open space and some older residential areas. Substantial infill development begins. Some multifamily housing is built, and many land parcels originally passed over for office space are developed. At this stage, the edge city becomes firmly known as a destination. It also creates some controversy because of the growth problems it triggers. Congestion begins to build as the network of feeder roads, which was never intended to handle urban-level traffic, becomes increasingly burdened.

—*Stage 3*. Strong NIMBY (not-in-my-backyard) sentiment mounts in the local community, especially among surrounding homeowners. The edge city's ability to grow outward in a contiguous area becomes severely limited, and development is forced to go up. Some development spills out into small isolated clusters that are disconnected from but within several miles of the edge city. Many of the issues associated with land-constrained markets emerge. Building heights and costs rise. Expensive parking decks are built in place of surface parking to make more efficient use of land. The network of feeder roads becomes overwhelmed. An all-day rush hour results because workers make multiple automobile trips to run errands and go to lunch. The cost benefit of the edge city relative to that of the downtown has either substantially narrowed or disappeared altogether.

The Future of Edge Cities

Edge cities are still so new that even though some are in relative decline, none are in real decline. Despite their problems, most are still attracting new businesses, even if they are losing some ground in terms of office space to edgeless cities and downtowns. But many edge cities, especially the big, denser glamour galleries, are at a crossroads. To keep growing and remain competitive, they will have to change their land use and transportation practices to accommodate denser development. Much of the discussion at the first-ever National Edge City Conference held in June 2001 in the edge city of Schaumburg, Illinois, focused on the issue of how to turn these places into real, dynamic, multiuse centers. Sessions were devoted to how to improve edge cities through new urban design methods and promote connections to mass transit systems. Yet ultimately, economic forces will largely determine the fate of edge cities. That is where they face their greatest challenge.

As noted earlier, one reason that big downtowns remain relevant despite their costs and congestion is their agglomeration economies, which create efficiencies that lower the barriers of cost and inconvenience. Many edge cities lack an agglomeration economy, which might justify the cost of a massive retrofit of their infrastructure to accommodate greater density. There is little evidence that office tenants are willing to pay much higher rents to be in an edge city than they would pay to be an edgeless city. A recent survey conducted by the Building Owners and Managers Association (BOMA) and the Urban Land Institute (ULI) showed that less than half of the office tenants who are now in a suburban downtown (edge city) believe the location to be important, suggesting that they could move elsewhere when their lease is up. If edge cites begin to grow denser, driving up costs, they may lose tenants to edgeless cities. Meanwhile, it is hard to justify the types of costs and congestion that are typical of large CBDs because many tenants do not regard "a downtown suburban location . . . as a substitute for downtown."[18]

However, traditional big-city downtowns do not rely on market forces alone to ensure their success. Because they are deemed so important to their region's economic development, and perhaps more important, because they enjoy the political support of big-city mayors, downtowns benefit from a good deal of public funding. Edge cities may soon be in the same position to receive public largess, if they are not already. What they often lack is a strong partner in government. Most are in suburbs, which do not have a history of lobbying for public funds. Others, especially some big edge cities, lie in several jurisdictions. However, an edge city consciousness does seem to be emerging—evident in part in the conference in Schaumburg, which included several mayors of towns with edge cities. Perhaps the funds for the massive urban redesign of edge cities could be justified as a public good; if so, it would help edge cities make the critical improvements necessary to their continued growth without passing the costs along to businesses, which would then flee to lower-cost locations, often in edgeless cities.

In sum, edge cities face a potentially serious development dilemma. If they grow inward it raises costs and produces congestion; yet their opportunities to grow outward are curtailed by limited developable land and NIMBY opposition. Given their internal and external constraints, it would not be surprising to see edge cities lose considerable ground relative to both edgeless cities and downtowns over the next decade. Perhaps in twenty years or so, bailing out edge cities may be the twenty-first century equivalent of postwar federal urban renewal efforts, hopefully with better results.

Edge Cities: Product of Markets or Planning?

One of Garreau's central claims is that whether you like them or not, edge cities are products of the marketplace. That claim has been more or less accepted by even edge city critics such as Neil Peirce, who argues that we can do more than simply allow the market to determine the shape of our cities.[19] But what if, left to its own, the market does not routinely produce edge cities?

The Phoenix regional plan, in which the now widely accepted criteria for edge cities were first established, did not assume that edge cities

18. BOMA/ULI (1999), p. 20.
19. Peirce (1991).

(what it called urban villages) just happen. The concern in Phoenix was that office development was scattering far beyond a polycentric form. Pheonix's regional planners wanted to promote the growth of multiple large-scale, mixed-use business centers to capture most new office development, leading the region to adopt various land use policies, such as density bonuses, designed to promote urban village growth.[20] Ironically, Garreau's edge city criteria—filtered through Chris Leinberger, one of the Phoenix plan's authors—originated in a planning document that was drafted because the market was not generating edge cities.

It is also interesting that the origin of many of the nation's largest edge cities was in part a secondary effect of decisions made by Galleria developer Gerald Hines. Concerned that downscale versions of his malls would be built next to them and thus cut into their market area, Hines insisted that the land around his Galleria malls be zoned for office/commercial use. During the 1960s and 1970s a zone of office buildings sprang up around Hines's malls, including places such as Post Oak; this accounts for Garreau's observation that large malls anchor office development. It appears that in the case of some glamour gallerias, the very visible hand of an influential developer working through a zoning board replaced Adam Smith's "hidden hand of the marketplace."

Edgeless Cities: The Ultimate Stealth Cities

There appears to be a relationship—although it is impossible to statistically confirm given the limited number of cases in this study—between the higher-than-average share of edgeless city space and the smaller-than-average size of non-CBD buildings.[21] It may be that smaller buildings lend themselves better to widespread diffusion. Smaller building sites are easier to find, the financial risk of building them is much lower than that of building bigger ones, and more people have enough capital to build smaller buildings.[22]

Many edgeless city office buildings adjoin suburban subdivisions; NIMBY resistance may therefore limit the profile and size of these structures.[23] The typical edgeless city office building, which runs in the 50,000- to 60,000-square-foot range and is a couple of floors high, is in about the same size range as what the Urban Land Institute refers to as neighborhood retail centers (NRCs). These centers often sit just outside

20. Phoenix Planning Department (1984).
21. Building size was analyzed for this study, but the data are not presented in the book.
22. The author thanks Tony Downs for suggesting this point.
23. Fulton (1996); McGovern (1994).

subdivisions along the arterial roads that thread through the suburbs, the same location where most edgeless city office buildings can be found. NRCs are to edgeless cities what the glamour galleries are to the biggest edge cities. Most non-CBD office space does not encircle regional malls—it competes for the suburban street with convenience shopping centers. While most suburbanites can tolerate NRCs near their subdivision, anything larger is feared for the traffic it will generate.

Unlike edge cities, edgeless cities are not seen as destinations. They comprise what are essentially strip center office buildings or neighborhood office buildings. However, while the structure may fit within the scale of the neighborhood, its businesses do not necessarily serve the local residents the way those in an NRC do. Some of their employees live nearby, but others are scattered throughout the surrounding area, and most people travel farther from their home to reach an edgeless city office than to go to an NRC. The reason is simple. People have more choice in where to shop than in where to work.[24] The market area for an NRC is therefore smaller than the commuter shed of an edgeless city office. The policy implications of this simple observation will be discussed in more detail in chapter 8.

It is probable that one of the reasons edgeless cities have gained so much office space is that local residents often oppose the continued growth of edge cities. By contrast, edgeless cities have a lower profile, are more diffuse, and generate less local traffic than their counterparts. The country is now full of local horror stories about once livable suburban counties that have been "ruined" by overdevelopment.[25] In the Washington, D.C., region, most residents in the exurban county of Loudoun, Virginia, are not interested in becoming the next Fairfax County, which is home to Tysons Corner.[26] In fact, it is hard to imagine that too many more large edge cities are in formation. Most edge cities will be curbed well short of the space threshold needed to qualify as one.

24. Lang (2000b).

25. To the extent that the first generation of big edge cities sneaked up on suburbanites during the early 1980s, they were stealthy. But by now most suburban residents understand what edge cities are and would greatly prefer that they not be built in their backyards. In short, they will not get fooled again.

26. Fairfax and Loudoun both appear in an analysis of "growth counties," which looks at counties in the top-fifty metropolitan areas that have grown by double digits for each census since 1950 (Lang 2002a). Loudoun is grouped with "new metropolis" counties, which appear at the region's fringe and have been added to the metropolitan area only since 1971. These counties are decidedly less diverse and urban than the older and more established growth counties, such as Fairfax. Lang speculates that part of their development dynamic is driven by a desire not to evolve into counties like Fairfax.

CHAPTER 7

The Many Faces

of Sprawl

*In LA the very pattern of the city is the underlying problem, and the city is
stuck with it. It is stuck with its sprawling low-density, single-family house
monoculture communities . . . .*

—JAMES H. KUNSTLER (1993)

Kunstler's remark on Los Angeles is the standard rap on the region. For
such critics of the American metropolis, Los Angeles's supposed low-
density, sprawling cityscape is Exhibit A in the case for new urbanism.
Yet Los Angeles is among the most densely built metropolitan areas in
the United States. It may sprawl, but not at low density. If Kunstler
wanted to write about low-density sprawl, he should have visited
Atlanta or any of its Southern cousins, such as Charlotte, Birmingham,
Nashville, or Raleigh.

The problem with the word "sprawl" is that it can mean many
things, and too often it is taken to be synonymous with low-density
development. There are many dimensions to sprawl. It relates to everything from density, to land use, to pedestrian orientation. This chapter
considers those multiple dimensions in order to put office sprawl in context. It presents ways to measure the new metropolitan form, beginning
with housing sprawl in the same thirteen metropolitan areas for which
office data were analyzed. Next, an urban density index for the fifty
largest regions in the nation is presented to place these thirteen areas in
the national context, followed by a comparative analysis that looks at
all three spatial measures: office space, housing, and density. Edgeless
cities then are examined in the context of these measures. Finally, the
multiple dimensions of sprawl are looked at together and case examples
are presented.

Measuring Housing Sprawl

A team led by George Galster measured housing sprawl in the same thirteen metropolitan areas considered in this study. Housing data are much easier to work with than office data because, unlike the latter, housing data are collected and disseminated by the federal government. The housing data used in the Galster study are based on files provided to the U.S. Census Bureau by the Environmental Systems Research Institute.[1]

Galster's team looked at what the Census Bureau defines as an "urbanized area": the developed land within a metropolitan area that maintains a density of at least 1,000 people per square mile. The team extended that definition by adding land adjacent to an urbanized area that had at least 250 people per square mile (or about 100 housing units); this slight alteration allowed the team to track the low-density areas that make up the metropolitan fringe. The primary unit of analysis is the same one-mile square grid that MARC used for the office data maps. Galster's team also developed a multidimensional definition of urban sprawl, defining sprawl as follows:

> [A] pattern of land use in a UA [urbanized area] that exhibits low levels of some combination of eight distinct dimensions: density, continuity, concentration, compactness, centrality, nuclearity, diversity, and proximity.[2]

Unfortunately, the Galster team could not find data for two of these eight dimensions: continuity (which gauges leapfrog development) and diversity (which tracks mixed land uses) had to be left out of the study. The Galster study defined the six sprawl dimensions that could be measured as follows:

—*Density:* the average number of residential units per square mile of developable land in an urbanized area

—*Concentration:* the degree to which development is located disproportionately in relatively few square miles of the total urbanized area

—*Compactness:* the degree to which development has been "clustered" to minimize the amount of land in each square mile of developable land occupied by residential or nonresidential space

---

1. The author commissioned this study, based on data from the U.S. Census Bureau (1995), in order to provide a context for the office data. See Galster and others (2001) for a full description of the methodology.

2. Galster and others (2001).

Table 7-1. Urbanized Area Rankings on Sprawl Indicators

Urbanized area	Density	Concen-tration	Compact-ness	Centrality	Nuclearity	Proximity	Total	Rank
New York	1	1	3	1	1	1	8	1
Philadelphia	6	4	2	2	2	9	25	2
Chicago	4	6	4	9	4	3	30	3
Boston	10	2	6	3	3	6	30	3
Los Angeles	2	8	13	8	9	2	42	5
San Francisco	5	3	12	13	5	5	43	6
Houston	11	6	1	4	13	10	45	7
Washington, D.C.	8	9	6	5	8	11	47	8
Dallas	12	4	5	10	12	4	47	8
Denver	7	12	8	6	7	13	53	10
Detroit	9	10	10	11	6	7	53	10
Miami	3	11	8	12	11	12	57	12
Atlanta	13	13	11	7	10	8	62	13

Source: Galster, Hanson, Wolman, Coleman, and Freihage (2001).

—*Centrality:* the degree to which residential or nonresidential development is located close to the CBD of an urbanized area

—*Nuclearity:* the extent to which an urbanized area is characterized by a mononuclear in contrast to a polynuclear pattern of development

—*Proximity:* the degree to which observations of a single land use or different land uses are close to each other in an urbanized area.[3]

Table 7-1 shows the results of the Galster team's analysis. The thirteen metropolitan areas are ranked on all six dimensions of sprawl, with the top rank (1) on each dimension indicating the least amount of sprawl. The rankings are added together to create an overall sprawl score for each metropolitan area—or more accurately here, for its urbanized area.

According to the analysis, of the thirteen urbanized areas in the study New York sprawls the least and Atlanta sprawls the most. The overall housing sprawl scores line up for the most part with the measures of office decentralization. Older regions such as New York, Chicago, and Boston tend to sprawl less, while newer ones, such as Denver, Miami, and Atlanta, tend to sprawl more. But some metropolitan areas run

3. These definitions are fully operationalized in Galster and others (2001).

against this general pattern: Detroit, an older region, is ranked between Denver and Miami, and Los Angeles, a newer region, follows Boston.

The Philadelphia metropolitan area, which has an abundance of edgeless city office space, is the second-least-sprawling region in the Galster team's study. The region is the only one among the thirteen metropolitan areas in this study in which office decentralization does not at least roughly correlate with housing sprawl. However, on one key sprawl dimension, proximity, which measures the extent to which different land uses are adjacent to one another, Philadelphia's office development pattern is reasonably consistent with the findings of Galster's team.

A major finding in the Galster study is the fact that metropolitan density, which some use as a synonym for sprawl, does not fully correlate with the other dimensions of sprawl. For example, Miami is the third-densest urbanized area in the study, but overall it ranks as the second most sprawling. Conversely, Boston has relatively low density, but on other dimensions it sprawls less: overall Boston is the forth-least-sprawling region of the thirteen urbanized areas.

The other dimensions of sprawl shown in table 7-1 also reveal some surprising findings. For instance, Houston registers as the most "compact" region in the study. Recall that compactness measures the degree of "clustering" among housing units—housing can be clustered yet still scattered widely. Apparently, much of Houston's housing clusters into nodes, conserving land in the region. It may be that wetlands prevent housing from diffusing into much of the open space or that open space has been preserved between and within large subdivisions through master planning. Also note that Houston's office space was developed in nodes, often as master-planned projects. However, the "proximity" indicator in table 7-1 suggests that most housing and office nodes are not near one another.

The Miami and Los Angeles metropolitan areas, described as kindred regions in chapter 4, also show some notable parallels in the sprawl rankings. Both places are dense, and their ratings on "concentration," "compactness," "centrality," and "nuclearity" are lower than average for the thirteen areas. In terms of "proximity," however, Miami and Los Angeles differ widely: Los Angeles has high proximity, and Miami has low proximity. Los Angeles is dense, and its different land uses (such as residences, offices, and stores) are located close to one another. Miami also is dense, but its different land uses lie far apart. Nevertheless, Los Angeles's proximate development pattern does not mean that the region is pedestrian friendly. While the region's different land uses are proxi-

mate, its urban design, which features wide boulevards and ample parking, still encourages auto use. New York, the only region in the study
that exceeds Los Angeles in terms of both density and proximity, is much
more likely to have urban environments that accommodate pedestrians.

It is important to remember that the Galster team's analysis measures
overall sprawl within an urbanized area but that it does not indicate the
differences that exist within a region. For example, New York's urbanized area received a low sprawl score, but a big part of that score comes
from New York's dense regional core. What cannot be known from the
data presented here is the extent to which the edges of the New York
metropolitan area sprawl in a way that resembles Atlanta more than the
center of the region.

Metropolitan Density Index

In order to put the thirteen metropolitan areas in the study in a national
context, an index was developed that ranks the fifty most populous
regions in the United States in terms of how dense they are and how
their density has changed from 1982 to 1997. Here density is treated as
both a condition and a process by including static and dynamic measures. The data for the index come from the National Resources Inventory (NRI), compiled by the U.S. Department of Agriculture.[4]

In the past, urban density measures often were derived from inappropriate units of analysis.[5] Some measured density by dividing metropolitan area population by county land area. But land within the outer
reaches of metropolitan counties often is rural, and the density denomi-
nator therefore may be distorted. Consider the eastern counties in
greater Los Angeles, which span miles of open desert to the Colorado
River. Density estimates for the Los Angeles metropolitan area based on
a county-unit calculation drop dramatically because the area includes
deep rural land.

One way to exclude deep rural land from urban density measures is
to base metropolitan density on urbanized area. However, some rural
land within metropolitan counties is developed at nearly "urbanized"
densities, for example, as large-lot subdivisions, and that land should be
included in the built-up part of a metropolitan area. Galster's team
addressed the problem by adding land that had 250 people per square

4. U.S. Department of Agriculture (2001).
5. Gordon and Richardson (1997).

mile to the urbanized area. Another way to estimate almost urbanized rural development is through the NRI data, which report urbanized acreage per county. The inventory includes any land converted from agricultural to urban use regardless of density.[6]

Table 7-2 shows a density index based on NRI data for the fifty most populous metropolitan areas in the United States, excluding San Juan, Puerto Rico.[7] Each score includes two density measures: the first is population density per square acre (using 1997 population data); the second is the percent change in the first measure from 1982 to 1997.[8] Each metropolitan area is ranked on these two measures from 1 to 50, and the two rankings are then combined. The maximum score that a metropolitan area could receive is 100 (most dense); the lowest score is two (least dense). The following are the key findings from table 7-2:

—Almost all of the nation's largest metropolitan areas lost density during the 1980s and 1990s, but three in the West gained density.

—Nashville (density score 5) has the lowest and Los Angeles (density score 95) has the highest density score.

—The South accounts for eight of the ten lowest density scores (Nashville, Richmond, Louisville, Oklahoma City, Charlotte, Greensboro, Memphis, and Raleigh).

—The West accounts for six of the ten highest density scores (Los Angeles, Las Vegas, Phoenix, San Francisco, San Diego, and Sacramento).

—Two of the ten metropolitan areas with the highest density scores are found in the South (Miami and San Antonio).

—None of the twenty-five metropolitan areas with the lowest density scores are found in the West.

—Northeast/Midwest density scores are grouped for the most part in the middle of the index.

Table 7-3 shows the thirteen metropolitan areas considered in this study. While Atlanta ranks the lowest among the group of thirteen on the density index, it ranks fifteenth among the nation's fifty largest regions. Atlanta may have low density for a very large region, but clearly there are places that already are less dense and are losing density faster than Atlanta, and most of these are in the Southeast (except for South Florida). New York and Los Angeles again are the densest metropolitan areas, but New York lost density over the last two decades, while Los Angeles grew denser. Eight of the thirteen metropolitan areas

6. U.S. Department of Agriculture (2001).
7. All of these regions, except Richmond, Virginia, had more than a million residents.
8. The author thanks Rolf Pendall and Karen Danielsen for supplying the NRI data.

Table 7-2. Density Index, Top Fifty U.S. Metropolitan Areas[a]

Top 50 rank	Metropolitan area	State(s)	Census region[b]	Density score	Density (1982)	Density (1997)	Rank (1997)	Percentage change (1982–87)[c]
1	Nashville	TN	South	5	4.14	2.72	3	−34.3
2	Richmond	VA	South	10	3.89	2.82	5	−27.6
3	Louisville	KY, IN	South	14	5.12	3.43	11	−33.0
3	Oklahoma City	OK	South	14	3.93	2.99	7	−23.8
5	Charlotte	NC	South	15	3.02	2.41	1	−20.1
6	Greensboro	NC	South	17	3.44	2.74	4	−20.4
7	Memphis	TN, AR, MS	South	18	5.00	3.50	14	−30.0
7	Pittsburgh	PA	NE/MW	18	5.76	3.72	17	−35.4
9	Raleigh	NC	South	19	3.22	2.66	2	−17.4
10	Cincinnati	OH, KY, IN	NE/MW	28	4.79	3.77	18	−21.2
11	Minneapolis	MN	NE/MW	30	4.96	3.85	21	−22.4
12	Cleveland	OH	NE/MW	33	5.28	4.03	25	−23.7
13	Indianapolis	IN	NE/MW	34	4.24	3.58	16	−15.6
13	Jacksonville	FL	South	34	3.67	3.16	9	−14.0
15	Atlanta	GA	South	38	3.20	2.84	6	−11.4
16	Grand Rapids	MI	NE/MW	39	3.80	3.32	10	−12.5
17	Kansas City	MO, KS	NE/MW	42	4.41	3.78	19	−14.2
17	St. Louis	MO, IL	NE/MW	42	4.59	3.89	23	−15.3
19	Norfolk	VA, NC	South	43	5.21	4.22	28	−19.1
20	Detroit	MI	NE/MW	45	5.26	4.27	29	−18.7
21	Boston	MA, NH	NE/MW	46	7.78	5.65	40	−27.4
21	Milwaukee	WI	NE/MW	46	4.60	3.93	24	−14.7
21	Philadelphia	PA, NJ, DE	NE/MW	46	6.37	5.03	34	−21.1
24	Columbus	OH	NE/MW	46	3.99	3.53	15	−11.5
25	New Orleans	LA	South	50	7.15	5.64	39	−21.1
26	Houston	TX	South	52	3.79	3.47	13	−8.4
27	Rochester	NY	NE/MW	54	5.13	4.41	30	−14.1
28	Tampa	FL	South	55	4.35	3.86	22	−11.3
29	Austin	TX	South	56	2.68	3.12	8	16.2
30	Salt Lake City	UT	West	59	5.79	5.00	33	−13.7
30	West Palm Beach	FL	South	59	3.14	3.47	12	10.5
32	Buffalo	NY	NE/MW	61	6.75	5.74	41	−14.9
33	Hartford	CT	NE/MW	63	4.65	4.16	27	−10.6
33	Orlando	FL	South	63	4.50	4.07	26	−9.7
35	Dallas-Fort Worth	TX	South	64	3.92	3.78	20	−3.5
35	Washington-Baltimore	DC, MD, VA, WV	NE/MW	64	6.31	5.50	37	−12.8
37	Seattle	WA	West	66	5.78	5.10	36	−11.8
38	Denver	CO	West	69	4.91	4.47	31	−9.0
38	Portland	OR, WA	West	69	5.75	5.10	35	−11.3
40	Chicago	IL, IN, WI	NE/MW	71	6.89	6.02	43	−12.7
40	New York	NY, NJ, CT, PA	NE/MW	71	10.04	8.57	50	−14.7
42	San Antonio	TX	South	72	4.89	4.53	32	−7.3
43	Providence	RI, MA	NE/MW	77	6.66	5.93	42	−10.9
44	Sacramento	CA	West	83	5.71	5.55	38	−2.8
45	San Diego	CA	West	87	7.84	7.50	46	−4.3
46	Miami-Fort Lauderdale	FL	South	89	8.25	7.93	47	−3.8
47	San Francisco	CA	West	91	8.28	7.96	48	−3.8
48	Las Vegas	NV, AZ	West	94	4.42	6.67	44	50.9
48	Phoenix	AZ	West	94	5.91	7.20	45	21.8
50	Los Angeles	CA	West	95	8.09	8.31	49	2.7

Source: National Resources Inventory, U.S. Department of Agriculture.

a. Density: number of people per acre, from least (1) to most dense (50).

b. NE: Northeast; MW: Midwest.

c. Percent change in the number of people per acre from 1982 to 1997.

score in the top third of the index, with five among the top-ten regions. Of the thirteen metropolitan areas studied, all but one—Los Angeles—lost density from 1982 to 1997.

Comparing Metropolitan Areas

The data presented show that metropolitan density patterns diverge in different regions. A broader discussion follows of metropolitan density as it manifests itself in the eastern and western parts of the United States and in the wet and dry Sun Belt.

East versus West

The data in tables 7-2 and 7-3 clearly show a distinct difference in metropolitan density in the eastern and western halves of the United States. The difference can be illustrated more fully by comparing case examples. The typology in table 7-4 shows the relationship between population and density changes in three metropolitan areas. Note that no area—East or West—is losing population while maintaining density.

The Wet versus Dry Sun Belt

A key finding that emerges in the NRI density index is the difference between the metropolitan density of the southwestern United States (the dry Sun Belt) and that of the southeastern United States (the wet Sun Belt). The dry Sun Belt, on the measure used here, contains the densest, large metropolitan areas in the nation; the wet Sun Belt contains the least dense areas.[9] Two of the metropolitan areas in the case comparison—Atlanta and Los Angeles—illustrate the differences in development patterns in the wet and dry Sun Belts. Consider the forces that affect urban density in these fast-growing metropolitan areas:

In Atlanta,

—the climate is wet, and those who live in its exurbs can use wells and septic tanks.

—the city is surrounded by land owned for the most part by private parties.

—the terrain is hilly, but it has few severe slopes.

In Los Angeles,

—the climate is dry; most water must be piped from the Colorado River and the Owens Valley.

9. For more details on the reasons for the difference, see Lang (2002b).

Table 7-3. Density Index, Thirteen Metropolitan Areas[a]

Thirteen metropolitan area rank	Top 50 rank	Metropolitan area	State(s)	Census region[b]	Density score	Density (1982)	Density (1997)	Rank (1997)	Percentage change[c] (1982–97)
1	15	Atlanta	GA	South	38	3.20	2.84	6	−11.4
2	20	Detroit	MI	NE/MW	45	5.26	4.27	29	−18.7
3	21	Boston	MA, NH	NE/MW	46	7.78	5.65	40	−27.4
3	21	Philadelphia	PA, NJ, DE	NE/MW	46	6.37	5.03	34	−21.1
5	26	Houston	TX	South	52	3.79	3.47	13	−8.4
6	35	Dallas-Fort Worth	TX	South	64	3.92	3.78	20	−3.5
6	35	Washington-Baltimore	DC, MD, VA, WV	NE/MW	64	6.31	5.50	37	−12.8
8	39	Denver	CO	West	69	4.91	4.47	31	−9.0
9	40	Chicago	IL, IN, WI	NE/MW	71	6.89	6.02	43	−12.7
9	40	New York	NY, NJ, CT, PA	NE/MW	71	10.04	8.57	50	−14.7
11	46	Miami-Fort Lauderdale	FL	South	89	8.25	7.93	47	−3.8
12	47	San Francisco	CA	West	91	8.28	7.96	48	−3.8
13	50	Los Angeles	CA	West	95	8.09	8.31	49	2.7

Source: National Resources Inventory, U.S. Department of Agriculture.

a. Density: the number of people per acre, from least (1) to most dense (13).

b. NE: Northeast; MW: Midwest.

c. Percent change in the number of people per acre from 1982 to 1997.

—the city faces deserts to the east that contain public lands.

—the terrain includes steep mountains that enclose the area on three sides.

The result is that metropolitan Los Angeles has some limits; Atlanta, in contrast, seems limitless. Los Angeles has a relatively sharp edge—the metropolitan area ends in master-planned communities that often contain modest-sized lots, and beyond them lies open desert or mountains. Metropolitan Atlanta has a more diffuse edge. It slowly fades in almost imperceptible increments into a rural hinterland.

The growth of both Los Angeles and Atlanta boomed during the post–World War II years, built on automobiles, interstate highways, FHA mortgages, and tract housing.[10] Superficially they seem the same, but they differ in at least one critical way: Los Angeles's urban space is more than two-and-a-half times as dense as Atlanta's.

According to urban historian Sam Bass Warner, growth patterns throughout the nation are similar at any one point in time because they

10. Fishman (2000).

Table 7-4. Metropolitan Typology[a]

Population	Losing density	Gaining density
Gaining population	Atlanta	Los Angeles
Maintaining population	Detroit	None

a. Based on metropolitan area population and density change from 1982 through 1997.

are determined by the prevailing market "fashions" (for example, archi-tectural styles) and "feasibilities" (for example, transportation technol-ogy.[11] But perhaps Warner's observation holds true only as long as cities also share approximately the same physical environment. In the case of Atlanta and Los Angeles, two places that grew up together but differently, the environmental setting may have proven more crucial than timing.

Atlanta and Los Angeles do exhibit some similarities, and an impor-tant one is that both are auto dependent. However, Atlanta is auto dependent because of its low density, while Los Angeles, despite its high density, remains auto dependent in part because many areas (except on the West Side) lack mixed-use development or an urban design that accommodates pedestrians.

Comparing Metropolitan Spatial Measures

Table 7-5 compares the thirteen metropolitan areas studied on the three spatial measures presented in this book.[12] The first, which measures office sprawl, was discussed in chapter 4. A comparison of the office space in primary downtowns and edgeless cities resulted in four cate-gories for the thirteen metropolitan areas: core-dominated, balanced, dispersed, and edgeless. The housing sprawl index shown in table 7-1 provides a sprawl score, which can be characterized as high, medium, or low. Finally, the density measure shows the rank by density in 1997 of the thirteen metropolitan areas among the largest fifty areas in the nation; their density also can be categorized as high, medium, or low.

Table 7-5 indicates that New York and Chicago are very similar; both are core dominated, and both have low sprawl and high density (or in the case of Chicago, medium-high density). Los Angeles and San Fran-cisco are almost identical. Both score in the medium range in sprawl and in the high range in density, and both have a balanced distribution of

11. Warner (1972).
12. The author thanks Bill Fulton for suggesting this table and analysis.

Table 7-5. Comparison of Spatial Measures, Thirteen Metropolitan Areas[a]

Metropolitan area	Office sprawl typology	Sprawl index	Sprawl score	Density index	Density rank
Atlanta	Dispersed	High	62	Low	6
Boston	Balanced	Low	30	Medium	40
Chicago	Core	Low	30	Medium	43
Dallas	Dispersed	Medium	47	Low	20
Denver	Balanced	High	53	Medium	31
Detroit	Dispersed	High	53	Medium	29
Houston	Dispersed	Medium	45	Low	13
Los Angeles	Balanced	Medium	42	High	49
Miami	Edgeless	High	57	High	47
New York	Core	Low	8	High	50
Philadelphia	Edgeless	Low	25	Medium	34
San Francisco	Balanced	Medium	43	High	48
Washington, D.C.	Balanced	Medium	47	Medium	37

a. Office typology from percentage of office space in primary downtowns and edgeless cities; see table 4-17. Sprawl index from Galster (scores range from "low sprawl" of 8 to "high sprawl" of 62); see table 7-1. Density index from NRI data (scores range from "low density" of 6 to "high density" of 50); see table 7-3. Office typology data from 1999; sprawl index data from 1995; density index data from 1997.

office space. Washington, D.C., and Denver also are similar, as are Dallas and Houston.

Perhaps most interesting is that Atlanta and Detroit are comparable, with the former being a somewhat more sprawling version of the latter. As shown in chapter 5, both also have modest-sized downtowns, surrounded by two or three large non-CBD clusters and lots of edgeless office space. Detroit is a three-star (CBD and two big edge cities) and Atlanta is a four-star metropolis (CBD and three big edge cities).

While similarities in metropolitan area seem logical for New York and Chicago, Los Angeles and San Francisco, Dallas and Houston, and, perhaps stretching a bit, Washington, D.C., and Denver, the fact that Atlanta and Detroit are comparable is a bit odd. The first is the quintessential Sun Belt area, while the second is a Midwestern Rust Belt metropolis. Some metropolitan areas share similarities on some measures but differ significantly on others. Boston and Philadelphia are similar in terms of sprawl and density, but differ significantly in their spatial structure of office space. The same is true of Boston and Chicago. In contrast, Miami and Philadelphia are similar in terms of office space distribution but nothing else.

Comparing Measures: Implications for Edgeless Cities

The metropolitan sprawl and density data show that edgeless cities are situated in different kinds of metropolises—some are in high-sprawl and others in low-sprawl regions. Most are in metropolitan areas that are losing density, but the rate of loss varies tremendously.

In the East, outpost edgeless cities may be better able to gobble up land at the periphery and project a region's commuter shed deeply into rural hinterland. In the West, they would more likely form part of the dense urban fabric. In Los Angeles, edgeless city office space is just another commercial land use on the crowded boulevard. It is edgeless because for the most part it is isolated from other office buildings and so does not form a cluster. In the East, however, edgeless city office space can be the "office in the dell"—the forward bunker of the region and a spearhead of sprawl. Because of that, edgeless cities in general may be a bigger public policy concern in the East than the West. They also happen to be quite prevalent in the East.

Finally, some metropolitan areas have a balanced or dispersed office typology (dispersed being edge city–oriented), as well as medium or low sprawl and high density. In these areas, edgeless city development may not be as big an issue. The metropolitan areas that meet these criteria are Los Angeles, San Francisco, Denver, and Washington, D.C. In such a regional context there is a better opportunity to fit edgeless office space into the urban fabric.

Putting It All Together

The office data and sprawl analysis suggest that a complicated relationship exists between land uses and built density. Some places are dense and have mixed uses; others are dense but do not have them. Still more places are just plain low-density. One way to organize this relationship is on a hierarchical scale, commonly known to researchers as Guttman scaling.[13] This scaling could help critics of sprawl such as Kunstler focus on what aspects of the built environment they find most offensive and on what specifically they seek to improve.

Consider the relationship between high built densities, mixed land uses (including retail and office), and pedestrian friendliness (a measure not presented here that can be inferred for illustrative purposes). These

13. Babbie (1986).

Table 7-6. Density, Land Use, and Pedestrian Orientation in Selected Areas

Place	High density	Mixed-use retail	Pedestrian friendly	Mixed-use office
Back Bay (Boston)	X	X	X	X
Adams Morgan (Washington, D.C.)	X	X	X	
West Side (Los Angeles)	X	X		
Suburban Miami	X			
Suburban Atlanta				

three urban elements are the holy grail of the new urbanist and smart growth crowd. Most of their designs and policy proposals aim to move metropolitan America closer to a world in which all three qualities intersect in one place. Table 7-6 shows their relationship in Boston, Washington, Los Angeles, Miami, and Atlanta.

Compare the relationship of the features listed in table 7-6, starting with the Back Bay of Boston. The Back Bay has it all: housing, shopping, and office employment, all laid out in an atmosphere that is pedestrian friendly (except in the dead of winter). People live, work, and play in the same area. Back Bay is a new urbanist dream. Washington, D.C.'s Adams Morgan neighborhood has all the elements of Back Bay, minus office space.[14] People may have to commute to work by car or public transit, but local trips, such as running out for milk, are done on foot.

Throughout much of Los Angeles's West Side, two of the four conditions also exist.[15] This part of the city is relatively dense, with small-lot single-family homes, modest-sized apartment buildings, and retail stores lining its boulevards. The problem, however, is that the boulevards often are wide, multilane roads that were built for cars, not people. A pedestrian feels overwhelmed by the auto-dominated street. Also, the stores along the boulevards are mini-malls with parking out front; they have lost the classic main street connection with the sidewalk.[16] The structure of L.A.'s streets and stores encourages people to drive, even to pick up a carton of milk, but at least the milk run often is just around the block.

14. The author lived for six years in this neighborhood.
15. The author lived for a year in the West Side of Los Angeles.
16. L.A.'s mini-malls are not the typical suburban variety retail strip. Often they are smaller, but they are packed with ethnic eateries and specialty shops reflecting the region's diverse population.

Miami, as the data show, has a relatively high built density across much of its region. Houses often occupy small lots, and the whole area presses up against the federally mandated Everglades urban growth boundary. But mixed uses are not especially prevalent in South Florida, where subdivisions stand isolated from neighborhood shopping centers. It is indeed very rare for adults to arrive on foot at one of these neighborhood centers; if they do, a neighbor may ask whether their car broke down and they need a lift.

Atlanta, as the data show, lacks any of the crucial urban elements. It has low-density suburbs that for the most part lack mixed uses, and pedestrians are an endangered species. Most of suburban Atlanta is a new urbanist nightmare.[17]

Now consider the public policies that relate to all five places in terms of making them match the goals of smart growth and new urbanism. In Back Bay, the built environment is fine; policymakers there just worry about gentrification. The same is true for Adams Morgan. The West Side of Los Angeles has an urban design problem. Measures might be taken to improve the pedestrian orientation of the street, and some sidewalk cafés could be thrown in for good measure, perhaps by adapting the mini-mall parking lots. Miami is more of a problem. It needs to have retail stores that are better integrated into its subdivisions and an improved streetscape within them. Then there is Atlanta. First you must build more densely, then integrate stores, then focus on the street—or, more likely, start from scratch.

17. Interestingly, the photo of Atlanta's Perimeter Center in chapter 3 shows subdivisions bumped up against this edge city. But a person living and working in an adjacent office must get in a car, loop out on the interstate, and drive several miles to gain access.

CHAPTER 8

Facing the Reality

of the Elusive Metropolis

The existence of edgeless cities challenges policymakers and practitioners who favor more compact regions to rethink some of their planning strategies. New urbanist architects, smart growth advocates, transportation and land use planners, environmentalists, politicians interested in regional social equity, and many others are directing much of their attention to curbing the type of urban sprawl that edgeless cities are part of and may contribute to. This chapter considers the effects of edgeless cities on a host of regional growth issues, and it also explores the market and investment conditions that edgeless cities present. However, it should be noted again that the data analysis and the categories reported in this book are preliminary and will be further refined. It is really too early to make definitive recommendations on how to fix edgeless cities.

Nevertheless, the impulse to fix edgeless cities is so irresistible to planners and designers that the work already has begun. Even though only a preliminary form of the edgeless city research reported in this book was published in fall 2000,[1] several organizations have started to develop plans to improve edgeless cities based on that research. The Lincoln Institute of Land Policy held a meeting in October 2001 entitled "Redesigning the Edgeless City," and the Regional Plan Association of New York is developing a new handbook with the same title.[2] And the

1. Lang (2000c).
2. Lane (2002).

Urban Land Institute (ULI) recently published a book, *Transforming Suburban Business Districts*,[3] based on the typology of suburban office space developed in the preliminary report and a paper presented at New York University that has been posted on the Taub Center's website.[4] Many of the policies and practices suggested in the book focus on ways to increase the density of suburban business districts, mix more uses within them, and make them more pedestrian friendly.

Diverse challenges confront metropolitan America, and there are no one-size-fits-all solutions to them. The same is true for office space in edgeless cities. Does it constitute a problem? It depends on where it is situated, how it relates to the rest of the built environment, and variables such as the structure of local jurisdictions in the region. For example, an edgeless city could spread valuable tax ratables across multiple municipalities, helping local budgets. At the same time, an outpost edgeless city could extend commuter ranges deep into the rural hinterland and eat up open space. Edgeless cities are not all good or all bad. The point is that they have been ignored or overlooked.

General Impacts

Clearly, the relevance to public policy of the findings presented here is so broad that a full exploration would constitute a separate book in its own right. The data can be read and interpreted in many different ways. However, some general impacts are likely to be associated with edgeless cities. Below is a summary of the possible impacts that edgeless city growth *could* have on ten major metropolitan issues. The interpretations offered here certainly are not incontestable. Some of the predicted outcomes are more likely than others. In general, the impacts on the environment, open space, and transportation seem more probable than those related to fiscal matters, employment, and social equity. The analysis does not include quality of life and aesthetic impacts, which are more subjective.

The impacts vary by issue. In some cases, the expansion of edgeless city office space may actually be a desirable goal compared with expansion of space in the other office location categories. In other cases, edgeless city expansion is likely to have a mostly negative impact; that is

3. Booth (2001).

4. The ULI book categorizes non-CBD development as "compact" (secondary downtown), "fragmented" (edge city), and "dispersed" (edgeless city) office space (www. informationcity.org/events/dec13-lang/Edgeless-Cities.htm [October 24, 2002]).

especially true for the environment and transportation. The categories below hardly exhaust the range of possible impacts, but they do represent those that have been at the center of the public policy debate over sprawl.[5] Also, most problems specifically concern outpost edgeless cities, which add to sprawl at the metropolitan edge.

Environment/Land Use

There is a possible link between expansion of outpost edgeless cities and lower-density development, especially in metropolitan areas of the eastern United States. To the extent that urban space sprawls into natural habitat, it increases the scale of environmental impact. On the other hand, there are those who argue that when low-density growth spreads to an area, its effects are not as intense as those of high-density growth.[6] The trade-off is that a region can have a compact but intense environmental impact or a more diffuse but less intense one.

Open Space Preservation

Outpost edgeless city expansion can promote growth at the periphery and thereby consume open space. While the loss of open space at the metropolitan fringe may be partly offset by increased space between developments in built-up areas, such space often consists of smaller private parcels and very little of it is developed as parkland.[7] Again there is a trade-off. A region can build densely, as Portland did in order to preserve nearby access to open space, or it can build the city in the country, as Atlanta has.[8] Curbing outpost edgeless cities promotes the former; expanding them promotes the latter.

Public Transportation

When it comes to opportunities to provide public transportation, most edgeless cities fall far short of even edge cities. One can imagine that a dense, maturing edge city might be well integrated into a bus or even a light-rail system,[9] but edgeless cities—at least outposts and in-betweeners—offer no such prospect. As the percentage of office space in these edgeless city categories rises, the percentage of people who can

5. Burchell and others (1998); Ewing (1994).
6. Gordon and Richardson (1997).
7. Downs (1994).
8. Abbott (1997); Lang and Hornburg (1997).
9. Frank and Pivo (1994).

commute by mass transit drops. In most of these places, even paratransit service, such as private vans, would be difficult.

Private Transportation

As the percentage of regional office space in most edgeless cities (except in-towners) expands, reliance on automobiles to commute to work grows, as does commuting distance. However, some observers point out that while diffusion of office space may add to the length of commutes, it also reduces congestion and increases speed, thereby barely altering commuting time.[10] Edgeless city expansions also may lessen some of the congestion problems around big edge cities.[11]

Job Location

Growth in the percentage of office space that is found in outpost edgeless cities may help draw jobs away from regional cores. If growth of office space in edgeless cities slows relative to that of office space in downtowns and edge cities, it may indicate a reconcentration of jobs in or near regional cores. In contrast, an increase in office locations at the periphery serves to extend commuter sheds deep into the rural hinterland.[12]

Jobs/Housing Balance

The jobs/housing balance may actually improve in many suburbs as in-betweener and in-towner edgeless cities grow because office space may disperse deeper into residential areas. But the reduction of commuting distances, which is the goal of maintaining a jobs/housing balance, may not occur.[13] That paradox results from the fact that a local edgeless city building may not be a local commuter's destination. Given that edgeless cities are not concentrated employment centers or "destinations," it is probable that the people living nearby do not work there. There is, however, a gender-based difference in the probability: studies have shown that the commuter sheds of working mothers often are smaller than those of men.[14] These women are more likely to be employed locally and therefore could benefit from edgeless cities.

10. Gordon and Richardson (1994).
11. Crane (1996).
12. Louv (1985); Lessinger (1987); Lewis (1995).
13. Cervero (1996); Cervero and Gorham (1995).
14. Kasarda and Ting (1996).

Jobs/Spatial Mismatch

The jobs/spatial mismatch hypothesis holds that in the absence of effective fair and affordable housing efforts, growth in suburban employment has put lower-income and minority households that remain in cities at a disadvantage.[15] To the extent that most edgeless city growth occurs far from regional cores, it exacerbates the mismatch. However, edgeless cities also are built in a wide variety of non-CBD locations and may be found outside the "favored quarter" in less affluent suburbs that increasingly are home to lower-income and minority households;[16] the mismatch hypothesis has been criticized for not recognizing this aspect of the new metropolis.[17] Many edgeless cities scatter so widely that they spill into the unfavored three-quarters of a metropolitan area, whereas edge cities for the most part are found in the more affluent suburbs.[18] The expansion of edgeless cities may be one of the reasons why the favored quarter phenomenon does not apply to every region. In this counterintuitive way, edgeless cities may be reducing the jobs/spatial mismatch problem in many metropolitan areas, especially if there has been substantial suburbanization of lower-income households.

Municipal Budgets

Because edgeless cities are distributed so widely, they may help some suburban municipal budgets by adding valuable office space to the local tax base; high-tech research parks in particular can do wonders for municipal budgets.[19] Of course, edgeless cities also may increase traffic and require additional infrastructure. If edgeless cities are built in areas that are less affluent than those where edge cities are built, their presence may improve the distribution of the tax base across a region; however, regional revenue sharing is likely to prove a better method of distributing tax resources among municipalities than having office development sprawl.

Public Costs

Office development has costs as well as benefits. If edgeless cities are built in low-density settings, the costs in roads and other infrastructure

15. Kain (1992).
16. Leinberger (1996).
17. Ihlanfeldt and Sjoquist (1998).
18. Garreau (1991); Leinberger (1996); Orfield (2002).
19. Burchell, Listokin, and Dolphin (1997).

may be higher than if they are concentrated in already built-up areas.[20] Often, the higher costs are borne by all levels of government. Many localities hesitate to charge impact fees to office development because it is such a high ratable. However, some regions—especially the Bay Area, where job growth has so outpaced housing development—are more resistant to new office development.[21]

Fiscal Equity

To the degree that edgeless city growth occurs at the regional fringe, it pulls resources from the regional core. Research has shown that the metropolitan periphery has received far more investment than the center, including the inner ring of suburbs.[22] The entire region pays the public subsidies that are required for outpost edgeless city infrastructure and road projects. If outpost edgeless cities capture a growing share of a region's office development, they will add to existing regional inequalities in public infrastructure expenditures.

Edgeless Cities and Metropolitan Growth Policy

The emergence of edgeless cities is especially important to the policy debate on metropolitan growth. The proposals offered for changing growth patterns so far have not considered the policy implications of a post-polycentric metropolitan form.

Edgeless Cities and Smart Growth

Smart growth advocates prescribe more mixed-use development, especially development that combines job locations and housing;[23] one often-cited reason is the reduced commuting time that results when they are close to each other. Yet regional commuting patterns have grown so complicated that transportation engineers equipped with supercomputers have a hard time figuring them out.[24] As the office data in this study indicate, a significant percentage of jobs have decamped from regional cores, and people increasingly commute from one dispersed location to another.[25] Even the concept of well-defined suburban edge cities seems a

20. Burchell (1997).
21. McGovern (1994).
22. Orfield (1997).
23. Danielsen, Lang, and Fulton (1999).
24. Maher (1992); Lang (2000b).
25. Gordon and Richardson (1997).

bit out of date as some metropolitan areas become increasingly post-polycentric or edgeless.

The main concern for most metropolitan residents is whether jobs, services, friends, and fun can be easily reached from their home.[26] To ensure maximum opportunity in the regional job market, people must be most flexible about where they are willing to work. If the job location is near their home, fine, but if not, many seem willing to make long commutes (the major exception, cited above, being working mothers). In large regions, the likelihood is slim that a job location is very near home or that home and job location both are near mass transit. Developers can build offices and houses together (and in edgeless cities they often are fairly close), but many people will work far from their home if they find a better opportunity elsewhere—and chances are that there will be no public transportation available to make the commute.

Even though the odds of reducing commutes are poor, not all is lost. Most household trips are not commutes; local roads are clogged with people simply taking care of daily tasks, such as picking up their children or dropping off dry cleaning. While the new metropolis presents real challenges for altering commuting patterns, a much better job can be done of mixing neighborhood retail into residential areas to provide some pedestrian access and reduce the number of trips.[27] Certainly there are challenges to enacting such a proposal, such as overcoming NIMBY opposition, changing zoning regulations, and getting mixed-use projects financed.[28] But given the realities of current metropolitan form, it seems like a reasonable first step toward mixing land uses in edgeless cities.

Urban Growth Boundaries—A Sure Way to Slow Outpost Edgeless City Growth?

One way to slow outpost edgeless city growth may be through urban growth boundaries (UGBs), which limit opportunities for low-density growth.[29] UGBs are not without their critics, who see them as potentially distorting land markets and reducing housing affordability.[30] The most famous UGB surrounds Portland, Oregon.[31] Interestingly, Portland

---

26. Fishman (1990).

27. Lang (2000b); Crane (1996).

28. Lang (2000b).

29. For a more detailed definition and a discussion of the public policy issues surrounding UGBs, see Danielsen, Lang, and Fulton (1999).

30. See Fischel (1997); Lang and Hornburg (1997).

31. Abbott (1997).

has one of the largest percentages of CBD office space compared with that of non-CBD space of any region in the country, and that percentage is the highest in the West.[32] Although outpost edgeless cities typically consume a lot of land, edgeless cities also thrive in relatively high-density metropolitan environments, such as Los Angeles. There are regions where, due to either physical or regulatory constraints, edgeless cities per se do not cause sprawl. To the extent that a metropolitan area can rein in the growth on its edge, it dampens the ability of outpost edgeless cities to grow and flourish.

Investment and Market Implications of Edgeless Cities

This book has been written from a social science perspective; its purpose is to describe and measure office development in order to improve knowledge of the new metropolitan form. But its findings also have definite market and investment implications—they are, after all, based on commercial data sources. The analysis does not include such market-sensitive data as rents, vacancy rates, and absorption rates, which are beyond its scope. Yet such data are available, and the analysis eventually can be translated with more precision into market indicators that track real estate performance of rental office space. The most important market and investment dimension of this research is the office development categories. Given the contrast between their office environments, it is very likely that edge cities and edgeless cities experience variations in their market performance.

Commercial real estate firms such as Cushman and Wakefield, CB Richard Ellis, and Grubb and Ellis have delineated some office markets; however, most still are unsystematically derived from traditional categories.[33] The metropolitan submarkets many real estate firms use in their research often reflect local convention and typically mix edge cities and edgeless cities together.

If there is a meaningful distinction between edge cities and edgeless cities, then an analysis of their separate market conditions is advisable. Given that suburban property is now the target of most real estate investment, it makes sense to have better categories to gauge suburban

32. Cushman and Wakefield, *Pacific Northwest: Real Estate Forecast and Review* (1997).
33. Equitable Real Estate Management (1999); Cushman and Wakefield, *Real Estate Forecast and Review,* various cities (1997).

investment opportunities.[34] One useful tool would be an index of large edge cities (or the glamour gallerias, those with more than 10 million square feet of office space and mixed land uses); another would be an edgeless city index to track office environments that fall under edge cities. There is not yet enough information to declare that edge cities of between 5 and 10 million square feet of office space fully constitute a distinct market.

The lack of good empirical information and analytical models has not prevented real estate "experts" from making pronouncements about investment opportunities in suburban office markets, and some of the advice seems to be strongly against investing in edgeless cities. A recent report put out by PricewaterhouseCoopers advises that "fringe suburban office space, away from subcities [edge cities], should be off limits."[35] No statistics on office space performance or absorption are offered to support that assertion.

In time, the analysis of office mapping that ameregis is performing may yield empirically based analytic categories that are consistent around the country; investments then could rationally target one type of office environment over another. Investors also could determine relative performance on rents and space absorption. Eventually, real estate investment trusts (REITs) could emerge that specialize in a particular type of non-CBD office investment—for example, mid-sized suburban clusters that fall below the level of edge cities but have more density than scattered office space does. It may turn out that such places perform better than edge cities because they face less land pressure.

The only current market indicator that separates types of non-CBD office development is the Urban Land Institute's "suburban high-rise and low-rise office rent forecasts."[36] The local real estate industry professionals who contribute to ULI market reports determine the distinction between high-rise and low-rise properties, which means that they are not based on systematic criteria. Of the dozen property categories that ULI tracks (which range from shopping malls to single-family homes), three cover office development. Of those, downtown currently performs best (third among twelve), followed by low-rise suburban space (fourth among twelve) and high-rise suburban space (sixth among twelve).

---

34. Equitable Real Estate Management (1999); ULI (2000).
35. PricewaterhouseCoopers (2002, p. 19).
36. ULI (2000).

The ULI vacancy index very roughly parallels the office categories developed in this study—the high-rise suburban group corresponds to edge cities and the low-rise group to edgeless cities. Based on ULI's current assessment of market conditions, both downtowns and edgeless cities are doing better than edge cities, a finding consistent with the analysis in this book. Ultimately, the market performance of an office space type will translate into the amount of space that is constructed. The ULI index is yet another hint that some edge cities may be heading for trouble.

The Elusive Metropolis: The Twenty-First Century Urban Project

Even though many developers, practitioners, planners, academics, and public officials have focused much of their attention on the problems of cities, the restructuring and reordering of the elusive metropolis is the great project of the twenty-first century. In the nineteenth century, Americans created a vast, coast-to-coast network of cities. By 1900, the core of every major American region, except Las Vegas, was established.[37] During the twentieth century, especially in the post–World War II years, growth spread from the urban cores, giving us our now vast metropolitan areas.

The elusive metropolis seems to keep evolving. To some, it represents a radical departure from traditional city building; to others, it is a continuation of a metropolitan decentralizing process that dates back to the mid-nineteenth century. Either way, designing public policy for the elusive metropolis will not be easy, in part because America's metropolitan areas differ substantially from one another in terms of density, form, environment, and mix of land uses. Policymakers need to understand and work with those differences, because no one model or set of practices can be universally applied to all metropolitan areas. It is hoped that this book will shed some light on how the elusive metropolis is structured.

37. Warner (1972).

Data Sources

Office market statistics are not collected by government agencies but by a variety of real estate brokers, consulting firms, realty and building associations, and office guide publishers.[1] Given the diversity of sources, with their correspondingly varied focuses and interests, no uniform guidelines exist for determining even basic attributes of office markets, such as total size. In fact, there is not even general agreement on what should be categorized as an office building. Therefore any compilation of office statistics must to some extent be customized and data selected on the basis of their relevance to the task at hand.

The major source for office data in this study is *Black's Guide to Office Leasing*, a directory of office space published by a company based in Gaithersburg, Maryland. Data from Cushman and Wakefield, a national commercial realtor, also were used. *Black's Guide* and Cushman and Wakefield's data were folded into a common online data source, Reality IQ, which is now out of business. Data for the maps came from CB Richard Ellis and were compiled by the Metropolitan Area Research Corporation in Minneapolis.

Black's Guide Office Data

At the time this study began, *Black's Guide* was the only national source of office data that, because it lists buildings by address, allowed

1. ULI (1999).

researchers to use any geographic unit of analysis they choose. *Black's Guide* lists multi-tenant rental office buildings of 15,000 square feet or more that are identified as existing, under construction, or proposed. Inventory data, which determine total market size, include buildings under construction at the time of the survey but not those proposed, even if a starting date is given. *Black's Guide* surveys even the smallest suburban office markets, making it possible to compare data across regions. Buildings are listed in the publication at no cost to owners or developers, and the guide is distributed free to companies and institutions involved in office leasing. *Black's Guide*'s primary source of revenue is display advertising.

Cushman and Wakefield's Office Data

Cushman and Wakefield's survey of office buildings is based on a two-tier categorization of the market that distinguishes between class A space, the primary market, and class B space, the secondary market. Class A buildings generally have 200,000 or more rentable square feet, are professionally managed, are located in prime locations, are finished with superior materials (such as marble in lobbies), and command higher rents. Class B offices are of any size, even as small as 15,000 square feet. Further, they are not located in prime areas and charge moderate rents. Cushman and Wakefield surveys both class A and B space; however, because its research focuses on the higher end of the market, class A space is overrepresented in its reports.

Like *Black's Guide,* Cushman and Wakefield surveys only multi-tenanted offices. Inventory calculations also exclude owner-occupied buildings, government and medical facilities, and proposed projects. Buildings under construction are included if they have a certificate of occupancy as of November 15 of the year they are reported. Owner-occupied properties can be included in both *Black's Guide* and Cushman and Wakefield's survey if they are partially leased out to other companies. In such instances, the entire building, not just the leased portion, is factored into the rental office inventory.

Only rental building data were used in this study because there are no comprehensive office reports that survey owner-occupied structures. The commercial real estate firms that follow the office market are concerned primarily with brokering leases, so they have little reason to follow owner-occupied inventory. Reports that survey all buildings, including exclusively owner-occupied ones, show rental structures to compose a much larger share of the total market and to be constructed at a faster rate.[2] Further, owner-occupied inventory can decline as companies that once used their entire building offer even a small amount of space for lease. It therefore can be assumed that the office data reported in this study constitute the majority of gross space in metropolitan America. However, on the individual market level there are select cases in which owner-occupied structures do account for a substantial proportion of total office space. It also is important to consider that owner-occupied office space is not located in the same pattern as rental space. Owner-occupied buildings, especially those of large firms, tend to be more scattered and isolated because their owners can provide many amenities on site and therefore need not locate in clusters with like businesses. Many large, owner-occupied corporate campuses sit at the edge of a region, where land is plentiful.

CB Richard Ellis Office Data

The data for the maps come from CB Richard Ellis, a national real estate firm that tracks rental office space. The company categorizes four classes of office space: A, B, C, and D. Class A space is prime office space that is professionally managed and commands high rents. B space is a slightly scaled down version of A space, with slightly lower rents. C space is found in smaller buildings that are not in prime locations. D space is a diverse category that captures warehouse conversions and flex-office space.

In some markets, such as San Francisco, CB Richard Ellis gives more coverage to class D space than in places such as Chicago, which accounts for why the Bay Area's total office inventory exceeds Chicago's in its survey. In comparison, both *Black's Guide* and Cushman and Wakefield's survey show Chicago's metropolitan area exceeding San Francisco's. Many of the city of San Francisco's high-tech enterprises are housed in class C and D space, which CB Richard Ellis shows in abundance in the CBD.

Because CB Richard Ellis geocodes its data and makes the data available electronically, its office inventory was used for mapping. In the near future, all of the commercial data on office location will be geocoded and available online, which will greatly enhance future research efforts on metropolitan development.

2. ULI (1999).

Office Markets and Submarkets

Commercial real estate firms such as Cushman and Wakefield, CB Richard Ellis, and Grubb and Ellis have delineated some office markets; however, most are still unsystematically derived from traditional categories. The metropolitan submarkets many real estate firms use in their research often reflect local convention and typically mix edge cities and edgeless cities together.

The only published market indicator that separates types of non-CBD office development is the Urban Land Institute's "suburban high-rise and low-rise office rent forecasts."[3] The local real estate industry professionals who contribute to ULI's market reports determine the distinction between high-rise and low-rise buildings, which means that it is not based on systematic criteria. Of the dozen property categories that ULI tracks (which range from shopping malls to single-family homes), three cover office development. The ULI office vacancy index very roughly parallels the office categories developed in this study—the high-rise suburban category corresponds to edge cities and the low-rise category to edgeless cities.

Many office data sources report their inventory by what is typically referred to as submarkets, which vary tremendously by data source.[4] Consensus usually exists on what office space constitutes the CBD submarket, but beyond that there is little agreement on how many submarkets exist and where they are. Often there is little consistency among different metropolitan reports from the same data source. For example, Cushman and Wakefield lists each county in northern New Jersey as an office submarket. In Houston, however, Cushman and Wakefield uses many smaller, submunicipal geographic units to define submarkets. Some non-CBD submarkets are recognizable to those who follow the nation's major edge cities. For instance, Tysons Corner is a submarket, as is Post Oak. The problem is that most other non-CBD submarkets are really the creation of real estate firms that need to establish data reporting categories and have to draw the line somewhere.[5] Large patches of metropolitan America turn up as non-CBD office submarkets. Such places are where one finds edgeless cities.

3. ULI (2000).
4. ULI (1999).
5. ULI (2000).

Submarkets were ruled out as potential research units in this study because they lack any analytical basis and vary considerably from region to region. However, where submarkets are located and how they are configured reflects the expert opinions of real estate professionals who study office markets, and their opinions should not be dismissed. Submarkets therefore are used to inform and shape the analytically derived categories in this study's data analysis.

Research Methods

Secondary analysis of existing data was the main research method used in the study reported in this book. The data used were from commercial sources, making them expensive and difficult to work with. Given the nature of the study and the research questions addressed, there was simply no way around the hard reality that data collection would consume considerable time and resources.

Black's Guide was selected as the primary data source because it lists and then maps all of its data. Most important, the data are listed in disaggregated form, enabling construction of a metropolitan office geography specific to the theory and methods developed for this study. Reassembling *Black's Guide* data was painstaking because the data were not available in electronic form and so had to be manually entered into thirteen spreadsheets, one for each of the metropolitan areas studied.

The building entries in *Black's Guide* contain a wealth of information on everything from parking to leasing terms. The information selected for this study included such key variables as building size, age, and location. Other data were considered but subsequently rejected because of inconsistent reporting. For example, the figures for parking space relative to building square footage could have been useful because they show the extent to which an office development accommodates automobiles, but data of this type were spotty.

Historical Analysis

Black's Guide data were gathered only for 1999. Before the mid-1990s, the guide surveyed just a handful of major markets, so it would have been impossible to gather data for all the cities in the study at different time intervals. For example, there was no *Black's Guide* for Detroit or Denver in 1980 that listed then-current office inventory. However, *Black's Guide* does include "year built" for virtually every building in its survey, allowing for historical analysis of the existing inventory. From the year a particular building was completed, the age of current office space can be determined.

It cannot be known from current inventory what the exact office space figure was for any one year because buildings that existed then may have subsequently cycled out of the current inventory. That is not really a problem for most suburban office markets because they are so new that few buildings have fallen out of use. By contrast, much of the urban stock that was present in 1970 or 1980 has by now turned over. It also is safe to assume that, given the life span of office buildings, little of the space added in the last two decades of the twentieth century has dropped from the inventory. There was substantial overbuilding, especially in Sun Belt markets during the 1980s, but most of that space has since been occupied.[1] In sum, almost all of the buildings added during the period analyzed here remain occupied as office space. While there are limits to what historical analysis of current inventory allows, it still provides important information about building trends and evolving metropolitan growth patterns.

Another term for this type of analysis is "cohort study" (or "panel study"); such analysis examines populations as they change over time. In this case the study is really a reverse cohort, because the data start at an endpoint and look back. To be included in the study, a building must have existed in 1999. An assessment then was made as to when it was built. For example, if a building existed in 1999 and was built in 1985, it was counted in the 1989 inventory. There are of course buildings that existed in 1989 that no longer exist and so cannot be counted because there is no way to track them.

1. ULI (1996).

Data Quality Control

The data in spreadsheets were entered in the order that they appeared in *Black's Guide*. Because such a procedure can result in errors, several quality control steps were taken. The first was to check the office space inventory totals from the spreadsheet against those reported in *Black's Guide*. In some cases there were substantial discrepancies between the two figures. In the process of checking the spreadsheets, it was determined that at times the *Black's* totals were wrong. In follow-up conversations with *Black's Guide*, I was informed that the error was likely to have occurred at their end because the totals were not "electronically derived."

Another quality control measure involved randomly sampling the spreadsheet entries and checking them against the data in *Black's Guide*; this process showed that the most common type of error was made in recording office space. All space entries then were rechecked. Thus the office inventories were entered, sampled for error, and reconfirmed. Any procedure that entails a massive transfer of data involving thousands of entries is bound to include some errors. However, with careful entry and systematic quality control, the errors hopefully have been kept to a minimum.

Given the errors found in the *Black's Guide* space totals, there was some concern that other data in the guide contained errors. It was especially important that the individual entries contain accurate information. In order to determine their accuracy, I checked the information in the *Black's Guide* listings with the building managers of twenty-five buildings; while not a scientific sample, they provided at least a check on the correctness of the data. Starting with the building that I was working in during 1999, I found that the entries were highly accurate. On reflection, I was able to reconcile *Black's Guide* accuracy in one area with its inaccuracy in another. Its main business is to provide commercial real estate brokers with a guide to a region's rental office space; the accuracy of data such as the location and size of a specific office are therefore quite important to its reputation. However, information such as total inventory is less critical because *Black's Guide* is not conducting research on office markets. Thus, *Black's Guide* is highly accurate in the area that is most important for the purposes of this study—the individual entry. Combining Black's detailed listing with quality-controlled data entry yielded the most comprehensive and accurate office inventory database possible in 1999.

Use of Median Measures

In some parts of the data analysis, medians were calculated even though the number of cases was very small. In those instances, averages are the preferred summary calculation. However, New York, in particular Manhattan, is so large relative to the rest of the nation's office stock that it would have greatly distorted average calculations. Therefore medians were sometimes used instead.

Downtown and Edge Cities:

Comparison of the Lang

and Garreau Categories

Metropolitan area	Lang	Garreau
Atlanta	**Downtown**	**Downtown**
	Atlanta	Atlanta
	Buckhead	**Edge city**
	Edge city	Buckhead
	Cumberland/Galleria	Cumberland Mall
	Perimeter Center	Gwinnett Place Mall
		Midtown
		Perimeter Center
Boston	**Downtown**	**Downtown**
	Boston	Boston
	Cambridge	**Edge city**
	Edge city	Alewife T Station in Cambridge
	Burlington/Woburn	Attleboro/Mansfield/Foxboro
	Framingham/Natick	Burlington Mall
	Quincy/Braintree	East Cambridge/Kendall Square
	Waltham/Newton	Framingham
		I-495 at Mass. Turnpike
		Nashua
		Peabody/Danvers
		Route 128 at Mass. Turnpike
		Quincy

Metropolitan area	Lang	Garreau
Chicago	**Downtown** Chicago **Edge city** Chicago O'Hare Deerfield/Northbrook Lombard Naperville Oakbrook Schaumburg	**Downtown** Chicago **Edge city** Chicago O'Hare Edens Expressway Lombard Naperville Oakbrook Schaumburg
Dallas	**Downtown** Dallas Fort Worth **Edge city** Far North Dallas Las Colinas LBJ Corridor Oaklawn (Midtown) Plano/Richardson Stemmons Freeway	**Downtown** Dallas Fort Worth **Edge city** Galleria/LBJ Freeway North Central Expressway Plano Stemmons Freeway Turtle Creek/Oak Lawn
Denver	**Downtown** Boulder Denver **Edge city** Cherry Creek Denver Technology Center Greenwood Plaza Inverness/Centennial Airport	**Downtown** Denver **Edge city** Cherry Creek Denver Technology Center
Detroit	**Downtown** Detroit **Edge city** Southfield Troy	**Downtown** Detroit **Edge city** Auburn Hills Dearborn/Fairlane Village Farmington Hills/Livonia/Novi Southfield/Northland Mall Southfield/Prudential Town Center Troy

Metropolitan area	Lang	Garreau
Houston	**Downtown** Houston **Edge city** Clearlake Greenspoint Greenway Plaza Katy Freeway Post Oak Westchase	**Downtown** Houston **Edge city** Clearlake/NASA FM 1960 Galleria/Post Oak Greenspoint Greenway Plaza Northwest Freeway Sharpstown Mall/Highway 59 Texas Medical Center Westheimer/Westchase West Houston Energy Cooridor
Los Angeles	**Downtown** Beverly Hills Glendale Long Beach Los Angeles Pasadena Santa Monica Mid Wilshire **Edge city** Costa Mesa/Irvine/Newport Santa Ana Sherman Oaks South Bay/LAX West Los Angeles Woodland Hills	**Downtown** Long Beach Los Angeles **Edge city** Beverly Hills/Century City Burbank/North Hollywood Calbasas/101 Freeway Culver City/Marina Del Ray Encino/Sherman Oaks Glendale Irvine Spectrum I-5 South Orange County Irwindale/Covina LAX/El Segundo Mid-Wilshire Newport Beach/Fashion Island North Orange County/Fullerton Pasadena Ontario/Rancho Cucamonga Riverside San Bernardino Santa Ana Freeway/Anaheim Santa Ana Freeway/Santa Ana Santa Monica South Coast Metroplex/Irvine Thousand Oaks/West Lake Village Universal City Valencia Ventura/Coastal Plain Warner Center/Woodland Hills

Metropolitan area	Lang	Garreau
Los Angeles		West Hollywood
		West Los Angeles
		Westminster/Huntington Beach

Miami	**Downtown**	**Downtown**
	Fort Lauderdale	Fort Lauderdale
	Miami	Miami
	Edge city	**Edge city**
	Boca Raton	Boca Raton
	Miami Airport	Coral Gables
		Cypress Creek
		Miami Airport

New York	**Downtown**	**Downtown**
	Manhattan	Newark
	Brooklyn	New York/Downtown
	Jersey City	New York/Midtown
	Newark	Trenton
	New Haven	**Edge city**
	Stamford	Fort Lee
	White Plains	Garden City/Mitchell Field
	Edge city	Great Neck/Lake Success
	Garden City	Greenwich
	Franklin/Piscataway	I-80/287 Parsippany/Fairfield
	Lake Success	I-287/78 Bridgewater Mall
	Melville	Mahwah
	Morristown	Meadowlands
	Parsippany	Morristown
		Paramus
		Princeton/Route 1
		Route 110/Melville
		Stamford
		Tarrytown
		White Plains/Purchase
		Woodbridge/Metropark

Philadelphia	**Downtown**	**Downtown**
	Philadelphia	Philadelphia
	Wilmington	Wilmington
	Edge city	**Edge city**
	King of Prussia	Cherry Hill
	Malvern/Paoli/Wayne	Christiana Mall
		King of Prussia/Route 202
		Malvern/Paoli/Wayne

Metropolitan area	Lang	Garreau
San Francisco	**Downtown** Oakland San Francisco San Jose **Edge city** North San Jose Pleasanton San Ramon Walnut Creek	**Downtown** San Francisco Oakland **Edge city** Airport/San Mateo Berkeley Bishop Ranch Concord Dublin/Pleasanton Menlo Park/Stanford Palo Alto/Sunnyvale Pleasant Hills Redwood City San Jose San Rafael Santa Clara Walnut Creek
Washington, D.C.	**Downtown** Alexandria Arlington–Rosslyn/Court House Arlington–Ballston/Clarendon Bethesda Silver Spring Washington **Edge city** Greenbelt Chantilly/Dulles Crystal City Fairfax Center Reston Rockville/North Bethesda Shady Grove Tysons Corner	**Downtown** Washington **Edge city** Alexandria Bethesda/Chevy Chase Crystal City Dulles-Route 28 Eisenhower Valley Fairfax Center I-270 Gaithersburg/Germantown I-270 Rockville I-270 Shady Grove I-395 Area Lanham/Landover Laurel/I-95 Merrifield Reston/Herndon Rosslyn/Ballston Corridor Silver Spring Tysons Corner

References

Abbott, Carl. 1990. "Southwestern Cityscapes: Approaches to an American Urban Environment." In *Essays on Sunbelt Cities and Recent Urban America*, edited by Raymond A Mohl and others, 59–86. College Station, Tex.: Texas A&M University Press.

———. 1991. "To Boldly Go Where No Data Have Gone Before." *Journal of Urban History* 19 (3): 139–45.

———. 1997. "Portland: Where City and Suburbs Talk to Each Other—and Often Agree." *Housing Policy Debate* 8 (1): 11–51.

Alonso, William. 1960. "A Theory of Urban Land Markets." *Regional Science Association Journal* 6: 149–58.

Babbie, Earl. 1986. *The Practice of Social Research*. Belmont, Calif.: Wadsworth.

Baerwald, Thomas. 1978. "Emergence of A New 'Downtown.'" *Geographical Review* 68 (3): 309–18.

———. 1982. "Land Use Change in Suburban Clusters and Corridors." *Transportation Research Record* 861: 7–12.

———. 1983. "Major Diversified Centers in Midwestern Metropolises." Paper presented to the West Lakes Division of the Association of American Geographers.

Baldassare, Mark. 1986. *Trouble in Paradise: The Suburban Transformation of America*. Columbia University Press.

Baldassare, Mark, and C. Katz. 1987. "Disurbia Emerges as the Successor to Suburbia." *Newsday* (August 14): p. 1.

Barnett, Jonathan. 1992. "Accidental Cities: The Deadly Grip of Outmoded Zoning." *Architectural Record* 180 (2): 94–101.

Bateman, Michael. 1985. *Office Development: A Geographical Analysis*. St. Martin's Press.

Beauregard, Robert A. 1995. "Edge Cities: Peripheralizing the Center." *Urban Geography* 16 (8): 708–21.

Black's Guide. 1999. *Black's Guide to Office Leasing: Atlanta Office Space Market*. Gaithersburg, Md.: Black's Guide Publishing.

———. 1999. *Black's Guide to Office Leasing: Boston Office Space Market*. Gaithersburg, Md.: Black's Guide Publishing.

———. 1999. *Black's Guide to Office Leasing: Chicago Office Space Market*. Gaithersburg, Md.: Black's Guide Publishing.

———. 1999. *Black's Guide to Office Leasing: Connecticut/New York Suburbs Office Space Market*. Gaithersburg, Md.: Black's Guide Publishing.

———. 1999. *Black's Guide to Office Leasing: Dallas/Fort Worth Office Space Market*. Gaithersburg, Md.: Black's Guide Publishing.

———. 1999. *Black's Guide to Office Leasing: Denver Office Space Market*. Gaithersburg, Md.: Black's Guide Publishing.

———. 1999. *Black's Guide to Office Leasing: Detroit Office Space Market*. Gaithersburg, Md.: Black's Guide Publishing.

———. 1999. *Black's Guide to Office Leasing: Houston Office Space Market*. Gaithersburg, Md.: Black's Guide Publishing.

———. 1999. *Black's Guide to Office Leasing: Los Angeles/Orange County Office Space Market*. Gaithersburg, Md.: Black's Guide Publishing.

———. 1999. *Black's Guide to Office Leasing: New Jersey Office Space Market*. Gaithersburg, Md.: Black's Guide Publishing.

———. 1999. *Black's Guide to Office Leasing: Philadelphia Office Space Market*. Gaithersburg, Md.: Black's Guide Publishing.

———. 1999. *Black's Guide to Office Leasing: San Francisco Office Space Market*. Gaithersburg, Md.: Black's Guide Publishing.

———. 1999. *Black's Guide to Office Leasing: South Florida Office Space Market*. Gaithersburg, Md.: Black's Guide Publishing.

———. 1999. *Black's Guide to Office Leasing: Washington, D.C. Metro Area Office Space Market*. Gaithersburg, Md.: Black's Guide Publishing.

BOMA/ULI. 1999. *What Office Tenants Want: Office Tenant Survey Report*. Washington: Building Owners and Managers Association/Urban Land Institute.

Booth, Geoffrey. 2001. *Transforming Suburban Business Districts*. Washington. Urban Land Institute.

Bourchert, James. 1996. "Residential City Suburbs: The Emergence of a New Suburban Type, 1880–1930." *Journal of Urban History* 22 (3): 283–307.

Breckenfeld, Gurney. 1972. "'Downtown' Has Fled to the Suburbs." *Fortune* (October): 80–87, 158, 162.

Brekhus, Wayne. 1998. "A Sociology of the Unmarked: Redirecting Our Focus." *Sociological Theory* 16 (1): 1–40.

Brookings Institution. 1999. "A Region Divided: The State of Growth in Greater Washington, D.C." Center on Urban and Metropolitan Policy.

Brown, Joeseph E., and Michael E. Hickok. 1990. "Beyond Gridlock: Looking for the New Suburban City." *Development* (July/August):17–20.

Bruegmann, Robert. 1995. "The American City: Urban Aberration or Glimpse of the Future?" In *Preparing for the Urban Future: Global Pressures and Local Forces*, edited by Michael A. Cohen and others, 336–67. Washington: Woodrow Wilson Center Press.

Bruegmann, Robert, and Tim Davis. 1992. "New Centers on the Periphery." *Center: A Journal for Architecture in America* 7 (1): 25–43.

Burchell, Robert W. 1997. *South Carolina Infrastructure Study: Projections of Statewide Infrastructure Costs 1995–2015*. Rutgers University, Center for Urban Policy Research.

Burchell, Robert W., David Listokin, and William R. Dolphin. 1997. *The Development Impact Assessment Handbook*. Washington: Urban Land Institute.

Burchell, Robert, and others. 1998. *The Costs of Sprawl—Revisited*. Washington: National Academy Press.

Bureau of Labor Statistics. 1998. *The Employment Situation: September 1998*. U.S. Department of Labor.

Burgess, Ernest W. 1925. *Urban Community: Selected Papers from the Proceedings of the American Sociological Society*. University of Chicago Press.

Cervero, Robert. 1986. "Unlocking Suburban Gridlock." *Journal of the American Planning Association* 52 (4): 389–406.

———. 1989. *America's Suburban Center: The Land Use Transportation Link*. Boston: Unwin.

Cervero, Robert, and Robert Gorham. 1995. "Commuting in Transit versus Automobile Neighborhoods." *Journal of the American Planning Association* 61 (2): 210–25.

Church, George. 1987. "The Boom Towns." *Time* (June 15): 14–17.

Clarke, Paul Walker. 1992. "Review of *Edge City: Life on the New Frontier*." *Design Book Review* 26 (3): 12–17.

Columbia University. 1992. "Cities on the Edge: New American Dream or Post-Industrial Nightmare?" Conference held in New York, April 30.

Congress for the New Urbanism (CNU). 2000. *Charter of the New Urbanism*. McGraw-Hill.

Crane, Randall. 1996. "Cars and Drivers in the New Suburb: Linking Access to Travel in Neo-Traditional Planning." *Journal of the American Planning Association* 62 (1): 51–65.

Cushman & Wakefield, Inc. 1997. *Atlanta: Real Estate Forecast & Review*. New York.

———. 1997. *Dallas: Real Estate Forecast & Review*. New York.

————. 1997. *Denver: Real Estate Forecast & Review.* New York.

————. 1997. *Florida: Real Estate Forecast & Review.* New York.

————. 1997. *Houston: Real Estate Forecast & Review.* New York.

————. 1997. *Metropolitan Washington, D.C.: Real Estate Forecast & Review.* New York.

————. 1997. *Midwest: Real Estate Forecast & Review.* New York.

————. 1997. *New England: Real Estate Forecast & Review.* New York.

————. 1997. *New York Area: Real Estate Forecast & Review.* New York.

————. 1997. *Northern California: Real Estate Forecast & Review.* New York.

————. 1997. *Pacific Northwest: Real Estate Forecast & Review.* New York.

————. 1997. *Philadelphia: Real Estate Forecast & Review.* New York.

————. 1997. *Phoenix: Real Estate Forecast & Review.* New York.

————. 1997. *Southern California: Real Estate Forecast & Review.* New York.

————. 1989. *Focus on Marketrends.* New York.

Daniels, Peter W. 1985. *Services Industries: A Geographical Appraisal.* New York: Methuen.

————. 1991. "Producer Services and the Development of the Space Economy." In *The Changing Geography of Advanced Producer Services*, edited by Peter W. Daniels. London: Belhaven Press.

Danielsen, Karen A., and Robert E. Lang. 1998. "The Case for Higher-Density Housing: A Key to Smart Growth?" In *ULI in the Future*, edited by Gayle Berens and Dean Schwanke, 20–27. Washington: Urban Land Institute

Danielsen, Karen A., Robert Lang, and William Fulton. 1999. "Retracting Suburbia: Smart Growth and the Future of Housing." *Housing Policy Debate* 10 (3): 513–40.

Delany, Charles J. 1993. Review of *Edge City: Life on the New Frontier. Journal of Real Estate Literature* 1 (1): 83–85.

Ding, Chengri, and Richard D. Bingham. 2000. "Beyond Edge Cities: Job Decentralization and Urban Sprawl." *Urban Affairs Review* 35 (6): 837–55.

Doherty, James C. 1984. *Growth Management in Countrified Cities.* Alexandria, Va.: Vert Million Press.

Downs, Anthony. 1994. *New Visions for Metropolitan America.* Brookings Institution Press.

Erickson, Rodney A. 1983. "The Evolution of the Suburban Office Space Economy." *Urban Geography* 4(1): 95–121.

————. 1985. "Multinucleation in Metropolitan Economies." *Annals of the Association of American Geographers* 76 (3): 331–46.

Erickson, Rodney A., and Marylynn Gentry. 1985. "Suburban Nucleations." *Geographical Review* 75 (1):19–31.

Equitable Real Estate Investment Management. 1999. *Emerging Trends in Real Estate: 1999.* Chicago: Real Estate Research Corporation.

Ewing, Reid. 1994. "Characteristics, Causes, and Effects of Sprawl: A Literature Review." *Environmental and Urban Issues* (Winter): 1–15.

————. 1995. "Beyond Density, Mode Choice, and Single-Purpose Trips." *Transportation Quarterly* 49 (4): 15–24.

Fischel, William A. 1997. "Comment on Carl Abbott's 'The Portland Region: Where City and Suburbs Talk to Each Other—and Often Agree.'" *Housing Policy Debate* 8 (1): 65–73.

Fischer, Claude. 1975. "Toward a Subcultural Theory of Urbanism." *American Journal of Sociology* 80 (6): 1319–41.

Fishman, Robert. 1987. *Bourgeois Utopias: The Rise and Fall of Suburbia.* New York: Basic Books.

————. 1990. "America's New City: Megalopolis Unbound." *Wilson Quarterly* 14 (1): 24–45.

————. (2000). "The American Metropolis at Century's End: Past and Future Influences." *Housing Policy Debate* 11(1): 199–213.

Florida, Richard. 2002. *The Rise of the Creative Class and How It's Transforming Work, Leisure, Community, and Everyday Life.* New York: Basic Books.

Frank, L. D., and Gary Pivo. 1994. *The Relationship between Land Use and Travel Behavior in the Puget Sound Region.* WA-RD351.1. Washington State Department of Transportation.

French, Steven P., Lawrence D. Frank, and William Bachman. 2000. "Land Use Patterns in the Atlanta Metropolitan Region." Paper presented at the Association of Collegiate Schools of Planning Conference, Atlanta, November 2.

Fulton, William. 1986. "The Once and Future Suburbs." *Planning* 52 (7): 13–17.

————. 1996. "Are Edge Cities Losing Their Edge?" *Planning* 60 (5): 4–7.

————. 1997. *The Reluctant Metropolis: The Politics of Urban Growth in Los Angeles.* Berkeley, Calif.: Solano Press Books.

Galster, George, and others. 2001. "Wrestling Sprawl to the Ground: Defining and Measuring an Elusive Concept." *Housing Policy Debate* 12 (4): 681–717.

Garreau, Joel. 1991. *Edge City: Life on the New Frontier.* Doubleday.

Gillham, Oliver. 2002. *The Limitless City: A Primer on the Urban Sprawl Debate.* Washington: Island Press.

Glaeser, Edward L. 1994. "Cities, Information, and Economic Growth." *Cityscape* 1(1): 9–47.

Goldberger, Paul. 1987. "When Suburban Sprawl Meets Upward Mobility." *New York Times* (July 26): sec. 2, pp. 1, 30.

Gordon, Peter, and Harry W. Richardson. 1996. "Beyond Polycentricity: The Dispersed Metropolis, Los Angeles, 1970–1990." *Journal of the American Planning Association* 62: 285–89.

————. 1997. "Are Compact Cities a Desirable Planning Goal?" *Journal of the American Planning Association* 63 (1): 95–106.

Hall, Peter. 1998. *Globalization and World Cities.* London: Allen & Unwin.

————. 1982. *Urban and Regional Planning.* London: Allen & Unwin.

Harris, Chauncy D., and Edward L. Ulman. 1945. "The Nature of Cities." *Annals of the American Acadamy of Political and Social Science* 242: 7–17.

Hartshorn, Truman A., and Peter Muller. 1986. *Suburban Business Centers: Employment Implications*. Washington, D.C.: Association of American Geographers.

———. 1989. "Suburban Downtowns and the Transformation of Metropolitan Atlanta's Business Landscape." *Urban Geography* 10: 375–379.

Herbers, John. 1986. *The New Heartland: America's Flight beyond the Suburbs and How It Is Changing Our Future*. New York: Times Books.

Howard, Ebenezer. 1965 [1902]. *Garden Cities of Tomorrow*. MIT Press.

Hoyt, Homer. 1939. *The Structure and Growth of Residential Neighborhoods in American Cities*. Federal Housing Administration; Government Printing Office.

Hughes, James W., K. Tyler Miller, and Robert E. Lang. 1992. *The New Geography of Services and Office Buildings*. Rutgers University, Center for Urban Policy Research.

Hughes, James W., and George Sternlieb. 1986. "The Suburban Growth Corridors." *American Demographics* 8 (4): 34–37.

Huth, Mary Jo. 1983. "Towards a Multi-Nodal Urban Structure." *Transportation Quarterly* 37 (2): 245–62.

Hutton, Thomas A., and H. Craig Davis. 1985. "The Role of Office Location in Regional Town Center Planning and Metropolitan Multinucleation." *Canadian Journal of Regional Science* (Spring): 17–34.

Huxtable, Ada Louise. 1973. "An Alternative to the Slurbs." In *The Urbanization of the Suburbs*, edited by Louis H. Masotti and Jeffery K. Hadden. Beverly Hills, Calif.: Sage Publications.

Ihlanfeldt, Keith R., and David L. Sjoquist. 1998. "The Spatial Mismatch Hypothesis: A Review of Recent Studies and Their Implications for Welfare Reform." *Housing Policy Debate* 9 (4): 849–92

Jackson, Kenneth. 1985. *Crabgrass Frontier: The Suburbanization of the United States*. Oxford University Press.

Jacobs, Jane. 1961. *The Death and Life of Great American Cities*. New York: Vintage.

Kain, John. 1992. "The Spatial Mismatch Hypothesis: Three Decades Later." *Housing Policy Debate* 3 (2): 371–459.

Kasarda, John D., and Kwok-fai Ting. 1996. "Joblessness and Poverty in America's Central Cities: Causes and Policy Prescriptions." *Housing Policy Debate* 7 (2): 387–419.

Knack, Ruth Eckdish. 2000. "Contrarians." *Planning* 12(66): 20.

Knox, Paul. 1992. *The Packaged Landscape of Postsuburban America*. Working Paper 91-5. Blacksburg, Va.: Virginia Polytechnic Institute and State University, Center for Urban and Regional Studies.

Kostof, Spiro. 1992. *The City Assembled: The Elements of Urban Form through History*. Little Brown.

Kunstler, James Howard. 1993. *The Geography of Nowhere: The Rise and Decline of America's Manmade Landscape*. New York: Touchstone Books.

Lane, Robert. 2002. *Redesigning the Edgeless City*. New York: Regional Plan. Association (forthcoming).

Lang, Robert E. 1994a. *Beyond the Office Park: A Typology of New Jersey's Business Centers*. Report. Rutgers University, Center for Urban Policy Research.

———. 1994b. *Subregional Variation in New Jersey Development Patterns: A Classification Analysis of Recent Trends*. Report. Rutgers University, Center for Urban Policy Research.

———. 2000a. "Office Sprawl: The Evolving Geography of Business." Center on Urban and Metropolitan Policy Survey Paper Series (October). Brookings.

———. 2000b. "The Store Next Door." *Urban Land* 59 (7): 50–51.

———. 2000c. "Why Are Western Metropolitan Areas Denser than Eastern Ones?" Lecture given at the symposium *Metropolitan Frontiers of the American West: Lessons for the East?* Washington, National Building Museum, April 17.

———. 2002a. "Growth Counties." *Housing Facts and Findings* 4 (3): 2–3.

———. 2002b. "Open Spaces, Bounded Places: Does the American West's Arid Landscape Yield Dense Metropolitan Growth?" *Housing Policy Debate* 13 (4) (forthcoming).

Lang, Robert E., Deborah Epstein Popper, and Frank J. Popper. 1997. "Is There Still a Frontier?: The 1890 U.S. Census and the Modern American West." *Journal of Rural Studies* 13 (3): 377–86

Lang, Robert E., and Steven P. Hornburg. 1997. "Planning Portland Style: Pitfalls and Possibilities." *Housing Policy Debate* 8 (1): 1–10.

Lang, Robert E., and Patrick A. Simmons. 2001. "Boomburbs: The Emergence of Large, Fast-Growing Cities in the U.S." Census Note Series (June). Washington: Fannie Mae Foundation.

Langdon, Philip. 1990. "Pumping Up New Downtowns." *Planning* 56 (7): 22–28.

Leinberger, Christopher B. 1984. "New Shape of Cities Will Impact Corporate Locations." *National Real Estate Investor* 26 (14): 40, 140.

———. 1988. "The Six Types of Urban Village Cores." *Urban Land* 47 (5): 24–27.

———. 1989. "Malls: Magnets for Urban Cores." *Chain Store Age Executive* 65 (11): 94–102.

———. 1990. "Urban Cores: Development Trends and Real Estate Opportunities in the 1990s." *Urban Land* 49 (12): 4–9.

———. 1995. "The Changing Location of Development and Investment Opportunity." *Urban Land* 54 (5): 31–36.

———. 1996. "Metropolitan Development Trends of the Late 1990s: Social and Environmental Implications." In *Land Use in America*, edited by Henry L.

Diamond and Patrick F. Noonan, 203–22. Cambridge, Mass.: Lincoln Institute of Land Policy.

———. 2001. *Financing Progressive Development*. Brookings.

Leinberger, Christopher B., and Charles Lockwood. 1986. "How Business Is Reshaping America." *Atlantic Monthly* 258 (10): 43–52.

Lessinger, Jack. 1962. "The Case for Scatteration." *Journal of the American Institute of Planners* 28 (3): 159–69.

———. 1987. "Penturbia." *American Demographics* 9 (6): 31–39.

Levin, Charles L. 1988. "Post-Industrial Regional Change and the New Urban Geography." In *America's New Market Geography: Nation, Region and Metropolis*, edited by George Sternleib and James W. Hughes. Rutgers University, Center for Urban Policy Research.

Lewis, Pierce F. 1983. "The Galactic Metropolis." In *Beyond the Urban Fringe*, edited by R. H. Pratt and G. Macinko. Minneapolis: University of Minnesota Press.

———. 1995. "The Urban Invasion of Rural America: The Emergence of the Galactic City." In *The Changing American Countryside: Rural People and Places*, edited by Emery N. Castle, 39–62. Lawrence, Kans.: University Press of Kansas.

Lockwood, Charles, and Christopher Leinberger. 1988. "Los Angeles Comes of Age." *Atlantic Monthly* (October): 43–52.

Louv, Richard. 1985. *America II*. New York: Penguin Books.

Lynch, Kevin. 1961. "The Dispersed Sheet, Urban Galaxy, and the Multinucleated Net." In *The Pattern of the Metropolis*, edited by Lloyd Rodwin. New York: George Braziller.

Maher, Ian. 1992. "Commuting Calculations." *Journal of the American Planning Association* 58 (4): 386–87.

Malin, Steve R. 1988. "Serv-Urbs, U.S.A." *Across the Board* (February): 23–27.

McGovern, Patrick A. 1994. "Contra Costa County Edge Cities: The Political Economy of Planning." Ph.D. dissertation. Berkeley, Calif.: University of California.

Meltzer, Jack. 1984. *Metropolis to Metroplex: The Social and Spatial Planning of Cities*. Johns Hopkins University Press.

Mills, Edwin. 1988. "Service Sector Suburbanization." In *America's New Market Geography: National, Regional, Metropolis*, edited by George Sternlieb and James W. Hughes. Rutgers University, Center for Urban Policy Research.

Moss, Mitchell L., and Andrew Dunau. 1987. "Will Cities Lose Their Back Offices?" *Real Estate Review* 17 (1): 31–47.

Muller, Peter O. 1976. *Outer City: Geographical Consequences of the Urbanization of the United States*. Resource Paper for College Geography. American Association of Geography.

Orfield, Myron. 1997. *Metropolitics: A Regional Agenda for Community and Stability*. Brookings.

———. 2002. *American Metropolitics: The New Suburban Reality*. Brookings.

Orski, Kenneth C. 1985. "Suburban Mobility: The Coming Transportation Crisis?" *Transportation Quarterly* 39 (2): 283–96.

Packard, Vance. 1972. *A Nation of Strangers*. New York: David McKay.

Palen, John C. 1995. *The Suburbs*. McGraw-Hill.

Peirce, Neal. 1991. "Edge City: The Best America Can Do?" *Nation's Cities Weekly* 14 (40): 5.

Phoenix Planning Department. 1984. "Urban Villages/Council Districts—The Future . . . or Frustration?" Research Report, Fourth Phoenix Town Hall.

Pivo, Gary. 1990. "The Net of Mixed Beads: Suburban Office Development in Six Regions." *Journal of the American Planning Association* 56 (4): 457–69.

Porter, Douglas. 1997. *Profiles in Growth Management*. Washington: Urban Land Institute.

Pressman, Neil. 1985. "Forces for Spatial Change." In *The Future of Urban Form: The Impact of New Technology*, edited by John Brotchie. London: Croom Helm.

PricewaterhouseCoopers. 2002. *Emerging Trends in Real Estate*. New York.

Raines, Franklin D. 2000. "Playing from Strength: The Market Power of Cities." *Brookings Review* 18 (3): 14–17.

Regional Plan Association. 1960. *Plan for Greater New York*. New York.

Romanos, Michael C., Carla Chifos, and Tony Fenner. 1989. "Emergence of Metrotowns in the American Metropolitan Scene: Definitition and Evolution of the Concept." In *The City of the 21st Century*, edited by Michael C. Romanos. University of Cincinnati.

Sassen, Saskia. 1994. *The Impact of the New Technologies and Globalization on Cities*. Thousand Oaks, Calif.: Sage.

Saxenian, Anna Lee. 1996. "Inside-Out: Regional Networks and Industrial Adaptation in Silicon Valley and Route 128." *Cityscape* 2 (2): 41–60.

Scheer, Brenda Case, and Mintcho Petkov. 1998. "Edge City Morphology: A Comparison of Commercial Centers." *Journal of the American Planning Association* 64 (3): 298–310.

Sharpe, William, and Leonard Wallach. 1992. "The Edge of the New Frontier." *Journal of the American Planning Association* 58 (3): 393–95.

———. 1994. "Bold New City or Built-Up 'Burb'?" *American Quarterly* 46 (1): 1–30.

Sohmer, Rebecca R., and Robert E. Lang. 2000. "From Seaside to Southside: New Urbanism's Quest to Save the Inner City." *Housing Policy Debate* 11(4): 751–60.

Soja, Edward. 1989. *Postmodern Geographies*. London: Verso Press.

———. 1997. "Inside Exopolis: Scenes from Orange County. In *Variations on a Theme Park: The New American City and the End of Public Space*, edited by Michael Sorkin. New York: Hill and Wang.

Stevens, William K. 1987. "Beyond the Mall: Suburbs Evolving into 'Outer Cities.'" *New York Times*, November 8, sec. 3, pp. 1, 5.

Taylor, Graham R. 1915. *Satellite Cities: A Case Study of Industrial Suburbs.* New York: Ayer Company.

Urban Land Institute (ULI). 1996–99. *ULI Market Profiles: North America.* Washington.

———. 2000. *ULI 2000 Real Estate Forecast.* Washington.

———. 2002. *ULI 2002 Real Estate Forecast.* Washington.

U.S. Department of Agriculture. 2001. *National Resources Inventory: Highlights* (January). Washington.

Vance, James E., Jr. 1964. *Geography and Urban Evolution in the San Francisco Bay Area.* University of California–Berkeley, Institute of Governmental Studies.

———. 1977. *This Scene of Man: Role and Structure of the City in the Geography of Western Civilization.* Harper Press.

Warner, Sam Bass, Jr. 1972. *The Urban Wilderness.* Harper and Row.

Webber, Melvin M. 1967. "The Urban Place and the Non-Place Urban Realm." In *Explorations in Urban Structure*, edited by Melvin M. Webber. University of Pennsylvania Press.

Index

Figures, tables, and color plates are indicated with *f, t,* and *map.*

149